D1123007

NO LONGER PROPERTY OF
SEATTLE PUBLIC LIBRARY

THE GOVERNMENT VS. *Erotica*

THE GOVERNMENT VS. *Erotica*

The Siege of Adam & Eve™

PHILIP D. HARVEY

FOREWORD BY NADINE STROSSEN
PRESIDENT, AMERICAN CIVIL LIBERTIES UNION

Prometheus Books

59 John Glenn Drive
Amherst, New York 14228-2197

Published 2001 by Prometheus Books

The Government vs. Erotica: The Siege of Adam and Eve. Copyright © 2001 by Philip D. Harvey. All rights reserved. No part of this publication may be reproduced, stored in a retrieval system, or transmitted in any form or by any means, digital, electronic, mechanical, photocopying, recording, or otherwise, or conveyed via the Internet or a Web site without prior written permission of the publisher, except in the case of brief quotations embodied in critical articles and reviews.

Inquiries should be addressed to
Prometheus Books
59 John Glenn Drive
Amherst, New York 14228–2197
VOICE: 716–691–0133, ext. 207
FAX: 716–564–2711
WWW.PROMETHEUSBOOKS.COM

05 04 03 02 01   5 4 3 2 1

Library of Congress Cataloging-in-Publication Data

Harvey, Philip D., 1938–
    The government vs. erotica : the siege of Adam & Eve / Philip D. Harvey ; foreword by Nadine Strossen.
        p. cm.
    Includes bibliographical references and index.
    ISBN 1–57392–881–X (alk. paper)
    1. Sex and law—United States. 2. Sex crimes—United States. 3. Obscenity (Law)—United States. 4. Crimes without victims—United States. I. Title: Government versus erotica. II. Title.

KF9325 .H37 2001
323.44'3'0973—dc21   00–065317

Printed in Canada on acid-free paper

For Bruce Ennis
(1940–2000)

CONTENTS

7

ACKNOWLEDGMENTS

Bruce Ennis is one of the heroes of this book. He died in July 2000 at the age of sixty, from complications relating to leukemia.

Bruce was perhaps the finest First Amendment attorney in the United States. The skill and determination he brought to our case—the case described in this book—was dazzling. And ours was but one of many dozens of cases that Bruce managed and argued that have helped establish and maintain essential individual liberties in America.

Bruce argued sixteen cases before the U.S. Supreme Court, where he was well known and highly respected. Supreme Court Justice Ruth Bader Ginsberg stated, "[Bruce Ennis] earned the respect of my colleagues for the reliability of the briefs bearing his name, and for his engaging, hardly ever at a loss, conversations with us at oral argument."

I, and many others, are very much in his debt.

Others have contributed very substantially to this volume. My thanks to Dave Rudolf for scrutinizing the text from a lawyer's point of view, to him and to Wade Smith, Joe Cheshire, John Mintz, David Ogden, Peggy Oettinger, A.C. Bushnell, Skip Loy, Lloyd Sinclair, David Schnarch, Jerry Mooney, Fred Harwell and, especially, Marty Klein for submitting to interviews that provided essential material for this work.

Thank you, Sara Blackburn, for thorough and imaginative editing and thanks to Michele Thorburn for intensive and often detailed research in finding original source citations, to Rebecca DeVost for typing endless iterations of the book and for helping organize it, and to Sean Rowe for research assistance.

FOREWORD
Nadine Strossen

"[T]he government is . . . very dangerous . . . to deal with and it has enormous power. It has an endless supply of money. And if it wants you, if your government truly wants you, your government will have you."

—Wade M. Smith, one of Phil Harvey's attorneys

"I became convinced . . . that I no longer lived in a free country."

—Phil Harvey, describing his reaction to the third massive government raid of his company's offices in seven years

"In the long run the public gets just as much freedom of speech as it really wants."

—Zechariah Chafee, former Harvard Law School professor

The *Government vs. Erotica* is a gripping account of an important series of battles over free speech and other fundamental rights, which is both infuriating and inspiring. It is infuriating that our government waged a concerted campaign to deny adults access to constitutionally protected expressive materials concerning a subject of enormous significance to all of us—sexuality. Worse yet, in their crusade to crush First Amendment rights, government zealots also rode roughshod over a host of other rights, from the Fourth Amendment right to be free from "unreasonable searches and seizures" to the Sixth Amendment right "to have the assistance of counsel" in defending against criminal charges. Thus, far from serving "we the people," our "public servants" were abusing our fundamental rights—not to mention misusing our tax dollars in the process.

Yet this true-life "David and Goliath" tale is ultimately inspiring because one courageous individual fought back successfully, notwithstanding the seemingly limitless zeal and resources amassed against him. Phil Harvey not

Nadine Strossen is the president of the American Civil Liberties Union and professor at New York Law School. For research assistance, Professor Strossen gratefully acknowledges her academic assistant, Kathy Davis, and her research assistants Mara Levy, Janice Purvis, and Daniel Curtin.

11

only survived the government's relentless efforts to bully him out of business, as it had done to other businesspeople who also sold constitutionally protected materials to adults who sought those materials. Even more inspiringly, Phil Harvey and his impressive legal team secured new legal precedents and prosecutorial policies that will protect other individuals and businesses from similar government harassment and oppression.

Phil Harvey's harrowing ordeal and ultimate triumph have broad significance on several levels. First, this saga exemplifies the ongoing struggle for free speech and against government suppression in the area of sexual expression, which always has been especially embattled in the United States, with our puritanical heritage. In the words of humorist Garrison Keillor: "My ancestors were Puritans from England, [who] arrived here in 1648 in the hope of finding greater restrictions than were permissible under English law at the time."[1]

Now, several centuries later, in our brave new world of cybercommunications, we still have to fight against fearful old attitudes toward sexual expression. Our federal government has passed two cybercensorship laws, both aimed at online sexual expression. Five states have passed cybercensorship laws, all but one of which also have targeted sexual expression. Likewise, sexual expression has been the preeminent target of the many proposed policies—some of which have been implemented—to bar individuals from accessing certain online content, through blocking software, in public libraries and schools.

Despite its demonization by too many politicians, most sexual expression is constitutionally protected, and much of it has serious value. Indeed, the first time the U.S. Supreme Court considered the First Amendment status of sexually oriented expression, the justices eloquently extolled the importance of sexuality—and, hence, of words and images about sexuality: "Sex, a great and mysterious motive force in human life, has indisputably been a subject of absorbing interest to mankind through the ages; it is one of the vital problems of human interest and public concern."[2] Consistent with its recognition of the importance of sex for individuals and society alike, the Court has struck down many laws restricting sexual expression. In May 2000, it invalidated a federal law that curbed sexually oriented cable TV programs. Perhaps of greatest long-range significance, given the burgeoning of cybercommunications, is the Court's 1997 decision reviewing Congress's first cybercensorship law, *Reno* v. *ACLU*. In that historic ruling, the Court unanimously rejected the government's argument that it should have more power to regulate sexual expression online than in print.

The fact that the Supreme Court has protected most sexual expression against persistent attempts to stifle it illustrates another significant theme that *The Government vs. Erotica* highlights: the crucial role of our judicial system in protecting individual rights against government repression. State and federal prosecutors launched multiple investigations and prosecutions against Phil Harvey and his business, Adam & Eve, in state and federal courts in four different states, from Alabama to Utah. They followed the tactic of "forum shopping" for communities where they reasonably expected the judges and jurors to be especially intolerant of sexual expression and especially unsympathetic toward free-speech rights. Nonetheless, the prosecution—and persecution— failed in every single forum.

Judges are often assumed to be more protective of constitutional rights than juries. After all, judges are schooled in constitutional principles, including the core notion that the Constitution ensures freedom even for ideas or expression that the majority of the community finds offensive. In stark contrast, juries are intended to reflect the community consensus. Moreover, federal judges are generally assumed to be more protective of constitutional rights than state judges, since most state judges are subject to elections (initially and/or for retention) and therefore are at least potentially influenced by political pressures. The U.S. Constitution deliberately insulates federal judges from such majoritarian pressures by providing that they are appointed, in effect, for life; they can be removed only through the extraordinary process of impeachment, only if they fall afoul of the constitutional standard of "good behavior."

In light of these constitutional considerations, perhaps it should not be surprising that the federal courts that ruled on various aspects of the government's campaign to intimidate Phil Harvey consistently upheld his constitutional rights. It is noteworthy, though, that the courts did so firmly and forcefully, using unusually strong language to condemn the government's abusive, bad-faith tactics as—for example—"intrusive and intimidating," "harassment," "prosecutorial misconduct," and "vindictiveness."[3]

What is even more noteworthy is that the same rights-protective results were also reached by jurors even in the state court of a county that is probably one of the more socially and culturally conservative in the country: Alamance County, North Carolina. As a Raleigh, North Carolina, newspaper editorialized, castigating the government's continuing persecution of Phil Harvey and his company: "Alamance County is not exactly the Vegas of the Piedmont," and the jury consisted of "a cross-section of average citizens," including "a housewife, a minister's son, and a church choir member." Yet in only one hour, that jury unanimously repudiated the government's charges against Adam & Eve. Indeed, the jury foreman publicly stated that the jury actually reached its verdict in five minutes but continued its discussion for an hour to avoid embarrassing the prosecutors. He also stated that the jury had considered apologizing to Phil Harvey for the ordeal he had undergone.

In short, while the prosecutors who hounded Phil Harvey embody government at its worst—abusing its power to oppress citizens' rights—the judges and jurors who heard the claims embody government at its best—curbing present abuses, punishing past ones, and preventing future ones. The courts lived up to their intended constitutional role as the safety net for individual rights when other government agencies or officials violate them.

In upholding freedom of expression even for sexual expression, despite the persistent political stigmatizing and scapegoating of such expression, the courts that were involved in the Adam & Eve litigation are typical. The same pattern of political attack followed by judicial reprieve has characterized the current campaigns concerning sexual expression in cyberspace.

The ACLU has brought constitutional challenges to five cybercensorship laws targeting online sexual expression, all of which were passed by overwhelming bipartisan margins in Congress and the state legislatures, and championed by the Clinton administration and the state governors. Indeed, in several states, the cybercensorship measures passed unanimously in at least one house of the legislature. In short, our lobbying efforts have failed abysmally. In stark contrast, our litigation efforts have been stunningly successful; we have won all the lawsuits challenging all these laws, in every trial and appellate court that has ruled on them. Moreover, these cases have been ruled on by twenty-five different judges, who span the entire ideological spectrum. They were appointed by the last six presidents—going all the way back to Richard Nixon. Despite all their differences on constitutional issues, all of these judges—including all nine Supreme Court justices—have endorsed the ACLU's position in this litigation, upholding free speech for online sexual expression.

When it comes to distinguishing those government officials who favor censorship of sexual expression from those who favor freedom of speech, the crucial dividing line is not between Republicans and Democrats, or between conservatives and liberals. Rather, the critical divide is between politicians who must stand for election and judges who are relatively insulated from the pressures of electoral politics.

One abiding lesson to be drawn from *The Government vs. Erotica*, then, is the importance of defending our independent judicial system against the persistent attacks it faces. In recent years, for example, Congress has held repeated hearings on a range of proposals to curb the power of federal courts to enforce constitutional rights. One proposal, which was initially suggested in a book by Judge Robert Bork, would amend the Constitution to give Congress the power to overturn any court decision by a majority vote. In 1997, one congressional leader went so far as to call for the impeachment of various federal judges who actually honored their oath to uphold the Constitution, which all members of Congress and other elected officials also take, but too often honor in the breach. House Majority Whip Tom Delay (R-TX) advocated impeaching judges who were faithful to this oath, and to the Constitution, by invalidating government actions that violated constitutional rights.

Another abiding lesson to be drawn from *The Government vs. Erotica* is even more important because it teaches that even an independent judicial system cannot curb government oppression or enforce individual rights. Standing alone, courts are impotent. Courts that are independent in the sense of being relatively insulated from political or majoritarian pressures are not independent in the sense of having power to initiate even investigations of government abuses, let alone corrective actions to counter them. To the contrary, courts may only act—or, more accurately, *react*—when and if litigants file complaints and institute lawsuits. If Phil Harvey had decided not to incur the enormous financial costs—not to mention the enormous psychic and other intangible costs—required to defend against the government's massive, multifront attack, no judge or juror would have had the opportunity to reject the government's charges on their (de)merits.

Wade Smith's statement, quoted at the outset of this foreword, underscores that it would be completely rational even for a completely innocent target of such a government onslaught to waive his defenses—and, in the process, his constitutional rights, not to mention the constitutional rights of the many other citizens that are at stake. Even if one somehow emerged as a legal winner against every one of the government's relentless prosecutions, launched simultaneously or in rapid succession—itself a dubious proposition in light of the difficulty of adequately preparing against all such charges—one would inevitably be a loser at least in economic terms, and no doubt in psychic terms as well.

Consider Phil Harvey's reaction to his initial obscenity indictment: "Even though I believed the charges against me to be preposterously unfounded, the very fact of having been charged made me feel deeply vulnerable, isolated, and pushed out of the social fabric." Surely most of us would share these reactions were we, too, charged with criminal conduct and threatened with lengthy prison terms and fines; the government's first prosecution against Phil Harvey menaced him with imprisonment for up to forty-five years. In light of these considerations, it is understandable that other individuals who faced the same multiple-prosecution and harassing tactics as those aimed at Phil Harvey entered into plea agreements. Quite understandably, they concluded that they had no choice but to go out of business, and therefore succumbed to extortionate government demands that they cease selling even such mainstream material as *Playboy* and *The Joy of Sex*, rather than playing David to the governmental Goliath.

Harder to understand—especially from the perspective of the proverbial "rational man" posited by economic theory—are Phil Harvey's decisions not only to defend against the government's cumulative prosecutions, but also to take the even bolder, more courageous step of initiating affirmative litigation against the government, seeking to halt further abuses. After all, among his many other accomplishments, Phil Harvey is a successful businessman who has lectured at prominent business schools. In addition, though, Phil Harvey is a committed freedom fighter who originally launched his business as an offshoot of academic and activist work on behalf of reproductive freedom, which he still carries out through not-for-profit agencies that he also founded. Ultimately, as a matter of principle, Phil Harvey "just said no" to further government coercion, deciding that his—and our—priceless liberties are worth the price tag of bankrolling their defense (he was forced to spend $3 million in legal fees alone).

I consider Phil Harvey a hero for deciding that he would take up his slingshot against the governmental giant, despite the well-taken warning of Wade Smith. The litigation was an isolated effort to resist a nationwide campaign, launched by the U.S. Justice Department under Attorney General Ed Meese, to drive constitutionally protected sexual expression from the market. This campaign, and Phil Harvey's countercampaign, were chronicled in a 1991 ACLU report, *Above the Law: The Justice Department's War against the First Amendment.*

I also described this struggle in a 1995 book about censorship of sexual expression, *Defending Pornography: Free Speech, Sex, and the Fight for Women's Rights.* In fact, I first had the honor of meeting Phil Harvey when he attended a 1995 forum about the book in Washington, D.C. I still recall the thrill I felt when he stood up in the audience to ask a question and stated his name. Before I answered his question, I seized the opportunity to publicly thank him for his signal role in opposing the censorship and other rights violations that I had discussed in my book and oral presentation.

I recount this history in part to stress that my enormous admiration and respect for Phil Harvey—and my enduring gratitude to him—are based on the facts of the litigation, and not on any self-congratulations in *The Government vs. Erotica.* He was a hero to me before I met him, and long before he wrote the book. Far from engaging in braggadocio, Phil Harvey's book describes his own role in understated, modest terms, repeatedly giving credit to others who encouraged and facilitated his standing up to the government, including his legal team and his business colleagues.

To be sure, these other individuals also deserve our great respect and gratitude for their significant contributions of not only moral courage but also legal and strategic acumen. For example, such bold, imaginative legal strategies as initiating a civil action to enjoin the government's overreaching were crafted and carried out under the leadership of Bruce Ennis, whom I knew from other experience (including his distinguished service as the ACLU's Legal Director, 1977–82) to be one of the nation's premier lawyers. Superb lawyering by Bruce Ennis and other members of Phil Harvey's dedicated legal team led to an unprecedented ruling by the federal appellate court in Salt Lake City, Utah. It was the first time in history that an appellate court had intervened in an obscenity prosecution before trial, ruling that the government's coercive tactics had "tainted" the proceedings to such an extent that the defendant's constitutional rights would be jeopardized even by having to mount a defense at trial.

While Phil Harvey could not have withstood the government's siege without the aid of his lawyers and others, they certainly could not have undertaken any action at all without his determination to proceed. Phil Harvey's lawyers and other colleagues could—and did—advise, counsel, argue, and cajole, but the ultimate decision about whether to proceed with the litigation rested with Phil Harvey alone. He alone had to say yes or no about whether to defend against the government's criminal charges or to plea-bargain, and whether or not to pursue the novel approach of instituting affirmative civil litigation against the government. In the process, Phil Harvey had to wrestle with many competing considerations, including his concerns about the impact of any decision on his business partners and employees, as well as their families. Also on his conscience were concerns about his customers and, last but not least, everyone in this country who has a stake in robust constitutional rights. The book recounts dramatic discussions and debates—within Phil Harvey's own mind, as well as between him and his various counselors—over these excruciatingly difficult choices.

The Government vs. Erotica describes a "defining moment" in Phil Harvey's decision to stand up against the government as triggered by a powerful question posed to him by one of his attorneys, David S. Rudolf:

> Goddammit, we're talking about the First Amendment here! If you don't stop the government, who will? . . . Someone's got to take a stand. If not PHE [Adam & Eve's parent company], who will?

Whether consciously or not, Dave Rudolf was echoing the justly celebrated rhetorical questions posed by the first-century Talmudic sage, Hillel the Elder:

"If I am not for myself, who will be for me? If I am not for others, what am I? And if not now, when?"

Neither the First Amendment nor any other constitutional guarantees are self-executing. The Constitution itself as well as Supreme Court decisions enforcing it are worth only the paper they are written on unless courageous individuals such as Phil Harvey take action to translate those rights into realities, not only for themselves, but also for the rest of us. Zechariah Chafee's powerful insight, quoted at the beginning of this foreword, applies not only to free speech, but also to all our other rights. If these rights are to flourish, "we the people" have to want them—and not just in a passive, abstract way. We must be aware of our rights, alert to government actions that violate them, and engaged in any necessary counter measures to terminate and rectify such violations.

In a more proactive or preventive mode, we have to forestall violations of our rights by electing government officials who are committed to respecting them, and who will appoint judges who share that commitment. Recall Wade Smith's sobering edict that "if your government truly wants you, your government will have you." But if "we the people" in turn "truly want" our rights, then by definition our government will not "truly want" to suppress those rights.

Paradoxically, it is the individuals who come face-to-face with government oppression, as Phil Harvey did, who are most likely to be galvanized into fighting for freedom. Thus, repression can give rise to resistance and, eventually, liberation.

There is a further paradox, though. Despite the positive conclusion of *The Government vs. Erotica*, this book tells a story that does not have a conventional "happy ending." This story is about freedom as an ongoing process, demanding not only "eternal vigilance," but also eternal activism. The prosecutors who laid siege to Adam & Eve are not the last government officials who will abuse their power and citizens' rights. Accordingly, I hope—and believe—that Phil Harvey is not the last individual to stand up against oppression and for freedom. So this inspiring account is yet another contribution by Phil Harvey to the ongoing fight for rights; it should encourage others to follow in his footsteps.

Kent Lakes, New York
June 2000

NOTES

1. Garrison Keillor, testimony before the Senate Subcommittee on Education, on NEA Grant Funding and Restrictions, March 29, 1990.

2. *Roth* v. *United States*, 354 U.S. 476, 487 (1957).

3. See *United States* v. *Adam & Eve,* 965 F. 2d 848 (10th Cir. 1992); *PHE, Inc.* v. *United States*, 743 F. Supp. 15 (D.D.C. 1990).

OUR CASE AND
ITS CONSEQUENCES

The day that thirty-seven armed law enforcement agents forced their way into our mail-order company in Carrboro, North Carolina, in 1986, I had only an inkling of the implications. I knew we were under attack and that agents from several federal jurisdictions, as well as state agents from North Carolina, believed we were doing something illegal. What I did not yet realize was that the right to read and view and think in accordance with the most fundamental First Amendment traditions was in jeopardy. A campaign by an overreaching federal government to force people into conformity with the moral views of a relative handful of people in and out of the Department of Justice at the time was under way, full speed ahead, and our business was a target.

The case was about sex. Our company, Adam & Eve, sold sexually oriented merchandise, everything from condoms to massage oils, from lingerie to erotic videos, from vibrators to books and magazines with sexual themes and content.

The agents who arrived that day contended that we were violating obscenity laws. Our belief then and now was that most material about sex is not only legal but useful, that depictions of positive sexuality between cheerfully consenting adults, without violence or degradation, provide a valuable service to thousands of couples and are not the business of the federal bureaucracy.

Throughout history, when governments seek to control the private behavior of their citizens, they edge toward tyranny. As a first step, they have often attempted to control sexuality and to proscribe people's sexual thoughts. I am not sure why this is so, but every despot in the twentieth century has seen imposing constraints on sexual behavior as vital in limiting the freedom of the people over whom they hold sway.

The threat of open tyranny is remote and unlikely for us in America. Far more dangerous is the slow erosion of our liberties, particularly freedom of speech and of thought, by fervent moralists who believe they are "improving" us. "Men born to freedom are naturally alert to repel invasion of their liberty

21

by evil-minded rulers," said Supreme Court Justice Louis Brandeis. "The greater dangers to liberty lurk in insidious encroachment by men of zeal, well-meaning but without understanding."[1] When such people hold the levers that control the massive power of the federal government, all citizens should be vigilant.

The story of the eight-year battle between the Adam & Eve mail-order company and the U.S. Department of Justice is a case study in this vital province. During the Reagan administration, an official who described himself as "a man of prayer" was in charge of the unit in the Justice Department in Washington called the National Obscenity Enforcement Unit, whose purpose was to "clean up" sexual viewing and reading materials. By the time the federal prosecutors invaded our little office/warehouse in North Carolina and subjected our employees to a nightmare that would have repercussions for years, a dozen other mail-order companies that sold sexually explicit videos and magazines had already been—or soon would be—put out of business. The campaign of government suppression was winning in Connecticut, Wisconsin, and California. Threatened with simultaneous multiple prosecutions in jurisdictions across the country, mail-order companies were giving up, closing down, and paying fines; sometimes their owners were going to jail.

We were as frightened and as intimidated by the federal juggernaut as any small company of law-abiding citizens might be expected to be. But we decided that we would not go out of business just by virtue of being threatened. And we would not plea-bargain away our constitutional rights to sell the sexually oriented materials that our one million customers were paying us to deliver to them. At the very least, we knew that the Constitution's First Amendment protected speech and that, as citizens of a free country, we had the right to our day in court.

Over the years that followed we were bounced along as though on a river, through a succession of boiling rapids and long, slow glides. The principal decisions that we made were decisions to continue the journey until we had seen it through. The fact that we saw it through—after eight years of court battles, including indictments in two states, a trial in one, and an extended lawsuit we brought against the U.S. Department of Justice—led to a significant victory for the right of Americans to read and to see the forms of entertainment that they wish to read and to see.

The U.S. obscenity laws under which we were prosecuted are still in place, strong, vague, and therefore still enforceable in differing and frequently unjust ways. Books and movies about sex remain as controversial as ever. But the federal government can no longer annihilate businesses, including bookstore chains, video producers, filmmakers, and others who sell or market entertainment throughout the United States, by threatening to exhaust their resources by prosecuting them simultaneously in half a dozen places. Our case has forged a permanent change in that policy, and in the legal precedents that govern it.

I and my many colleagues who were drawn into this drama were often frightened and angry as the prosecuting authorities persisted in their campaign, and we have been profoundly changed by this attack on our business and on our personal values. In the end, we were exhilarated by how we came to assert our cause and prevail against a federal force that was zealously determined and almost infinitely well financed. That this remains possible in the United States is our greatest hope for a free future.

NOTE

1. *Olmstead* v. *United States*, 277 U.S. 438, 479 (1928) (Brandeis, J., dissenting).

CHAPTER ONE

THE RAID

I was in New York on the morning of May 29, 1986, when the phone rang. It was just after nine A.M. Ken Miskie, our print production specialist in Carrboro, North Carolina, was talking excitedly. Ken was a man whose voice always seemed a little cautious even in the smoothest of times. Now, reflecting the turmoil going on around him, he reported tensely that thirty or forty law enforcement officers had just raided our business and shut it down, and that all our employees were being interrogated. He and other management and supervisory staff were being held in one room, and a massive sweep of our premises was in process.

I couldn't believe it. As the principal owner of a company that specialized in sexually oriented merchandise, I knew it was about obscenity, of course. But when the North Carolina obscenity law had been revised and made more restrictive six months before, I had consulted with our local district attorney about the changes in the law. We had gone through the Adam & Eve catalog together, and DA Carl Fox had recommended that we remove certain items, which we had done. Now came this incursion, which was wildly out of proportion to anything we ever had imagined.

I had already booked a seat on the next flight to Raleigh-Durham. Now I called an attorney, Grainger Barrett, in nearby Chapel Hill, and he was already on his way to the company. Locking the offices of PSI, our budding nonprofit group on the fifteenth floor of an East Fifty-sixth Street office building in Manhattan, I hit the ground running and hailed a cab. What would I find by the time I got to Carrboro? From what Ken had said, it sounded grim.

Affidavit testimony from some our employees reports what was going on while I was on my way to Raleigh-Durham.

Affidavit of Shirley Sell:

I was working at Adam & Eve on the morning of Thursday, May 29, 1986. At approximately 9:00 A.M., while I was on the telephone with a customer,

25

four or five men came into my work area with some sort of badges . . . and one of these men ordered me to hang up the telephone. When I told him I was on the phone with a customer, he said he didn't care and that I should get off or he would hang the phone up, so I hung up on the customer. I did not know who the men were, or what was going on. I felt very badly about hanging up on the customer.

An announcement was made over the public address system that all employees had to go to the warehouse. I asked the man who had made me get off the phone if there had been a bomb threat, and he said no, that I just had to go to the warehouse. I did not believe that I had any choice, so I went to the warehouse.

When I arrived at the warehouse, all of the other employees were there. We were told by one of the officers that they had a search warrant. One of the supervisors, Mr. Loy, came in and said that he was not permitted to talk to us, but that the agents did have a search warrant.

All of the employees and supervisors were told that we had to turn in any concealed weapons, that we would be questioned, that after we were questioned we would be brought to the back door of the warehouse, and that we could not leave the building until we had a [grand jury] subpoena. . . . There were armed guards at every door, and I was guarded when I went to the restroom. I was not permitted to bring my pocket-book into the stall in the restroom, and had to give it to the female agent who escorted me there.

I would learn later that thirty-seven armed law enforcement agents had descended on our premises on Highway 54, seven miles west of Carrboro, North Carolina. The group was comprised of a sheriff and sheriff's deputies from two counties, federal postal inspectors from the Eastern District of North Carolina and from the State of Utah, and agents from the North Carolina State Bureau of Investigation.

Our reception area at the Carrboro offices was designed to hold eight or ten people, and as the agents poured in, demanding entry to the building, tensions rose. Our receptionist, Jodi Klomser, had instructions not to admit unauthorized visitors unless they asked to see a particular individual, in which case the person would come to the reception area to meet them. But the agents gave her no name; instead, they showed their badges and demanded entry. Jodi recognized Sheriff Lindy Pendergrass of Orange County, who told her they had a search warrant and asked her to get a manager. As she described it:

A man in a brown suit stuck his head inside the window between the lobby and my work space and told me to open the door. I said no, just one moment please, and continued to try to find a manager, as Sheriff Pendergrass had requested. As I was concluding my conversation with one of the managers, who said he was on his way, the man in a brown suit said: "You tell him if you do not open the door immediately, we will kick it in." When Skip [the manager] arrived and opened the door, the men in suits swarmed into the building. . . .

I turned off my switchboard, picked up my purse and locked the file cabinet. I walked to the front lobby to get an applicant's employment form [filled out just moments before the raid began]. I checked the front door to see if it was locked. I found an armed guard looking in, so I was satisfied the door was secure. I went to the warehouse, along with three agents. . . .

The agents told us to form seven lines, and they asked for all of the managers to go to one group. They told us that we would have to be interviewed, or go before the grand jury. By this time I was very scared.

I was taken to the lunch room and asked questions. . . . I believed that I had to answer the questions before I could leave. The agent who interviewed me also gave me a grand jury subpoena.

After the interview, I was taken back to the warehouse, and one of the agents took my picture and then asked for my driver's license. I was told to leave through the back door, and had to show a Sheriff's deputy guarding the exit my subpoena before I was allowed to leave.

Melinda Ruley of the Chapel Hill *Independent* summed up the day's major events: "By the end of the day, 118 employees had been 'processed,' questioned, and photographed. Subpoenas were issued, pocketbooks searched, documents and computer ledgers confiscated. Law enforcement officers ordered employees to turn over their weapons and demanded to see the studio where sex videos were made. 'They acted like it was a drug raid, and I guess we were a real disappointment to them,' [said] Skip Loy, director of operations. . . . 'The only weapons people had were their boxcutter knives. And I had to tell the officers, I said, there's no videos produced here. We just got things in boxes.' "[1]

The operation was described as the "first strike of a federal-state pornography task force."[2] Many members of the raiding party clearly had expected to discover salacious carryings-on, including the production of adult videos, a matter they could easily have disabused themselves of by asking a few questions over the phone. They could also have made an appointment to visit us and received copies of any of our merchandise that they might have wanted. We had nothing to hide. At the time we were mailing more than eight million catalogs that described our sexually oriented merchandise every year to several million households throughout America and would have cheerfully provided both catalogs and any merchandise requested to any bona fide law enforcement person who chose to ask for or buy those items. In summary, there was nothing for this task force to uncover.

The search went on. Acting on a warrant issued by North Carolina Superior Court Judge Anthony Brannon and a similar federal warrant requested through the state attorney general's office by U.S. Attorney Sam Currin, the agents sealed off all entrances to our plant and went about their work.

Grainger Barrett, the attorney I had telephoned from New York, was a lawyer who had served for four years as the deputy town attorney and town attorney for Chapel Hill, during which time he was the police attorney, responsible for providing advice to the Chapel Hill Police Department on searches and seizures. He had accompanied the Chapel Hill police on searches on a number of occasions. He provided the following statement in a June 23, 1986, affidavit:

> I arrived at the company's building on Highway 54 in Carrboro at approximately 10:30 A.M.
>
> When I arrived at the building, I saw that there were guards posted at all of the doors. I identified myself to the guard at the front door as an attorney for the company and entered the front reception area.
>
> As I walked through the reception area and into the office area, Postal Inspector Charlton met me at the door. I told Inspector Charlton that I had been asked by the company to go out to the premises, and asked him to take me around briefly so that I could see what the agents were doing, assess the situation, and be in a position to give my clients legal advice. Agent Charlton immediately adopted a confrontational, hostile manner and told me, in substance, [that] they had a valid search warrant and that I was not going to interfere with or impede their search in any way. . . .
>
> After I arrived, one of the company's supervisors asked me if she could advise the employees that I was present and that they could speak to an attorney if they wished. I told her yes, and gave her some business cards to provide to employees. I felt it important to reassure them that an attorney for the company was in fact now on the premises and of my name. About two minutes later Inspector Charlton came up to me and told me he would not allow my cards to be handed out any further. I told Inspector Charlton that I wanted to let the employees know I was there and to let them know what their legal rights were if they wished this advice. I repeatedly assured him I would advise employees generally to be cooperative and that neither I nor the employees would interfere with or impede their search. Inspector Charlton told me something to the effect that the employees didn't have a

right to consult with an attorney since they weren't under arrest, and I asked him if he was saying that persons not under arrest didn't have the right to talk to an attorney. Charlton then said that he didn't have to let me talk to the employees since I wasn't their attorney, but rather the company's attorney. At no time did Inspector Charlton ever permit me to provide legal advice to any of the employees being detained in the warehouse, despite my specific request to be allowed to do this. . . . I heard one agent tell the employees in the warehouse that if they each talked to an attorney, they would be there all day and everyone would thus be greatly inconvenienced.

I left the premises of PHE, Inc. [Adam & Eve's corporate name] at approximately 1:30 P.M. At the time I left, there were still at least 10–12 employees being detained in the warehouse. I also was informed prior to leaving that the switchboard had been cut off. During the three hours I was at PHE, Inc., from 10:30 A.M. until 1:30 P.M., none of the employees to my knowledge were allowed to leave the building without being interviewed, searched, photographed, and given a subpoena. All of the employees were restrained in a custodial atmosphere and the search was as intrusive and general a search as I have witnessed. It was clear to me that the majority of employees held there were intimidated, [that they] repeatedly asked whether they were under arrest, and were extremely fearful and apprehensive about what was happening to them. I hope never again to be called upon to provide legal counsel under such distressing circumstances and conduct by Government officials.

Shirley Sell:

One of [our] supervisors stepped out of the conference room the supervisors were kept in, and announced that some attorneys had arrived. I said to the agent "our attorneys are here, can I speak to an attorney?" The agent said that I could not speak with an attorney, that it was "too late" and that the interview had already begun. I told the agent I was not sure I should be talking to him, and he told me if I had done nothing wrong I should not be concerned about talking to him. I was then asked numerous questions about my job and PHE, Inc. The interview lasted between 20 and 40 minutes. . . . Had I known that I did not have to give information to the agents, I would not have answered any questions.

After the postal inspector was through with me, I was taken by the agent back to the warehouse and told to wait in line to have my picture taken. . . . [T]he agent told me to take my purse to another agent to be searched. I asked why my purse had to be searched, and the agent said, "Because that's what we're going to do." . . . None of the employees were allowed to speak to the managers. The agents treated us like criminals, and tried to scare us.

By the time I arrived at around four P.M., this drama was largely over. There were still what I thought were two or three unmarked police cars, and one marked "Sheriff," in the parking lot, but the lot was otherwise empty. Our employees, with a few exceptions, had been processed and had gone home. While there were still at least a half dozen federal inspectors on the premises, they weren't being particularly aggressive at the moment. I saw that they had already broken open my desk and gone through its entire contents.

One of the strongest images I had from the moment I entered the plant was of Denise Long calmly standing at the Xerox machine copying hundreds of financial documents. Denise is a tall, stolid, and utterly unflappable woman who, at the time, was in charge of our company's financial records. The agents had been about to confiscate a great deal of our financial documentation, and to Denise, it was unthinkable that we should not have copies of our own financial data. How could we operate the company without it? I have no doubt that her opinion on this matter was so absolute that the agents acquiesced fairly quickly and permitted her to make the necessary copies. She had been at it, she told me, for nearly two hours and would continue for an hour more.

Despite these somewhat reassuring images, I was shaking inside, and probably a little bit outside, too. Our corporate persona had been invaded, our privacy torn to shreds by people who presumably despised us and whom we now despised in turn. I now had to confront five or six of these men who, I had now learned, had ridden roughshod over the rights of virtually all our employees. To my surprise, they didn't expect me to give them any information. "I suppose your lawyers won't let you answer any questions," one said. Indeed, by now we had three lawyers present, who had instructed me to give only my name and my position.

Our offices resembled a battlefield after the battle. Denise stood by her copier, which continued to flash, flash, flash as she compiled the records she felt we absolutely had to have. I got a few more firsthand reports from our vice president, A. C. Bushnell, and from one or two others, arranged to meet our attorney the following morning, and headed home. After a stiff belt of Jack Daniels, I considered what had happened.

I felt as though I had been shoved off the bank of a river into swirling water with very little to do but hang on, look for help, and grab on to anything that floated. We would be accused of obscenity, that much seemed clear. But there had been no indictments and no arrests. Each of the employees had been issued a subpoena to appear before a federal grand jury in Raleigh a few weeks later. This suggested that we would be indicted by the federal authorities in the Eastern District of North Carolina, which is headquartered in Raleigh. But that was only a possibility, we were advised, as federal postal inspectors from the State of Utah and State Bureau of Investigation agents from North Carolina had also been present. (Why hadn't they consulted with District Attorney Carl Fox? His office had not participated in the raid. He could have told them that I had conferred with him and was making a good-faith effort to conform with North Carolina's new obscenity law and we could have discussed all this. So what was the reason for the raid?)

I was furious with the way our employees had been treated, especially in light of the far more civilized treatment that was accorded to me. I was also frightened for our business. Having been treated as they were, I feared that many of our employees simply would not show up for work again. Could we carry on? Our lawyers had been reassuring that we could not be closed down without a trial, that official suspicion of obscenity did not permit the prior restraint of materials like videos, books, and magazines if they had not been found obscene through due process of law. If we could staff our company, therefore, we could probably stay open, which would provide the funds we needed to defend ourselves.

The following morning, nearly every one of our employees arrived for work. Not only were they there, they were angry. "What right have they got to do that to us?" "No one was breaking any laws!" "Haven't they heard of the First Amendment? Who the hell do they think they are?" I grinned from ear to ear, but partly from embarrassment. I had greatly underestimated these fine people. They didn't like being pushed around by a bunch of bullies any more than I did, and they weren't about to take it lying down.

I have never known morale in our company to be higher or productivity better than it was in those next few months. As Melinda Ruley recounted in the *Independent*, "Skip Loy, director of operations at the plant, is fond of telling how, the day after the raid, all but a handful of employees showed up for work as usual. Even a woman who had been filling out an application when the agents filed in came back, still hoping to be hired. 'It's a uniting experience,' Loy says of the legal trouble PHE and Phil Harvey have gone through. 'People have suffered through this thing together.'"[3]

For the next three months we waited anxiously for the other shoe to drop. To prepare for the charges we anticipated and in the hope that we might be able to resolve the issue and avoid an indictment, we began assembling a team of criminal defense attorneys. We were remarkably lucky in this endeavor. While our area of North Carolina did not at the time have a nationally known criminal defense attorney who specialized in obscenity law, I was convinced that, rather than importing them from New York or Ohio, we should retain local lawyers. I learned that a number of distinguished trial lawyers practiced in Raleigh and Chapel Hill, and a team began shaping up quickly. As there are always at least minor conflicts between the interests of individuals and a corporation, we decided that David Rudolf of Chapel Hill would represent PHE, Inc., the parent corporation of Adam & Eve; Wade Smith of Tharrington, Smith, and Hargrove in Raleigh would defend me personally; and Joe Cheshire of Cheshire, Parker, and Hughes in Raleigh would act as cocounsel for the company (and would later defend Peggy Oettinger, our marketing manager). These three attorneys were assisted by Adam Stein of Ferguson, Stein of Chapel Hill and by Wade's colleague Randall Roden.

None of the lawyers had defended an obscenity case before. But they all came naturally, instinctively, and enthusiastically to our First Amendment case, sharing a deep belief in fundamental freedoms—in the right to speak, to think, to read. They quickly learned the necessary law, and they were a colorful and impressive group.

Dave Rudolf had been practicing in Chapel Hill for eight years. A native New Yorker, he had served as a public defender in Brooklyn and in the Bronx. In Chapel Hill, he had taught at the University of North Carolina Law School, running the criminal law clinic whose students represented people charged with misdemeanors in Orange County.

Wade Smith was one of North Carolina's best-known defense attorneys. He had successfully defended former North Carolina Lt. Gov. General Jimmy Greene against bribery charges, and in an even higher-profile case, had been defense attorney for Jeffrey McDonald, the Green Beret doctor serving a life sentence for the murder of his wife and two daughters. Wade had practiced in Raleigh for many years. With his courtly Southern accent and country wit, he seemed the quintessential Carolina lawyer.

Joe Cheshire was also a Carolinian born and bred, the son of a prominent Raleigh attorney and a practitioner experienced in both civil and criminal cases. He had worked with Dave Rudolf on the defense of two North Carolina government officials accused of misusing funds in the state's CETA job training program in 1980. Like Wade, Joe Cheshire sounds Southern, treats his opponents respectfully, and defends his clients with a ferocious passion masked by an almost deferential politeness.

In the weeks immediately following the incursion, this group did everything it could to find out the motivation behind the raid, what the prosecutors had been looking for, and how we might be able to resolve the situation without an indictment. Wade Smith and Joe Cheshire both knew people in the Eastern North Carolina Federal District U.S. Attorney's Office in

Raleigh, and they did their best to learn what they could from Sam Currin, the U.S. attorney there, and from Douglas McCullough on Currin's staff. But we were still not clear whether the prosecutors intended to indict us in North Carolina under the federal jurisdiction in Raleigh, in North Carolina under state jurisdiction in Alamance County or elsewhere, or under federal jurisdiction in Utah.

What we didn't know at the time was that George Hunt, the district attorney of Alamance County, was getting impatient with the federal authorities. It slowly emerged that an indictment in Alamance County, under the North Carolina state obscenity laws, was likely to happen sooner than any federal action.

We met repeatedly with our team of attorneys. Sometimes we met in Wade's office in Raleigh, sometimes in Dave's in Chapel Hill, sometimes at the Adam & Eve offices. We also engaged Winston-Salem lawyer Fred Harwell to represent our nonmanagement employees, particularly those who had been subpoenaed during the raid to appear before the federal grand jury in Raleigh.

We speculated about who might be indicted. I was particularly concerned about the possible indictment of other senior-level people; I had made a point of seeing to it that several of our senior managers had become stockholders in our privately held company, a step which had seemed generous and appropriate at the time, but which I now feared would give them a higher profile and invite individual prosecution. I would be at the top of the list, and maybe that would provide some cover for them.

Spring turned to summer with no indictments. Three months after the raid, in August, I was hiking in New Hampshire with Harriet Lesser, my wife-to-be. We had made our way across the top of Mount Washington, which is subject to drastic turns of weather, and had an exhilarating weekend. From a phone booth outside a 7-Eleven along Highway 16, I called Wade Smith. While Harriet and I had been braving the elements on Mount Washington, Wade had stayed in close touch with the DA's office in Alamance as well as with the federal authorities. He came on the line right away, which was very unusual for him and which I took to be a bad sign. I was right. In his reassuring but no-longer-cheerful tone, he reported that indictments had been handed down in Alamance County.

My heart sank. "How many indictments?" I asked.

"Nine."

My heart sank even further. I assumed this meant that a total of nine employees would undergo prosecution. I was mercifully wrong about that; the nine indictments referred to nine separate Adam & Eve videos and magazines, and it was only I, individually, and PHE, as a corporation, that would be prosecuted. While I was hardly pleased to be in the center of the radar, I was relieved that all of the other employees, including Vice President A. C. Bushnell, Operations Manager Skip Loy (who had opened the door that day), and Marketing Director Anne Busenburg, would be spared the status of indictee, at least for this round. I was to be charged with nine felony counts of disseminating obscenity, one count for each of five videos and four magazines. The penalties, laid end-to-end, totaled forty-five years in jail, plus fines.

Wade informed me that the Alamance County district attorney,* George Hunt, had agreed that I could appear voluntarily to accept service of the indictments and be processed early the following month. This would be a formal procedure at which I would be charged with the commission of a crime and fingerprinted and photographed, all unpleasant symbolic procedures that I was told were of little long-term consequence unless one is found guilty by a jury, or pleads guilty, which I had no intention of doing. I knew that accused criminals are sometimes brought to such events in handcuffs and at times not of their choosing, so it was apparently something of a concession on George Hunt's part to let Wade and me appear voluntarily in at least a moderately civilized way. (It didn't seem like such a great concession at the time.)

I remember vividly the events of that day. Wade Smith is one of the finest men I know, one of the best courtroom defense attorneys in the state of North Carolina and perhaps in the United States, a man with a distinguished shock of thick white hair and a courtly demeanor of Southern charm and accent. He is also enormously funny and wise about the ways of human behavior. But he is chronically late. So I stood waiting in our parking lot as twenty, then thirty, minutes past the scheduled time went by. I paced, kicked rocks, and mumbled obscenities about Southern punctuality. I could not drive to the courthouse on my own for two reasons: it is essential to be represented by an attorney at such events, or so I assumed, and I didn't know where to go. As the minutes ticked by my visions grew more vivid. A paddy wagon would pull up at any minute, and I would be clamped into leg irons and marched off in front of all our employees. At the very least, our tardiness would mean no more concessions, no negotiating about terms for the trial, or its date or circumstances. I even became sure that Hunt would ask for a longer sentence than he might have had we been decently on time.

At last Wade pulled up in his Porsche, apologized perfunctorily, and we headed for Graham. For once, I was grateful for his predilection for fancy cars and fast driving. But I was both furious with him and at the same time utterly dependent on him for getting through this ordeal. Though the delay did not

---

*Alamance is adjacent to Orange County; our offices were in Orange. The Orange County district attorney was Carl Fox, the man I had consulted.

seem to matter at all to the police who conducted the subsequent procedures that day, I remained angry with Wade Smith for weeks.

The county police had located their photography equipment well inside the Alamance County jail, so that by design or not indictees would be required to walk past some of the worst prison cells I have seen either in person or on film. That day one of these dank cells was occupied by a mentally ill man, talking pathetically to himself and to the walls. Did I only imagine that the police officer who conducted me along this route was grinning? No doubt he meant to show me the sort of treatment I could expect if I chose to fool with the law in Alamance County. (While this struck me as cheap theatrics, I was so appalled by the conditions in the jail that I contacted the prison program people at the North Carolina Civil Liberties Union a few days later and sent a contribution to help them do whatever they could to improve conditions there. I was told that the Alamance jails were no worse than many others in the state.)

I was duly fingerprinted and photographed. Would these procedures affect my citizenship? My place in society? Even though the local press had not been unfriendly, even though I believed the charges against me to be preposterously unfounded, the very fact of having been charged made me feel vulnerable and isolated.

We were now to be confronted by a band of powerful true believers who were not only convinced that they were wise and right, but were determined to prove it through prosecution and trial. I knew their wisdom was deeply flawed, but I also knew they had the might of the Federal Justice Department behind them.

NOTES

1. Melinda Ruley, "Trouble in Paradise, Making a Federal Case Out of Adam & Eve's Sex Toys," *Chapel Hill (N.C.) Independent Weekly*, March 27, 1991, p. 8.

2. Sean Rowe, "A Long Way From Eden. Adam & Eve Challenges Porn Law," *Phoenix Student Newsweekly* (Chapel Hill, N.C.), November 13, 1986, p. 4.

3. Ruley, "Trouble in Paradise," p. 9.

CHAPTER TWO

IS PORNOGRAPHY HARMFUL?

S tatesville (N.C.) *Record & Landmark*, October 30, 1990:

PORNOGRAPHY PROBLEM TARGETED BY CAMPAIGN

Gov. James G. Martin has proclaimed Oct. 28–Nov. 4 as "Pornography Awareness Week." . . .

Gov. Martin's proclamation stresses how "pornography undermines our standards of decency, destroys the moral fabric of our society and does irreparable harm to individuals, families, and the general public.

"Pornography inflicts tremendous suffering and damage on individuals, families, children, marriages, business districts, and the nation," the proclamation states. "Pornography can even be blamed for the increase of sexual assaults on children by other children who imitate what they see.

"To satisfy their compulsion, those addicted to pornography degrade, abuse, and violate other men, women, and children."

Mormon Elder Dallin H. Oaks, September 6, 1973:

Pornography or erotic stories and pictures are worse than filthy or polluted food. The body has defenses to rid itself of unwholesome food. With a few fatal exceptions, bad food will only make you sick but do no permanent harm. In contrast, a person who feasts upon filthy stories or pornographic or erotic pictures and literature records them in [the] . . . brain. The brain won't vomit back filth. Once recorded it will always remain subject to recall, flashing its perverted images across your mind and drawing you away from the wholesome things in life.[1]

Spencer W. Kimball, president of the Church of Jesus Christ of Latter-Day Saints, 1982:

> Each person must keep himself clean and free from lusts. He must shun ugly, polluted thoughts and acts as he would an enemy. Pornography and erotic stories and pictures are worse than polluted food.[2]

Midwest Center for Psychotherapy and Sex Therapy
426 South Yellowstone Drive
Madison, Wisconsin

February 1, 1994

Philip D. Harvey, President PHE, Inc.
P.O. Box 400
Carrboro, N.C. 27510

Dear Mr. Harvey:
. . . The issue of sexual images and potential harmfulness to adults from their use has been the subject of extensive scientific inquiry. . . . In an effort to examine these issues under the rigor of science rather than the potential hazards of emotion, hundreds of experiments have been conducted at universities in the United States and other countries. . . .

The overwhelming conclusion of this research is that nonviolent, noncoercive sexual depictions, regardless of their explicitness, are not harmful to normal adult viewers, whether viewers are exposed to motion picture or print media, over extended periods of time or only briefly. This type of material generally results in no negative behavioral or attitudinal change in normal adult[s]. . . .

However, when violence or coercion is depicted with sexual content, some negative effects are seen in some viewers. Interestingly, when the violence and coercion are removed, the effects on adults from viewing these materials become neutral or mildly positive. These positive effects include an increase in the likelihood that viewers will talk about sex (a generally positive effect since most sexual partners benefit from these discussions), an increase for a day or so in the likelihood of sexual behavior which is within the range of normal sexual behavior for that viewer (a benefit due to the pleasure generally derived from such experiences), and the introduction of medically and relationally safe variety into couples' sexual interactions, something many long-term couples find helpful in maintaining sexual interest and pleasure in their relationships.

. . . There is a strong consensus among those familiar with the scientific literature on this topic. Perhaps ninety percent of qualified professionals agree with the preponderance of [the] literature which concludes the findings described above.

Sincerely,
Lloyd G. Sinclair, MSSW, ACSW

Lloyd Sinclair is certified as a sex therapist, sex educator, and supervisor by the 1,900-member American Association of Sex Educators, Counselors, and Therapists (AASECT). He is a member of the Academy of Certified Social Workers. In short, Sinclair is an expert on the subject of sexuality. Among other things, he knows, from firsthand experience with patients, how human sexual impulses can go wrong. He founded the Wisconsin Sex Offender Treatment Network, an organization that trains mental health clinicians to evaluate and treat sex offenders. The board of directors of this group includes Milwaukee Roman Catholic Archbishop Rembert Weakland; the director of the Wisconsin Department of Corrections Michael Sullivan; District Attorney Philip Koss; and the commander of the Sensitive Crimes Division of the Milwaukee Police Department, Darrel Rodgers. Sinclair himself has supervised the treatment of and counseled sex offenders—rapists, pederasts, and others who abuse through sexual means. Because he also treats sexual assault victims, he understands the tragic consequences of human sexuality gone wrong.

His conclusion about nonviolent adult pornography is that it is harmless, benign, and useful.

Who is right, then? Do the devastating indictments of "pornography" in Governor Martin's proclamation, or the teachings of the Mormon Church, refer only to the comingling of violent and sexual images of the kind that trouble Lloyd Sinclair? Unfortunately, they do not. The uneasiness, fear, and general condemnation of pornography by millions of Americans seems instead to be based on a matter of faith or instinct, something we just "know" to be true; somehow, explicit sexual images *must* be harmful. Although a substantial body of evidence demonstrates that nonviolent sexual depictions are benign, this finding simply does not register with most people. If it does register, they often dismiss it as irrelevant.

People who are most vehemently opposed to erotica usually prefer to believe that most sexually explicit material is violent and degrading. Yet the majority of sexually explicit materials being produced by the adult film and video industry in the United States has generally been of the kind that is nonviolent and nondegrading. Today PHE reviews more than seven hundred feature videos from the adult industry every year, and no more than 3 or 4 percent of them contain coercion or other such violent or degrading material that triggers a rejection by our reviewers. Indeed, erotic videos are among the *least* violent of American filmed entertainment.

Why do so many Americans maintain that all pornography must be harmful? Why is it so difficult for this subject to be rationally examined, and for the results of those examinations to be accepted? Here I address only those issues immediately confronted by PHE's managers, who have had to decide what their company would sell. In deciding what choices to make for a business, consulting objective experts makes more sense than accepting the views of those who simply "believe" that erotica is wrong. In selecting our products, we therefore have turned to sexuality professionals like Lloyd Sinclair and others with credible expertise in the field of human sexuality, just as we might have done in other controversial business fields.

We knew that those items of our merchandise that contain sexually explicit or other strong sexual components would be controversial. "Do we want to do this?" was a question that came up frequently, and the feelings of those of us running the business were often in conflict. On one hand, our customers clearly wanted sexually oriented material. On the other hand, we all had certain reservations, all the way from the what-does-your-mother-think? syndrome to possible legal implications to all the negative noise that is associated with sex and sex products in our culture. All of these had to be weighed in the balance. For example, I am sure that a great many talented people have passed up an opportunity to work for PHE, as many do (on a much larger scale, I think) for cigarette companies and other firms that sell controversial merchandise. The difference, strongly felt by many employees at PHE, is that our products do no harm, and indeed, seem to be of real benefit, while smoking cigarettes kills several hundred thousand people every year. I know several Adam & Eve copywriters and artists (who have, among other things, wondrously expanded the list of English terms for human genitalia and sexual intercourse), who would refuse to write copy promoting cigarettes unless their families were verging on starvation.

The grounds for our decisions about product content have been judiciously rational, I believe. While sexual depictions that exceed the guidelines set out in Lloyd Sinclair's letter might in fact be harmless when it comes to actions rather than attitudes (as the evidence suggests they generally are), the very controversiality of our product line, as well as the compelling legal issues, suggested strongly that we continue meeting our consumers' stated expectations and demands (statements very clear in the pattern of products they chose to buy) while at the same time censoring ourselves to the extent that our offerings would include only material that would meet the professional guidelines we had sought. We would sell only sexual depictions that portrayed persons who freely chose to participate in sexual situations without force, coercion, or any circumstance where one could not give consent freely. In other words, while we didn't believe in the censorship of any information or utterance,★ we accepted the fact that the controversial nature of sex and sexualia dictated certain compromises.

We decided to screen our materials strictly in accordance with the above guidelines, supported by the more than a dozen outside expert reviewers who have taken part in our review process since we established it in 1987. Not only does adherence to this standard assure a high degree of legal protection, it also makes it possible for us to feel good about our product line, to be proud of what we sell. This is a crucial component of the generally high level of morale among our three hundred employees and makes possible our relatively philosophical imperviousness to the onslaughts of those who disagree, often very vociferously, with our position on these issues. These objectors include numerous folks who call our business on the telephone and can sometimes make our phone operators' workday emotionally stressful.

EROTICA, PORNOGRAPHY, OBSCENITY

Standards and definitions in this area are elusive. The only relevant term with a formal definition is "obscenity" as defined by the Supreme Court under the 1973 *Miller* v. *California* decision (described more fully in chapter 3). According to *Miller*, obscenity is a form of expression that is legally unprotected by the First Amendment and contains depictions of sexual activity that are "patently offensive to contemporary community standards." Taken as a whole, the material must be found to appeal to a "prurient" interest, meaning an unnatural or morbid interest in sex, and must be judged to be without lit-

---

★There are exceptions. The "imminent danger" proscriptions laid down by the Supreme Court analogous to shouting "fire" in a crowded theater and laws prohibiting libel and slander, designed to harm other persons are, in my opinion, among the acceptable restrictions on free speech in a free society.

erary, artistic, scientific, or political value. Any sexual depiction that meets all these tests, at a jury trial, is illegal.

Pornography, on the other hand, is simply material designed to elicit a sexual response. The word might conceivably be applied to everything from lingerie to the cover of *Cosmopolitan*, but the term has taken on a derisive meaning in American culture. Nadine Strossen notes that "the word 'pornography' has assumed such negative connotations that it tends to be used as an epithet to describe—and condemn—whatever sexually oriented expression the person using it dislikes."[3] Marjorie Heins amplifies: "Sometimes people try to distinguish between pornography (naughty, ugly, no redeeming value, leering or prurient in character) and erotica (nice, arty, more middle-class, not prurient but open and wholesome). . . . In short, pornography is anything with sexual content that you disapprove of; erotica is sexual material that's okay."[4] Others have defined pornography to include only those kinds of sexual depictions involving the coercion/degradation of participants, reserving the terms erotica or adult entertainment for describing the kinds of depictions of cheerfully consenting adults sold by PHE and approved by reviewers certified by the American Association of Sex Educators, Counselors, and Therapists.

I will not belabor these definitions. I use many terms for sexual depictions in this book and have titled this chapter "Is Pornography Harmful?" because of the common usage of that term in our society and because those who believe all sexual depictions to be harmful invariably refer to sexual depictions as pornographic. When referring to the sexual content of material generally sold by PHE (nonviolent, nondegrading), I prefer the terms "adult video," "X-rated video," and the more generalized "sexually oriented material."

EARLY DAYS

Our mailing of sexually oriented products had begun in 1970 with selling condoms by mail. I was working toward my master's degree in family planning administration in the School of Public Health at the University of North Carolina in Chapel Hill. As part of my thesis work, I obtained permission from the university to experiment with the mail-order sale of condoms as part of an effort to find new ways of delivering contraceptives outside clinic-based networks.

My interest in "nonclinical" contraceptives was shared by Tim Black, a British physician who had just spent several years working in the jungles of Papua New Guinea and in rural areas of Nigeria. Tim and I had met during our first weeks in Chapel Hill and we were very excited about discovering ways of promoting family planning outside and beyond the hospitals and clinics that were providing those services in the United States. His conviction had arisen from his work in Asia and Africa, where he had observed the utter dearth of clinic and hospital facilities, the inability of medical facilities generally to meet family planning needs, and the fact that the very few medical facilities in developing countries were swamped with treating emergency cases of illness and injury. Given this, they could not conceivably provide adequate contraceptive services to millions of healthy couples who could hardly be expected to wait in line or travel long distances for such services, something people are willing to do only when motivated by pain or illness.

By 1970 my own background had included five years with CARE in India, where I had taken part in a massive program to provide lunches for school and preschool children. Every year we increased the size of the program, but every year we could see that there was more and more left undone. It became increasingly clear to me that providing family planning services would likely be a far more efficacious way to assist low-income Indians than bringing in thousands of tons of food which, in any event, competed with locally produced food and tended to depress local farmers' prices, just one more of those unintended consequences of well-meaning foreign assistance.

So when Tim and I met in North Carolina a real spark was struck. We were both excited about the prospects for nonmedical family planning. Tim had the medical credentials to credibly describe the limitations of the clinic/hospital approach to family planning, I had five years of administrative experience in the developing world, and we were both fired up to sell the "commercial" marketing approach to family planning to the donor community, those government and nongovernment organizations in the business of funding such programs and initiatives. Western government donors were just then beginning to support national family planning programs, and we were convinced that they would support this approach. We focused on a system for disseminating birth control called "social marketing," which had first been tried just two years before in India. The idea was to provide contraceptives that are packaged and branded just like any other consumer goods product, heavily advertised through mass media, and made available through commercial distribution and retailing networks, but at very low, subsidized prices that virtually anyone can afford. The result, when this approach works (and it has worked remarkably well) is that affordable contraceptives are available in nearly every little shop and store in developing countries, just like Coca-Cola and Lipton tea and beer and soap. We have subsequently succeeded in promoting, funding, and managing a large number of these social marketing programs in numerous developing countries, a story told in another book.[5]

We wanted to start with mail-order condoms. No condoms were being sold by mail in the United States because it was illegal. The notorious morals crusader Anthony Comstock had succeeded in codifying a federal law in 1873 that declared contraception and all information about contraception (and abortion) as "obscene" and therefore unmailable through the U.S. postal system. The absurdity of such a law was clear on its face, but it did call for several years of prison for those found guilty of this count, 18 U.S.C. 1461 (124.42, Postal Manual). Tim and I consulted several attorneys, including Planned Parenthood lawyers, who assured us, lawyerlike, that this law had been construed so as not to prohibit the mailing of literature and contraceptives "for a lawful purpose." No one was absolutely sure what a lawful purpose was, however. In the recently decided (1965) case of *Griswold* v. *Connecticut*, the U.S. Supreme Court had declared unconstitutional a state law which forbade the sale of contraceptives to married couples. Therefore it seemed clear that we could violate with impunity the federal Comstock Law if we were mailing our condoms only to married couples (i.e., lawful purpose). But of course there would be no way to be sure whether our customers were married or not, and, in any event, it was our avowed intent to make contraceptives more available to young unmarried people in an effort to stem what even then was a near epidemic of out-of-wedlock teenage pregnancies.

The Planned Parenthood lawyers took great care, as lawyers should, to warn us of the dire consequences should we be found guilty of violating this law, and Tim spent some long hours thinking about his wife and two young daughters and how they might fare if he should be thrown in the slammer (I had no wife or children at the time). In the end, the risk seemed reasonable, and we decided to go ahead.

Since that day I have several times asked myself if our start in the mail-order business in the face of such an inane and obviously outdated law has had any effect on my subsequent willingness to take legal risks. It is certainly true that dealing with a draconian federal law which, on its face, was so clearly deserving of being flouted has had some effect on my disrespectful attitude toward bad laws generally, particularly bad laws by which the government tries to prescribe "moral" behavior for us all. But while it is no doubt true that the existence of bad and selectively enforced laws has a tendency to spread contempt for all laws, it is also clear that reasonable people are well able to distinguish between bad laws that attempt to dictate private consensual behavior and those that are necessary for the conduct of a civilized and reasonably orderly society.

Because the Comstock Law had deterred virtually everyone else from selling condoms through the mail, we found a ready market. We began by

SEX IS YOUR BUSINESS
(BIRTH CONTROL IS OURS)

We believe you're entitled to your privacy when it comes to buying contraceptives. We're a nonprofit family planning agency and we offer you contraceptives through the privacy of the mails. We specialize in men's products (including two new European imports)—but we have nonprescription foam for women, too. And a wide assortment of books and pamphlets to answer your questions on birth control, family planning, the population problem and ecology. Want details? Write today:

105 N. Columbia St., Dept. F-2   , Chapel Hill, N. C. 27514

Gentlemen: Please send me full details without obligation:

Name_____

Address_____

City_____ State_____ Zip_____

WHAT WILL YOU GET HER THIS CHRISTMAS—

PREGNANT??

Don't. We've made it easy for you to get men's contraceptives privately. We're a nonprofit agency and we offer quality condoms—nationally known and luxury imports—through the privacy of the mails. We have British brands which are superior to anything at the corner drugstore. And, in keeping with the season, we've put together the world's first gift sampler of men's contraceptives. It contains three each of seven different brands in a handsome, tasteful package for only $9.50. Give yourself a little variety or give a friend something unique: PSI's exclusive contraceptive sampler.

105 N. Columbia St., Dept. G8   , Chapel Hill, N. C. 27514

Gentlemen: Please send me:
_____gift samplers in a plain wrapper at $9.50 each (remittance enclosed)
_____complete information about your services at no obligation

I understand that I may return any PSI products if I am not satisfied with their quality for a full refund.

Name_____

Address_____

City_____ State_____ Zip_____

Can we send a gift in your name?

Figure 2-1. Early ads for mail-order contraceptives were clever, but not as effective as "Condoms By Mail," which came later.

placing two-by-three-inch couponed ads (Fig. 2-1) in college newspapers, and the orders came pouring in. We had a wonderful time with headlines ("What Will You Get Her This Christmas, Pregnant?"; "Sex Is Your Business, Birth Control Is Ours") and, without any training or experience in the business world, we were nonetheless able to register the fact that there was more money coming in than going out. Neither Tim nor I had intended to turn my thesis work into a business enterprise, but it seemed too good to walk away from.

We incorporated as Population Planning Associates (thus separating the mail-order business from the nonprofit Population Services, Inc.), and began to place mail-order condom ads in some national magazines like *Penthouse* and *True*, and were on our way. Tim, accompanied by his wife and daughters, went to Africa to start our first PSI social marketing family planning project in Kenya, and then returned to England to found another international family planning organization, Marie Stopes International. Family planning in developing countries has continued to interest and to occupy both Tim and me during the twenty-five years since. Much of my share of the profits from PHE's* mail-order sales has gone to support these family planning and AIDS-prevention programs in such countries as Ethiopia, India, Vietnam, and China.

Meanwhile I frantically read business books, and particularly books about mail order. The best one was, and still is, Julian Simon's *How to Start and Operate a Mail-Order Business.*[6] It appeared that we had already done the

*Population Planning Associates was changed to PHE, Inc., in 1982.

hardest part of starting a mail-order business, identifying a product that could bring in large numbers of new customers from magazine and newspaper ads at an acceptably low cost—customers who could then be offered a variety of other products for more profitable back-end sales. We recognized early that selling half-gross boxes of Trojans to college fraternities (there were quite a few of those) would not support a rapidly growing business indefinitely and that we would need a much broader product line.

We began with books and publications about contraception and reproductive physiology. While some of these were fairly explicit in their descriptions and depictions of genitalia and the reproductive process, they lacked what some refer to as "below-the-belt" appeal; they did not elicit a sexual response. Then one day we included a couple of erotic magazines with some soft-focus nudity, and sales took off.

"The customer is always right" has been a business axiom for centuries. And even in the seventies management gurus and mail-order experts were already stressing what has by now become a mantra. "Listen to the customer" was the message we read and heard everywhere we looked. And that is exactly what we did.

We began adding more and more books and magazines with erotic content, taking care to include material we believed would appeal to both men and women.

We also tried nonsexual merchandise. We offered fashion accessories for men, leather belts and fancy belt buckles, ship-building and airplane-building kits, digital watches and clocks, and a variety of women's leisurewear in addition to lingerie. The lingerie sold pretty well; the other leisurewear did not. Nor did the belts, clocks, or ship-building kits. It became increasingly clear over those first years that people who bought condoms by mail expected other products related to sex. We saw no reason not to respond to this interest.

The advent of the VCR in the early eighties presented a new and compelling way of putting sexual images in front of interested customers, and the video cassette containing sexually oriented depictions quickly became one the mainstays of our business. Condoms continued to sell, and in the mid-1990s we were selling 3 to 4 million condoms a year. But by then that was only a small portion of the overall business.

Our move into explicit sexual materials, including video cassettes, was unaccompanied by adequate review and thought. To be blunt, I just didn't pay enough attention to the kinds of portrayals that began finding their way into our inventory. There had been few high-profile prosecutions for obscenity, and, without really thinking it through, neither I nor my fellow managers could see anything wrong with providing material that responded to some of the kinkier interests of our customers. A few bondage magazines crept into our offerings.

This too-casual policy toward the content of our materials ended in 1987. Partly in response to the raid in 1986 and our understanding that federal authorities had been reviewing our materials in great detail, and partly because we realized that our policies in this area were overdue for review anyway, we spent long hours with our team of attorneys and with experts like Lloyd Sinclair to ascertain the best ways to screen our material to make sure that nothing we sold was either harmful or illegal. In accordance with the Supreme Court's *Miller* standard, we wanted to be as sure as we could that the representatives of even conservative communities would not find our material "prurient," "patently offensive," and/or lacking in scientific, literary, artistic, or political value.

Fortuitously, the interests of the sexuality experts and the tests applied to define obscenity under the *Miller* decision coincided very substantially. This had become clear to me at an early stage when our local district attorney in Orange County, North Carolina,* Carl Fox, had provided to video stores, record stores, and book and magazine outlets, as well as our mail-order company a carefully drawn set of prosecution guidelines. He had done this shortly after the North Carolina obscenity statute was changed in late 1985 so that it closely coincided with the Supreme Court guidelines under *Miller*. Mr. Fox intended his guidelines to let retailers know that there were certain kinds of sexual depictions he would likely prosecute, the implication being that he would not "kick down doors" going after materials that did not fall under these special definitions. His list of materials that we should all avoid included anything involving underaged performers (an area we had always vigorously avoided in any case), sexual activity that showed sexual gratification from sadomasochistic behavior or from any combination of sex and excretory functions, and bestiality (see appendix A). These proscriptions coincided pretty much with our policies except for those few bondage titles that had crept in, and on Mr. Fox's advice we removed those.

In most important respects, these guidelines and the interpretation by our lawyers of the directives in *Miller* coincided remarkably well with Lloyd Sinclair's descriptions of troublesome material. The areas to be avoided were areas where sex was in any way mixed with force or coercion (or even lack of visible consent) on the part of any participant. The other categories, for the most part, had always been off-limits for us anyway.

The result of this was a review procedure in which all of our sexual materials—"expressive materials," as the lawyers term them, meaning visual or aural depictions—were to be sent for review to a minimum of two qualified sex ther-

---

*Orange County contains Chapel Hill (our starting address), nearby Carrboro (our interim location), and Hillsborough, our present site.

apists/counselors for review. If either of these sexuality experts found anything which they could not comfortably certify as benign from their point of view as therapists and counselors, that item would be rejected and never offered for sale. Consequently, since early 1987 our materials have consisted exclusively of sexual depictions of what I describe as cheerfully consenting adults. It depicts cheerful people engaged in mutually consensual activity in which men and women participate as equals, celebrating their sexuality and enjoying it.

When we confine our attention to this type of sexual material, the question "Is Pornography Harmful?" is relatively easy to answer: It is not.

ISSUES OF HARM

In assessing the potential impact of sexual materials on individuals and on society it is well to consider certain features in American society that we know to be harmful. Here is a list of elements and the varying degrees of harm they cause:

Deaths Per Annum Caused By:	
Cigarettes	400,000
Alcohol	105,000
Automobiles	49,000
Handguns	8,900
Lightning Strikes	45
Pornography	0

Cigarette-related deaths: U.S. Centers for Disease Control. Alcohol-related deaths: L. Heise, *World Watch* magazine, (July/August 1991). Automobile-related deaths: 1988 statistics, *U.S. Commerce Department Statistical Abstract*, 1991. Handgun-related deaths (homicides only): 1988 statistics, *New York Times*, December 9, 1990. Lightning strikes: 1987 statistics, *Journal of Intensive Care Medicine* (November/December 1988).

America prides itself on being a free society, and we do not want our government to so patronize us that we cannot engage in activities that are risky. We do not wish to be protected from ourselves by laws threatening fines or imprisonment for actions that do not affect other people.* We therefore permit the sale and use of cigarettes and of automobiles and of handguns

---

*As abolitionist Wendell Phillips reminded us two centuries ago, the price of liberty is "eternal vigilance." There are many laws and regulations that *do* puerilize Americans, from mandating censoring chips in our TV sets, to the size of plums we may buy and sell in the marketplace, to dangerous overregulation of useful drugs. Government always tends to bloat; its power over our lives always tends to increase. Working to prevent such encroachments is a full-time job.

(within narrowing limits) because we believe a free people should be free to do things even if those things are risky or harmful to themselves, so long as they do not harm others in the process. We permit dangerous sports like hang gliding and rock climbing because a free society lets people take risks. And we permit love, which, as Milos Forman pointed out in a speech at the National Press Club in 1997, can be very harmful indeed:

> . . . a study of human social history will unarguably disclose that one of our most noble emotions—love—has prompted more damage, more violence, more suicides, even more murders than can ever be ascribed to pornography. So, should we blame "Romeo and Juliet" or "West Side Story" every time an unhappy lover loses control and does something damaging because of the unbearable pain of love in his heart? Should we call on Hollywood to stop making these kinds of movies?[7]

In this context, it is difficult to understand the outlawing of explicit sexual depictions which, on the basis of a massive body of evidence, impose no harm on anyone at all.

JURIES

The ludicrousness of our obscenity laws, at least insofar as they are designed to prevent the dissemination of harmful materials, is revealed perhaps most starkly by our jurisprudential process on obscenity. Hundreds of juries, formed by thousands of ordinary adult Americans, have been convened over the years to decide whether or not some work is legally obscene. Since 1974 the law has required that jurors, ordinary people like you and me, be required to read putatively obscene books in their entirety or to peruse magazines from front cover to back cover, or, as in the case of the PHE trial (to be described in chapter 3), watch closely from beginning to end several hours of sexually explicit videotapes. The law requires that indicted materials be "taken as a whole" and not simply judged on the basis of single excerpts. This process reveals a singularly ironic bit of societal hypocrisy. The prosecutor, who is responsible for the convening of the jury and the compulsory reviewing process, is saying to American society that (a) we are indicting this sexually oriented material because we believe it is harmful to individuals and to society, but (b) it is not really harmful for we are going to compel you jurors to read or observe or view all of it from beginning to end and we are confident that you will not be harmed in the process.[8] This combination of facts makes one wonder if the prosecution of obscenity and the use of coercive government force to suppress "pornography" is an attempt to prevent harm to individuals or if it is instead an attempt to impose the moral beliefs of some citizens upon all.

GOVERNMENT COMMISSIONS

In addition to juries, numerous commissions have been convened by governments to reach conclusions and provide policy recommendations on pornography and obscenity. The participants in these commissions subject themselves to hundreds of hours of viewing all kinds of sexual depictions. The Meese Commission on Pornography, convened by the Reagan administration's attorney general, Edwin Meese, in 1986, was particularly selective of the kinds of materials it chose to view, focusing on the most dreadful forms of violent and kinky sexual activity. Park Dietz's impassioned statement preceding the commission's findings, a statement adopted by a majority of the commissioners prior to the release of the report, asserted that he had "no hesitation in condemning nearly every specimen of pornography that we have examined in the course of our deliberations as tasteless, offensive, lewd, and indecent."[9] But nowhere in the six-hundred-page report of this commission do we find even a hint that any of the eleven commissioners, subjected as they were to so many excruciating hours of "obscene" and "immoral" sexual depictions, were themselves in any way harmed by the process.[10]

It is difficult not to conclude that these commissions are telling us, "You are little children. We can watch all nature of horrific sexual depictions without it harming us. But you are not so strong as we. Therefore, we are going to recommend laws which protect you from the dire consequences that might result from *your* viewing pornographic material."

WHAT ABOUT (REAL) CHILDREN?

No studies have been done about the impact of exposing children to explicit sexual materials for the simple reason that most Americans believe such exposure *might* actually be harmful. Therefore, I and most responsible people who oppose the criminalization of erotic materials, nonetheless recommend that it be kept out of the hands of children. The harmful items enumerated in the table above—including automobiles, alcohol, and, of course, handguns—pose great danger to children. Children must likewise be protected from drugs and medicines, swimming pools, dangerous precipices, and even stairs. But we cannot operate our society by proscribing for us all everything that is unacceptable for children. We make this distinction routinely in our daily lives, and we should likewise make it for sexually oriented materials. The U.S. Supreme Court has reiterated this point on more than one occasion, most notably in 1983—"The level of discourse reaching a mailbox simply cannot be limited to that which would be suitable for a sandbox"[11]—and in 1989—"[The government may not] reduc[e] the adult population . . . to . . . only what is fit for children."[12] Subsequent Court decisions have reaffirmed this principle.

WHAT ABOUT "SOCIETY"?

Some maintain that even if pornographic images do not harm individuals directly (or at least there seems little evidence that they do), the availability of sexual materials still may degrade and debase our society in some significant way. We have an excellent case study that addresses the prospect that sexually explicit material, if left relatively unrestricted, will flood our communities and ruin the quality of daily life. In 1986 the Supreme Court of the State of Oregon declared that its state constitution forbade the criminalization of any form of speech including sexually explicit speech, excepting only child pornography. With this single stroke, all adult pornography in Oregon was made legal. Five years after this decision, I asked the writer Jean Lawrence to investigate its impact in Oregon. Here is her report, beginning with the background:

> By all accounts Earl Henry's small business was unobtrusive, a small adult bookstore tucked in the conservative, religious community of Redmond, Oregon. No garish displays, no minors allowed.
>
> The police took to raiding the place, seizing on the second try, 73 magazines, 142 paperbacks and nine films. Henry was charged with possession of obscene material under the state laws of Oregon. A jury sent him to jail for 60 days and fined him $1,000.
>
> Henry appealed. The case went to the Oregon Supreme Court. The kicker was that Oregon, in response to standards handed down by the United States Supreme Court, had recently passed a set of anti-obscenity statutes that went beyond the definitions specified by the Oregon Constitution. While the U.S. Constitution prohibits any law "abridging the freedom of speech or of the press," Oregon had gone farther, decreeing: "No law shall be passed restraining the free expression of opinion, or restricting the right to speak, write, or print freely on any subject whatever." In fact, the Oregon

court took pains to note, "Oregon's pioneers had brought with them a diversity of highly moral as well as irreverent views . . . being rugged and robust individuals."

Pretty robust and rugged themselves, the members of the Oregon court, in effect, declared that Oregon law protecting free speech had superseded the wimpier federal statutes. By fiat, the members of the court swept away Oregon's new obscenity statutes. (In the past, Oregon, one of the original states to adjudicate "Deep Throat" and find it not to be obscene, had discontinued the practice of zoning adult bookstores and theatres out of existence and stopped the prohibition of "expressive conduct" in public places. Still in place: statutes on child pornography.)

As for Mr. Henry, he unlocked his bookstore without comment and turned on the cash register.

But, you might ask, what of other stubborn entrepreneurs who might see Oregon as a potentially indulgent site of many another sexually oriented enterprise? Did the overthrow of the state's obscenity's statutes turn Oregon into a modern-day Gomorrah?

"Nothing changed," sums up Rex Armstong of the law firm of Bogle & Gates, who defended Henry. Although federal obscenity statutes remain in effect, he adds, "the climate in Oregon discourages the U.S. Attorney from going after people here. The case removed the possibility of people being harassed."

But won't this permissive climate attract a certain sort?

"We're not prosecuting any cases," agrees John Bradley, first assistant to the Portland district attorney. "We don't have a combat zone, just the usual areas of prostitution," Bradley adds. "And, no, I wouldn't say any more bookstores have opened since the Henry decision."

Donald McClave, head of the Portland Chamber of Commerce, on Henry: "Never heard of it."

The president of the Portland City Council: "No interest."

What's the implication here? That Oregon was already so licentious that repealing the state laws had no effect? No. Oregon has one of the highest standards of literacy in the country and is routinely rated as among the most desirable states to raise a family.

Could it be that the millions of dollars authorities spend every year to investigate, paper, and prosecute obscenity cases in the United States is being misspent, that the demand for adult materials is a matter of individual choice and is more effectively proscribed (if that is deemed desirable) by individual preference than by law?

OTHER OPINIONS

In addition to the available data attesting to the essential harmlessness of sexual depictions from our jury processes, our commissions, and the report about the state of Oregon,* a substantial number of studies have been conducted by governments around the world to ascertain whether or not exposure to sexually explicit materials causes harm by provoking antisocial behavior or otherwise. Their conclusions overwhelmingly have been that nonviolent sexual depictions are harmless.

The most important studies/commissions:

(1) U.S. Commission on Pornography and Obscenity, 1970. "[T]here is no warrant for continued governmental interference with the full freedom of adults to read, obtain or view whatever . . . material they wish."[13]

(2) The Meese Commission, 1985. While generally deploring "pornography," even this heavily biased group conceded that "the totality of the social science evidence . . . is slightly against the hypothesis that nonviolent and nondegrading materials bear a causal relationship to acts of sexual violence."[14]

(2a) Einsiedel Report. The Meese Commission requested Dr. Edna Einsiedel, an expert from the University of Calgary, to conduct an independent review. This review found no link between sexually explicit material and sex crimes, and did not support the conclusions or the policy recommendations that the Meese Commission later made.[15]

(2b) Dr. C. Everett Koop Report. The Commission also asked Surgeon General Koop to gather additional information. Conclusions: The links between pornography and changes in some perceptions, attitudes, and behaviors are "circumscribed, few in number and generally laboratory-based."[16]

(3) Dr. Joseph Scott and Loretta Schwalm, Ohio State University, 1988. These researchers found that rape rates correlate as strongly with the availability of outdoor magazines as with pornography.[17]

(4) Cynthia Gentry, 1991. Dr. Gentry, a researcher at Wake Forest University, found "no evidence of a relationship between popular sex magazines and violence against women."[18]

(5) Fraser Committee Report, 1984 (Canada). "There is no systematic research which suggests that increases in specific forms of deviant

---

*In addition to Oregon, the states of Alaska, Maine, New Mexico, and Vermont have no state obscenity laws (and Hawaii's law is very limited). There appears to be no correlation whatever between the absence or presence of such laws and the quality of civilization.

behavior, reflected in crime trend statistics (e.g., rape) are causally related to pornography."[19]

(6) Williams Committee, 1979 (Britain). "We unhesitatingly reject the suggestion that the available statistical information for England and Wales lends any support to the argument that pornography acts as a stimulus to the commission of sexual violence."[20]

(7) Dr. Berl Kutchinsky (1970, 1984, 1985, 1987, 1991). Retrospective studies in Europe found that sex crimes actually dropped in some cases when pornography became more easily available.[21]

(8) Dr. Milton Diamond, University of Hawaii, 1999. "[F]rom our data and analysis [it is clear] that a massive increase in available pornography in Japan has been correlated with a dramatic *decrease* in sexual crimes and most so among youngsters as perpetrators or victims."[22]

A more complete review of these investigations and findings, including two studies that came to different conclusions, is given in appendix B.

NOTES

1. Dallin H. Oaks, "Challenges for the Year Ahead," speech given at Brigham Young University, September 6, 1973. Quoted in "Statements by Leaders of the Church of Jesus Christ of Latter-Day Saints Concerning Pornography," Brochure, 1986, 1988, Corporation of the President of the Church of Jesus Christ of Latter-Day Saints.

2. Spencer Kimball, *The Teachings of Spencer W. Kimball* (Salt Lake City: BookCraft, 1982). Cited in "Statements by Leaders."

3. Nadine Strossen, *Defending Pornography: Free Speech, Sex, and the Fight for Women's Rights* (New York: Scribner, 1995), p. 18.

4. Marjorie Heins, *Sex, Sin, and Blasphemy: A Guide to America's Censorship Wars* (New York: New Press, 1993), p. 139.

5. Philip Harvey, *Let Every Child Be Wanted: How Social Marketing Is Revolutionizing Contraceptive Use Around the World* (Westport, Conn.: Greenwood Publishing Group, 1999).

6. Julian Simon, *How to Start and Operate a Mail-Order Business* (New York: McGraw-Hill, 1965).

7. Milos Forman, address to the National Press Club, January 31, 1997, National Press Club Speaker Series, 1997, p. 4.

8. One of the prosecutors in our Alamance trial, Zesily Haislip, managed to double-think his way into somehow blaming *us* for the coercive process he and his colleagues had initiated. In his closing argument he told the jurors, "If you consider the pornography you were forced to watch yesterday and this morning, there can't be a reasonable doubt that these defendants are guilty." He failed to mention that it was the prosecution that had done the forcing; we don't think people should be forced to watch any form of entertainment, sexual or otherwise.

9. Attorney General's Commission on Pornography, *Final Report* (Washington, D.C.: U.S. Department of Justice, 1986), p. 51.

10. A wag has suggested that exposure to so much sexual material may sometimes induce a tendency toward financial shenanigans. Antipornographer Charles Keating of the Lincoln Savings and Loan was ousted from his position and subsequently served jail time for financial irregularities with his own institution subsequent to viewing massive amounts of sexually explicit material as a member of the Meese Commission. Keating, ironically, had served on the 1970 commission that had recommended abolishing obscenity laws. Once Keating had realized the direction of that commission's recommendations, he tried to sabotage its findings, going so far as to file a lawsuit to prevent the publication of the 1970 commission report. When the report was finally released, it contained a forty-six page "Keating" dissent which was largely written by a young White House aide named Patrick J. Buchanan. Keating had argued that pornography was "capable of poisoning any mind at any age and of perverting our entire younger generation." The rising tide of obscenity, he argued, was clearly "part of the Communist Conspiracy" (Eric Schlosser, "The American Sex Industry" [unpublished, 1997], p. 32). Keating pleaded guilty to four counts of fraud in 1999, having served more than four years in jail previously ("Keating Pleads Guilty to 4 Counts of Fraud," *New York Times* on the Web, April 7, 1999.).

11. *Bolger v. Youngs Drug Products Corp.* 463 U.S. 60 (1983).

12. *Sable Communications of California, Inc. v. FCC*, 492 U.S. 115 (1989).

13. Commission on Obscenity and Pornography, *The Report of the Commission on Obscenity and Pornography* (Washington, D.C.: U.S. Government Printing Office, 1970), p. 52.

14. Attorney General's Commission, *Final Report*, p. 337.

15. Marcia Pally, *Sense & Censorship: The Vanity of Bonfires. Resource Materials on Sexually Explicit Material, Violent Material, and Censorship: Research and Public Policy Implications*, (New York: Americans for Constitutional Freedom, 1991), p. 13.

16. Report of the Surgeon General's Workshop on Pornography and Public Health, 1986, p. 35. Cited in ibid., p. 13.

17. Marcia Pally, *Sex and Sensibility*, (Hopewell, N.J.: Ecco Press, 1994), pp. 54–55.

18. Ibid.

19. Ibid, pp 57–8.

20. Ibid.

21. Ibid, pp 59–60.

22. Milton Diamond, "The Effects of Pornography: An International Perspective," in *Porn 101*, eds. J. Elias, V. D. Elias, V. L. Bullough, et al. (Amherst, N.Y.: Prometheus Books, 1999).

CHAPTER THREE

THE TRIAL

N otes from the trial:

Monday, March 9, 1987. Today I go on trial here in the Alamance County court-house in Graham. Our defense team is sure that men are better than women on obscenity juries, and most of the people in the jury pool look too old or too female.

The judge has just entered. Court is in session.

Our jury pool is polled; we start with 41 women and 32 men. One woman is excused because she lives in Orange County, one because of her son's surgery, and a man because of medical problems. Now we have 39 women, 31 men.

Could I have run from this? Copped a plea? Not with honor, and not with a sur-viving business. So I am here.

Most lawyers familiar with obscenity cases will tell you that judicious jury selection is more than half the battle. We have taken this very seriously. Pro-vided by the court with the names and addresses of the seventy- or eighty-member jury pool from which our jurors will be drawn, PHE employees have been driving by their homes in the hope of finding bumper stickers and any other clues that might indicate a propensity to tolerance or intolerance about matters sexual. We figure "Save the Whales" on a potential juror's bumper is a good sign; "Abortion is Murder" probably is not so good. Jurors who have a college education probably would be good for our case; it has been found through polling data that people with more education tend to be more tol-erant of what others wish to read and view. Nevertheless, education fre-quently does not correlate with affluence, and education levels cannot be measured from outside a residence.

We will have twelve preemptory challenges—twelve persons we can dis-miss without cause or explanation—and we want to make the best possible use of this privilege. The prosecution will also have twelve preemptory challenges, and the judge may dismiss as many jurors "for cause" as he likes—that is, those who, in his judgment, would not be able to weigh the evidence fairly.

In all, more than eighty jurors will be examined over the space of the first week of the trial. Judge Donald W. Stephens will dismiss more than forty of them for cause. Octavis White, the prosecutor, who is an athletic and professional-looking black man in his midthirties, will exercise ten of his challenges; we will use nine of ours. White is an assistant district attorney with a reputation for efficiency, thoroughness, and fair dealing in this county.

In a state trial in North Carolina, the prosecution and the defense attorneys are permitted to question prospective jurors, a privilege that neither side has in a federal trial, where only the judge may ask questions. The process during which jurors are questioned—voir dire, "to speak truthfully"[1]—is intended to probe for potential jurors' bias so that the jury finally selected will consist of persons who can judge the evidence with open minds. The most obvious causes of bias include an earlier relationship with the defendant or the prosecuting or defense attorneys, or a personal involvement in a situation similar to the one for which the defendant is on trial—no one whose close relative has been shot by a police officer, for example, would be permitted to sit on a jury trying a policeman for a similar crime.

As Judge Stephens will dismiss for cause anyone he believes cannot fairly judge the evidence, it is part of our job to illuminate that propensity in our questioning of the potential jurors who we believe will not be friendly to our side. The intense emotional feelings that people have about sex give us another concern as well; we will do our best to have Judge Stephens dismiss persons who are so uncomfortable with open depictions of sexuality that it causes them serious emotional distress. For example, Judge Stephens dismisses a couple of jurors who say that watching explicit sexual depictions on tape would offend their religious sensibilities. This is a civilized and humane response to a difficult situation, but their dismissal does not, of course, delight the prosecution, who would be happy to have them on the jury.

As our attorney, Joe Cheshire, questions the jurors, he is attempting simultaneously to ascertain any bias they may have against sexual expression and also to accustom them to the idea of watching many hours of sexually explicit videotape. He tells each juror that there will be depictions of oral sex, anal sex, vaginal sex, and group sex. The judge, repeating these descriptions dozens of times over the course of the week, goes through this litany rather fast, and it is clear that some jurors do not understand him. Informed in this style that there will be depictions of "arl-sex-anl-sex-grup-sex," some jurors just nod uncomprehendingly. In examining the potential jurors, Joe does his

Figure 3-1. Jury selection for the Adam & Eve trial was a jolt for some residents of conservative Graham, N.C.

best to make these things clear, as a result of which the local press refers to some of those being questioned as "swooning matrons," and one memorable cartoon depicts several elderly ladies collapsed in a faint outside the courtroom simply from hearing the descriptions of the depictions yet to come (Fig. 3-1).

All this was one more example of the looniness of how human sexuality is perceived in contemporary society. I was on trial with my very freedom at stake; our company, which then employed nearly two hundred people, was on trial and if convicted, could well be put out of business; the prosecutors, scowling intently, were determined to protect what they were maintaining was community decency and public morality; the judge was dedicated to executing even-handed justice; our attorneys were working around the clock to defend us with every fiber of their talent and resources; and, in the midst of all this, the readers of Alamance County newspapers were getting a good chuckle about people being shocked into insensibility by descriptions of explicit sexual depictions in a court of law.

Wade Smith has a particularly good eye for these ironic human dramas. He would later remark that he felt like he was in a Woody Allen movie. It is so unreal. We're talking about looking at pictures of people enjoying sex. And it's the "community standard" that must prevail. How can anyone know what the community standard is—how his neighbors feel about these subjects? You don't know how the 103,000 Alamance County residents feel about oral sex. This is just not the type of thing neighbors talk over when one is washing the car and another planting tomatoes.

Despite the levity of some of these descriptions, I was not smiling at the time—far from it. Every step of this process was a matter of intense concern and acute anxiety to me. Every potential juror who might conceivably be hostile to our situation, particularly if he or she might be forceful enough to influence other jurors, was a cause of real anguish.

Whether one can get rid of an unfriendly juror for "cause" becomes increasingly important. If, confronted by a potential juror we know would be bad for our side, we can bring out his or her bias sufficiently so that the judge will dismiss him for cause, then we do not have to "burn one"—that is, use one of our twelve preemptory challenges. Where the judge cannot be convinced of a potential juror's bias, but we are convinced that the juror will be more supportive of the prosecution, we have to use up one of our precious twelve challenges. Octavis White, of course, is faced with the same predicament.

Notes from the trial:

We're losing good ones. Two young men who know a couple of our employees — lost! Damn. His aunt and uncle work for us. . . . Now Octavis is knocking off another one of our good young men with a preemptory challenge. Here's another regular church-goer, church treasurer, Sunday school teacher, believes all sexual depictions are bad. God! But she's honest. Admits her own bias, says she couldn't be fair. Excused by the court. Halleluia.

Mr. ____. Taciturn. Sells VCRs but doesn't own one. Sells satellite systems. Saw some portion of a satellite film with explicit sex acts. Was there penetration? Yes, sir. Oral sex? Yes, sir. Anal sex? No, sir. Did he have an opinion about this case? "To some degree, yes, sir." Would it cause him to not be fair and impartial in this case? "I don't think so, sir." If he was shown four to five hours of sexually explicit tapes, could he view all that material and keep an open mind? "Yes, sir. Since it is the law, I think I would have to go with the law." Now comes Octavis White's list; he rattles off: vaginal intercourse, anal intercourse, oral intercourse, masturbation, group sex; O.W. is really helping us do our work. He's reading his list aggressively. We will have to decide about this Mr. ____. He's holding his ground.

Two potential jurors are so biased against pornography that they admit that they cannot be fair; two are so biased in our favor that they feel they can't be fair. Could this happen in any other kind of trial? This demonstrates dramatically the many separate "communities" the county contains.

Another young man—dismissed for cause. We think he was on our side, but he put "guilty" on his questionnaire, prejudging the case. We think he didn't know what the term meant. He has two close relatives employed at PHE. Judge dismisses him on the basis that "if you have an opinion about the case that it would be difficult for you to put aside [in rendering a judgment], it would not be appropriate for you to serve."

Prospective juror #29, a male. Never married. Has lived in Caswell and in Orange County. Deep voice. Works for Pine Hill Cemetery. Mebane Hosiery. Sweet Grove Church. Attends church "just whenever I get the mood." Saw X-rated film six or seven years ago. "In theaters, but never in a home. What people do behind closed doors" is OK. He'd be good. O.W. will probably let him go. At least he won't get him for cause (I think). But now he is going too far. "I don't think I could sit in judgment. I don't think I could be [fair]." Damn. Says he'd use his personal feelings instead of the law. We're going to lose him on cause. *Damn. Judge will try to save him ["Do you believe you could put aside your personal feelings and judge the evidence fairly, without bias to either side?"] but it won't work. Damn. He's gone.*

★   ★   ★

We continue:

A young blond woman, twenty-three. Husband is a coach. She looks scared. Has no opinion on sex. The judge extends his estimate of the length of the film to be shown when he sees a vulnerable-looking juror: "Five-six hours." But she professes no problems with the "list" of sex acts. Joe makes it clear: group sex; ejaculation; two women; penis into vagina; penis into rectum (of a female).

This woman is quick, has a mind of her own. Kept books for Winn Dixie, now a full-time "homemaker." Was a substitute adult advisor for the children's swim team. Has seen our catalog, a year and a half ago. "Somehow or another I got on their mailing list." No opinion about the company. No opinion about our guilt or innocence. Says she wouldn't even be "uncomfortable." Grove Park Baptist Church. "My membership is with First Baptist." "Seldom" attends church. She may be hiding for our side! She could be good. Saw an X-rated film in her home: VCR. Debbie Does Dallas. Someone gave it to her first husband. Remarried Saturday before last. Ex-husband is *, local car dealer. "I don't think I watched the whole thing." Did it show intercourse? "Yes"; unclothed genitals, "yes"; oral sex, "I think it did. I fell asleep. . . . I'm open-minded, I just don't care—I fell asleep." She'd be good. O.W. burns one to take her out. That makes seven that O.W. has used.*

Two new ones. James Holt should be OK. Ms. W.—NEVER, NEVER, NEVER in a thousand years, and she missed a trip to Florida this week because of jury duty.

Surprise: Holt was with the Oakland As in '74 when they went to the World Series, spent 7½ years in the majors, 18 years in pro baseball. A good moment for all of us: Octavis says he feels "honored" to have him in the courtroom. Judge says "I think you just got real popular in this room." A good laugh. We want this man! Please let him not say he can't be fair. Let him not reveal his bias! He's been to Venezuela. That is rare here. Read Playboy, but not since '76 or '77. Has a nephew charged with rape. O.W. gives his list now: "lesbian sex, masturbation, ejaculation(!)" (1st time O.W. mentions this). Has seen material from Adam & Eve—not in this state, Minnesota, or California. Discussed A&E at work. 2–3 weeks ago. He looks OK.

Jack Weible, a reporter for the Chapel Hill bureau of the *Durham (N.C.) Herald*, had followed our case in great detail. Here is an excerpt from one of his reports:

> Sometimes the communication problem [in voir dire] can even surmount the resourcefulness of an assistant district attorney. One elderly woman who cleaned houses for a living said she had never seen an X-rated film or a sexually explicit magazine and objected to abortion and birth control.
>
> Asked by White if she might object to a mail-order company that deals in contraceptives, she replied, "What do you mean when you say contraceptives?"
>
> Told in similar questioning that they were prophylactics, she replied, "What do you mean when you say prophylactics?"
>
> White sat silent for a moment trying to phrase the sentence in everyman's language. It wasn't easy. The woman grew increasingly frustrated at not understanding the terms she was told she would see flashed on the screen.
>
> "Why don't you just send me home?" she finally said in exasperation to Stephens and he granted her wish. "Too much for me," she said quietly while leaving the jury box.[2]

Notes from the trial:

Last juror in the pool! An attractive fortyish woman: "It's getting lonely downstairs." She could be trouble. Let's see. She's going to say that she can watch it, but she

may be lying. ("5–6 hours!") May be a big surprise here. Has seen The Sex Goddess *(one of the indicted tapes). Perhaps more important, says Wade, she belongs to
CWA, a tough union in an anti-union state. Wade says this means she has balls and
will be anti-establishment.*

No regular church.

No church since she's been remarried. She could be good. (But she could be lying.)

*Has been to our company. We're going to lose her! Hard to believe—has purchased
items from our catalog. SHIT! Make him burn one! Please. Her friend "purchased frequently," "gave the catalogs to me." I think she will stick to her guns. I think he'll have
to burn one. She knows no employees, has never actually purchased. There are tapes in
her home. Husb. has purchased, "like, 6." "If he has friends in, I leave the room."
"Sometimes we watch them together" (she and her husband). "My husband purchases
Penthouse, Forum, (others)."*

Do you look at those magazines?

"Yes."

Regular basis?

"No."

*The Sex Goddess? "I'm not sure I've seen that particular film." "It's very pos-
sible I've seen one or several of those listed films." She's good. He'll have to burn one
here. Burn, Octavis. Burn one! He's given up. Good, good, good. 8 for O.W.*

Will he take the ball player?? (I think he will. Holt would be the third *black male
O.W. rejects—that's part of the reason I don't think he'll do it.) Right. We've got
Holt!*

*The excruciating importance of each juror and of the nuances expressed by each one is
of such clear importance to our vindication that the tension for me and for our lawyers
(and for A. C. and the other employees when they are here) is palpable. Juror X, who
so strongly supported people's right to choose what they will see in their own homes,
has turned wimpy. He saw an X-rated film at the Old Circle-G theater a few years
ago but now protests that it wasn't his idea; it was a double date (his, blind!).*

We wept, of course, whenever the judge dismissed a juror who so believed in
free speech that he (it usually was a he) said he could not be fair to the prosecution. Conservative Alamance County held its fair share—something of a
surprise to me—of people who were adamantly opposed to obscenity laws
on the grounds of freedom of expression.

Luckily the judge dismissed people who would obviously have been very bad for us also. Potential juror B.G. asserted that he didn't believe that he could look at the material and that if he did look at it he would decide the case based on his religious beliefs rather than on a balanced view of the evidence. Clearly he would have voted for conviction, and the judge dismissed him for cause.

The jury selection process consumed nine days. From Monday, March 9, through Thursday, March 19, eighty-five sworn jurors were summoned and interviewed. Twelve jurors and two alternates were seated; more than forty jurors were dismissed by Judge Stephens for cause.

These are unusual numbers. In a federal trial for obscenity, for example, where only the judge can question potential jurors, it is quite typical for no more than three or four or five jurors to be dismissed before a jury is seated. This means that jurors who believe that pornography is the devil's excrement and who will automatically vote to convict anyone who sells sexually explicit materials can be accepted. It also means that First Amendment absolutists who believe, as I do, that a civilized society should have no laws proscribing the dissemination of visual or audiovisual sexual materials that do no one any discernible harm can be seated.

Our jury was composed of seven men and five women. The two alternates, both male, were never used.

We had our ball player, James Holt, whose view of the world was clearly broad; a young scientist named Jeff Gilliam, who seemed open-minded; and an insurance salesman, Robert West, who would turn out to be jury foreman. We also had a very young woman named Robin Allen (Wade was afraid the material would "blow her mind"), and two middle-aged women who were very hard to read. They expressed tolerance of other people's views, but seemed very conservative in their demeanor and general outlook. The "problem" jurors loomed large in my thoughts that night and I went to sleep thinking about both the good and bad turns that Vera McCallum and Frankie Whitesell (who we always referred to as "Ms. Whitesell") might take in the coming trial. But overall, we felt we had a pretty good group. At the very least our team believed that they could persuade three or four of the jurors to stand firm for acquittal, which would mean, at worst, a hung jury. That, in turn, might give us considerable negotiating leverage with the prosecution, if nothing else.

Friday morning, March 20, 1987:

They're all in the box now. It's 9:33. The courtroom is full. Our Adam & Eve employees fill half the room, about 30 of them. The jury had plenty of opportunity to see me chatting with them. All our attorneys feel it is important that I show a positive and supportive two-way relationship with our employees. The jury is quiet. Ms. Whitesell meets my glance—quickly. We both probably feel we shouldn't "greet."

OYEZ, OYEZ, OYEZ, THIS HONORABLE SUPERIOR COURT OF THE COUNTY OF ALAMANCE AND THE STATE OF NORTH CAROLINA IS NOW IN SESSION. GOD SAVE THE STATE AND THIS HONORABLE COURT.

Octavis White in his opening statement now attempts to undo what he perceives to be some of the damage caused during the jury selection process. He asks the jurors to "cleanse your minds of what you went through in jury selection." He reviews the sequence of events, the shipment of magazines and tapes from PHE into Alamance County. And he tries to simplify: "You are able to determine what is acceptable. . . . This is not a complicated animal. It is very simple," he tells the jurors.[3]

Then White moves to the heart of the matter, addressing the issues required under U.S. obscenity law.

As noted earlier, obscenity in the United States is defined by a standard established in the U.S. Supreme Court's 1973 decision, *Miller* v. *California*, 413 U.S. 15 (1973). It is an odd law in many respects and was born of decades of frustration in the Court over the subject of obscenity, a frustration most memorably summed up by Supreme Court Justice Potter Stewart when he said, about pornography in general, "I can't define it, but I know it when I see it." That was one of the problems. For many decades the Supreme Court defined obscenity, one of very few forms of speech not protected by the First Amendment, in such a way as to result in the occasional requirement that specific materials be reviewed by justices of the Court, a practice they very much wanted to avoid. Partly for this reason, the Court set up a three-pronged test. Two of the prongs relate to the standards of local (or state) communities rather than setting a common standard for the entire United States. Under *Miller*, in order for a book or a movie or another depiction to be found legally obscene it must:

(a) depict sex in a manner that is patently offensive to contemporary community standards;

(b) taken as a whole, appeal to a "prurient" interest in sex. A prurient interest, also to be considered in light of community standards, is generally defined as a morbid, shameful, or unhealthy interest in sex; and

(c) have no scientific, literary, artistic, or political value. This last definition must be based on a national rather than a community standard.

By any measure this standard is extraordinarily vague, and offers the potential for the suppression of a very broad range of expression. Indeed the *Miller* test is so vague that if it concerned anything but sex, it would probably be held unconstitutional (see appendix C).

Octavis White continued his efforts to make all this appear as simple as possible. Speaking calmly and smoothly, he told the jurors that our company and its president distributed "clearly offensive" materials in Alamance, despite the threat of prosecution. "The corporation and this individual had notice that if you send this material into Alamance County, you will be prosecuted. . . . But they sent it anyway."[4] Getting directly to the *Miller* issues, he asserted that the material the jury would see had no serious political, scientific, artistic, or literary value, and that it appealed to a "shameful, unhealthy, and morbid" interest in sex.

Then it was Joe Cheshire's turn. He spoke of football and freedom:

Ladies and Gentlemen, as we talked about in jury selection, this is an important case. This may be, we contend to you, the most important case that's ever been tried in Alamance County. . . .

. . . Do not forget during the course of this case that the issue is, are you going to find these materials obscene so that you will say to the community of Alamance County, to your neighbors and your friends, you cannot see this kind of material in the privacy of your own home.

. . . In order to convict, you must find that [the defendants] are guilty of each and every element to a moral certainty, beyond a reasonable doubt. . . .

I like to say it's like a football field. In a civil case it's the greater weight of the evidence. You just shift the evidence a little bit and one side wins. You only have to get, in other words, just across the fifty yard line. But in a criminal case, Ladies and Gentlemen, the prosecution has got to score a touchdown. He's got to get to the twenty, he's got to get another first down to get himself past the thirty, he's got to get to midfield, he's got to get down into where the scoring range is, hard between the twenty and the goal line. He's got to get there and he's got to get across. He can't stop at the one-foot line.

He can't do the sweep around right end and get knocked out of bounds right before he hits the goal post. He's got to score a touchdown. That's what reasonable doubt is about. . . .

PHE wanted to move into Alamance County at one time. They wanted to bring the tax revenue in here to the people of Alamance County. Now what happened? Some well-meaning—and I don't cast any aspersions on them—religious leaders determined without truly knowing the nature of the business, of what they did, they didn't want them here. And that's the beginning of this case, Ladies and Gentlemen. And that's why instead of engaging in conversation with these people, they [the government agents] surreptitiously opened up post office boxes, ordered whatever it was, got undercover agents to follow people from a post office box in Graham. This isn't stuff that the community rose up because they were getting all of this unordered. This is just from a law enforcement officer who set this whole case up. That's the reason we're here. That's all it is. Why? Why? Is it the vocal minority of people trying to impose their will on the majority?

The State has the burden of proving that this material appeals to an unhealthy interest, [in] sex, a prurient interest. I believe the judge said morbid, unhealthy, shameful interest in sex. I want you to listen to the witnesses that they call about this. . . . We contend to you, Ladies and Gentlemen, that this material does not appeal to a prurient interest, to an unhealthy . . . shameful interest in sex. As a matter of fact, it appeals to a healthy interest in sex because the evidence will show that sex, in itself, is not unhealthy. Joyful sex, which is what you will see, whether you like [the depictions] or not, among consenting adults is not unhealthy.

And, Ladies and Gentlemen, you will hear from people that this material, whether you like it or don't like it, helps people. For example, married couples that have sexual problems; that cannot talk about sex; that are afraid to disrobe in front of their partners; that are unable to have a healthy, happy sex life; that may be on the verge of breaking up their marriage; that this type of material can help—not everybody—but can help those types of people. It can bring their ability out to speak, to talk about, to share with, to act out, fantasize, to act out what they want to happen in their marriage or with their sexual partner. . . . And that is scientific value.

Ladies and Gentlemen, this is not an easy case. . . . This is a search for strength, acceptance, understanding, tolerance, privacy, and freedom. It is the most beautiful thing in the world to be free. And we live in the free-est, although certainly not perfect, country. And maybe sometimes, for freedom . . . you have to let people see what you don't necessarily like yourself. Maybe you have to be open and tolerant and loving and accepting. And that's what this case is.

At least one of these arguments turned out to have surprising resonance. The burden of proof and the presumption of innocence are, of course, standard defense ammunition. I have no doubt that Joe's football game has been introduced at many a North Carolina trial. But Joe Cheshire is a very successful defense attorney, and when Joe says, "The presumption of innocence is real and it's beautiful," as he did in his opening statement, you can be sure he means it.

We knew the issue of tolerance would resonate well from having done some early interviewing and surveying, including a mock trial we had held in nearby Chapel Hill a few weeks before the trial as part of our jury-selection research. These affirmed for us that Americans are generally very reluctant to dictate what their neighbors can do, and this certainly extends to their choice of reading and viewing matter, particularly when such experiences take place in the privacy of the home.

On the other hand, we had learned from our mock trial—and this was confirmed in subsequent research—that when it comes to strong sexual materials, juries have no patience with an argument that focuses on "artistic value." If the dominant content in a video or magazine is explicit sexual material (as opposed to, say, an occasional sexual scene in an otherwise aesthetically engaging work), artistic value is an empty argument for an obscenity defense, and therefore one we did not advance. Somewhat to our surprise, however, the argument that the materials in contention had intrinsic scientific value took on real traction in our trial. It is certainly a fact that explicit sexual materials—pornography, if you will—are used by couples and by individuals to overcome sexual problems, including lack of sexual communication, and to assist desired sexual arousal. Wade Smith returned to this theme quite movingly in his closing statement, and later at least two of the jurors remarked upon this point. One said that we could have helped our case by bringing on an expert to testify that the materials are known to help people. He said, "the jury believed that if you could show that this [material] would help just one person, then it wouldn't matter what other witnesses White would call."

Notes from the trial:

Special Agent [of the North Carolina State Bureau of Investigation] David Hedgcock now on the stand for the State. Sent $55.16 to order Gourmet Quickies *and* a *"foot-long double dong." These two items are now introduced into evidence. Why? I expect our lawyers to object to the introduction of the dildo but they do not; apparently the prosecution is permitted to put these things in for atmospherics. With the item draped on the witness stand beside him, Hedgcock, with his mild demeanor, horn-rimmed glasses, and soft-spoken, almost apologetic correctness, seems especially out of place. Now he reads aloud from the Adam & Eve catalog (Gourmet Quickies): "nearly two hours of orgasmic action . . . so hot there's a dozen climaxes in the credits alone!" But his heart just isn't in it.*

Three hours later the jury gets its first look at a large batch of brochures, envelopes, magazines, and the famous "double dong." The materials are passed around the jury box.

At this point the prosecution returned to what is usually the most crucial and often the most interesting part of almost any other criminal trial, but the most boring and unimportant part of an obscenity trial: establishing the facts. Defending a "not guilty" plea in virtually all other criminal trials, the defense attempts to cast doubt as to whether the defendant performed the deed of which he is accused. Almost uniquely in obscenity cases, the defense essentially concedes that the defendant disseminated or mailed or exhibited the magazine, or film, or the like, in question, but asserts that the dissemination or display was legal because the material at issue is not obscene, and that nothing bad or evil has occurred at all; indeed, all that has occurred is that a video or magazine or book which was ordered and paid for by the person doing the requesting was appropriately sent or otherwise made available, more or less the essence of voluntary commerce in a free society. If the material itself is found to be not legally obscene, then no one need be held guilty for selling it. With a finding that the material is not obscene, the purported "crime" simply dissolves into thin air. Nevertheless, as the burden of proof rests with the prosecution, they must establish the facts even if they will not be disputed.

So on Friday, March 20, after the jury had looked at two sexually explicit magazines, the prosecutors showed photos and diagrams of the PHE offices; receipts and postage-meter permits; photos of PHE warehouse shelves, storage bins, and film boxes, as well as photos of the magazines and videos at issue in the trial. The jurors paid close attention.

Before the court is adjourned for the week we spot a man we believe to be a ringer for the federal establishment, sitting in the courtroom and paying very close attention to our case. My fiancée, Harriet, who had arranged to be present from her teaching work in Washington during the first days of testimony, was the first person to notice him. His case full of legal documents and his frequent conferences with the prosecution suggested something out of the ordinary. He turned out to be Alan Sears, who had been executive director of the Reagan administration's Meese Commission on Pornography. His presence in this Alamance County courtroom signaled a high level of interest in our case at the Justice Department in Washington.

Sears was not the only representative of the federal establishment who was taking close interest in these proceedings. William Delahoyde, an assistant U.S. attorney for the U.S. Attorney's Office in Raleigh (an office that was represented in the raid), also was frequently present, conferring with both White and Sears. His presence made it even clearer that the federal government was paying close attention to us and apparently considered our prosecution an important test case in its crusade to shut down sexually expressive materials across the country.

Dave Rudolf now got an opportunity to cross-examine State Bureau of Investigation agent Hedgcock. I was concerned that Dave was too hard on Hedgcock, that we might seem like bullies, but later our postverdict juror interviews suggested otherwise. "You received no complaints?" "You knew of no one who had received this material [in Alamance County]?" "You have never seen this kind of material in this county?" Agent Hedgcock's answers to all of these questions were negative and strongly in our favor. These videos and magazines were in the county only because he, as an agent of the state, had ordered them.

Notes from the trial:
Monday afternoon.

O.W. calls Rachel Hackler. Hackler and Skip Loy, PHE employees, are represented by Tom Loughlin; we have kept our word that all employees will be represented by first-class lawyers, at our expense. As agreed last week (and firmly insisted upon by Tom Loughlin), they are granted immunity from prosecution in exchange for their testimony. On direct examination both Rachel and Skip testify as to certain facts the prosecution must establish—who picks up the mail in Graham, how orders are processed, etc.

On cross-examination Dave establishes that Rachel's father was on the highway patrol, that she has 75 "close relatives" in Alamance County. Rachel's testimony on the company, benefits, bonuses, is excellent. *Left a very good impression, I think.*

Dave is quiet now. We all talked at lunch. I tell all the lawyers that they will, perhaps, have to set aside their profound respect for each other at least enough so that they can criticize each other to keep a unified case. My sense this afternoon is that they are

working better as a team. Dave is quieter and more effective. Wade agrees "we're get-
ting in a groove." Back in the courtroom, Wade passes on examining Hunt and
Hackler. No questions. Skip testifies that at least a dozen people (including Skip) have
reviewed our films to weed out the material we didn't want to sell. Skip also reminds
us that two of the Alamance County commissioners came to the PHE plant and toured
the offices and warehouse under Skip's guidance. They said they had no "personal
opposition to your move" to Alamance County.

Now it was time for the Reverend Gregory Barkman to take the stand for
the prosecution. From the information we have dug up during our pretrial
research, we have high hopes that Mr. Barkman will actually help our case.
First, he had been the motivator behind the political opposition to our move
to Alamance County and we believe that the jury will find his influence with
the District Attorney and with other politically influential persons in the
county to be an improper reason for a criminal prosecution. Second is his
apparent intolerance toward fellow citizens who are supposedly tainted by
anything he considers to be immoral. We hope that he will reaffirm the con-
demnatory position set out in his *Beacon Baptist BEAM* in August 1985. This
newsletter had described Adam & Eve's plan to move into Alamance County
as follows:

> Now, Adam & Eve, a multi-million dollar mail-order pornography business
> . . . is planning to move into new and expanded facilities in Alamance
> County. They currently employ about 40 people. (How would you like to
> have people handling this filth 40 hours a week as your neighbors? Would
> you feel that your wife and children were safe?) Christians need to raise a
> STRONG voice in opposition to this intended move![5]

We hope we can get Reverend Barkman to express his intolerant position about our employees in front of the jury.

Octavis White wants Barkman's testimony in order to establish that we had
been put on notice that obscenity laws would be vigorously enforced in Alamance County. Barkman had sent me a letter advising us not to move into the
county and enclosing a copy of the letter he had received from District
Attorney George Hunt in response to Barkman's quest to stir up opposition to
Adam & Eve. But this "notification" was primarily concerned with opposition
to our move; it did not express opposition to our mailing materials into the
county—materials that were requested and paid for by Alamance residents.

As he usually does when preparing to cross-examine a clergyman, Wade has brought a Bible and placed it on the defendant's table in front of him. As the Reverend Barkman gives his testimony, Wade picks up the Bible and leafs through it from time to time, making sure of his chapter and verse citation and making equally sure that the jury can see the Bible and the attention he is giving to it.

After Reverend Barkman is turned over to the defense for cross-examination, Joe reads aloud the excerpt from the *BEAM* newsletter and asks if the Reverend Barkman stands behind these assertions. To the delight of the entire defense team, Barkman defends the statements; he is prepared to condemn, as unfit citizens, anyone who works at our company. As Joe transfers the witness over to Wade, I have the image of him as a volleyball player at mid-depth ever so gently setting up a spike shot for a teammate in the front line. Joe has carefully managed to clarify that the Reverend Barkman is supporting what is clearly a bigoted position and now hands him off to Wade to complete the point.

"I'm saying," Barkman testifies, "that no one can work in that environment day in and day out and not be affected in the mind." Wade presses on. Barkman asserts that such employees can not "be good citizens of our community."

Rachel Hackler and Skip Loy have appeared as witnesses earlier in the day. Each has strong family ties to the Alamance community. Both embody an impression of good citizenship under any circumstances, and they have certainly done so on the witness stand.

Wade prods further, and Barkman allows that at a prayer meeting five days before he asked the members of his church "to pray for the success of the prosecution in this case." Wade asks Barkman who is on trial, and the witness concedes that "the employees are not on trial in this case."

"But didn't you place them on trial in the Beacon Baptist Church?" Wade asks. He wonders aloud how Barkman could find the company guilty without hearing the facts of the case. "If you're talking about finding them guilty before God, yes," Barkman replies.

Fingering his Bible, Smith asks Barkman if he is familiar with the first verse of the seventh chapter of Matthew. Barkman says he is.

"What does it say?" Smith asks.

"Judge not that ye be not judged," Barkman says.

"Thank you very much," Smith says. "No further questions."

The depth of feeling that Reverend Barkman inspired among members of the jury was revealed in several postverdict interviews. One juror referred to Barkman as "about the biggest hypocrite there is . . . to say such things . . . as a Christian and a Baptist, it was awful." Another said, "the man is not fit to tell others what to do." A third juror simply said he was "bigoted, biased, and arrogant."

Tuesday A.M.

Two 21" TV screens directly in front of jury, one 45" screen (huge!) at a diagonal near judge's bench, facing diagonally out toward audience. The sets in front of the jury will keep me from seeing [jurors] McCallum & Turner. There's some laughing by [jurors] Meyers, Holt . . .

Joking by stenographer, Dave. Jury laughs. Susan Meyers is showing more smiles than I've ever seen. Nervous? Jury is really joking now, asks for popcorn! Now everyone settles down. Judge warns everyone not to misbehave while videos are shown. No one under 18. No standees.

Sequence:	Vanessa del Rio	*30 mins*
	Sex Goddess	*90 mins*
	Ultimate "O"	*85–90*
	Tina Marie	*120*

So he's going to hit them with the worst first.
Here comes Vanessa in all her glory.

It wasn't by accident that the video featuring Vanessa del Rio was chosen by the prosecution to begin the screenings. In this tape, she is lust personified; she epitomizes the kind of sexual performance that sexologist Marty Klein has described as especially threatening to the establishment because it demonstrates how women can be lusty without being bad. In these clips the performer's olive-skinned body, round buttocks, full red lips, pendulous breasts, and slick pudenda are accompanied by the depiction of an unbridled, even aggressive sexual appetite. The video shows her having sex with a series of men, most of whom she easily bests in acrobatics, enthusiasm, and pure heat.

I am acutely embarrassed in this context, with the jurors forced to watch all this material in our presence and in the company of each other.

The worst is first.

Vanessa: "Cock in my cunt my mouth my ass . . . you know how I love it."

Williams frowns. Turner looks bored. Allen isn't flinching.

(Much orgasmic screaming. Boy, will we be tired of that!) Boggs looks intently. The court clerk very attentive.

Is the worst over? The context of this is positively awful. Ms. Whitesell has stopped looking at the monitor in front of her and is watching the larger screen across the room. So is Boggs. *I'm a little worried about Whitesell now.* Meyers looks OK. Ford looks OK. Allen is hanging in there. *No averted eyes except to shift screens.*

The clerk & stenographer, *both young women, are riveted.*

If they can get through this one, it's all downhill.

1st episode over! Now the hospital sequence? No—not yet, more clinical close-ups.

Meyers *looks fine.* Ford *looks fine.* Allen *is hanging in there, though she sure doesn't look comfortable.*

(Now the hospital sequence. "I want it right up your ass.")

CUs [close-ups]. More of same. I'm flushed; why shouldn't the jury be?

(Vanessa says, "I go crazy with cock. Your cock feels so good!" 30 mins. of Vanessa is a long time.

They're all looking. *No averted eyes. But no smiles either.*

END OF VANESSA —

Now it gets easier.

Jury doesn't talk. All fidget nervously. They don't know that the worst is over.

State's Exhibit M21: The Sex Goddess.

It starts out pretty strong (pre-credits).

Now we have some dialog. The Sex Goddess *rolls. Ninety minutes to go.*

Herein some thoughts of a 48-yr-old man [me] on watching porn flicks (six hours of them!) in a windowless white-tiled courtroom, fluorescent lights bearing down, in front of a jury of five women and seven men who will decide whether or not he is guilty of disseminating obscenity.

It is acutely embarrassing. Strange thought: I know the hardest parts have already been shown; the jury doesn't. For another hour or so, they'll probably be braced for some "bad stuff." After that, boredom, we hope.

Wade says that the clerk and steno do not have to watch, are not expected to. The fact that they are both so interested (Curious? Learning something?) may mean that one or two of the younger jurors (maybe older ones, too?) feel the same way. People really do learn from these tapes . . . new positions, new things to say, new lust.

Now Traci's on top, showing her technique, simulating orgasms.

Judge is reading now.

Turner looks bored.

Williams is still frowning.

Whitesell starting to get bored?

All starting to get bored? Let's hope so!

My own embarrassment factor is receding now. They've seen it. No one's fainted. Roof hasn't caved in. No one is raping and pillaging. No murder & mayhem! There's really some quite nice sex here.

Ford and Turner are both almost asleep. Williams is transfixed. Meyers glances at me once in a while, so I have to be careful about looking at her.

Clerk & steno have reached boredom threshold. Steno yawns.

Meyers smiles faintly.

The sex is gentle and loving now. That helps.

Jurors are starting to look around now when someone enters or leaves the room. The actresses really do seem to be having fun in this film.

Judge YAWNS.

I yawn. Lawyers are working on jury instructions.

Steno reads book.

Boggs looks bored.

Geegan frowns. Meyers, Williams attentive.

Will the jurors think about the actresses? And "how their parents must feel?" Massey (clerk) expressed this view at the break. *"Strong stuff,"* she said. *Boggs, Ford, Whitesell look around. Malhum (steno/reporter) now has a Spiegel's catalog in her lap.*

How to fill this time? There is too much going on (twelve people watching a huge TV screen and two monitors with an X-rated film in the process of deciding whether I should go to jail or not) to concentrate on something else, yet what is going on is dull.

Bailiff walks to back of room. (Maybe he's getting bored?)

"The real secret is love," says Matthew, our hero. As incongruous as that seems in this context, it still sounds good. Then Matthew lets out an animal roar I never heard before. It's effective! Matthew & Olivia live happily ever after. Natch.

Judge is going to let the jury vote (majority) on whether to see half or all of the Tina Marie Story *today. If half, we leave around 4:30, if all we leave at 5:30. It's a 30-sec. decision. Mr. Ford says "Roll it! All of it." His tone of voice suggests no discomfort whatever.*

Apparently, remaining contents of the film are of no interest to anyone.

With the completion of the showing of the videos, Octavis White turns over the case to the defense, on what everyone assumes will be a temporary basis. White is holding in reserve a large number of witnesses—particularly local ministers, political leaders, and law enforcement persons—who we presume he will use to try to establish community standards. These witnesses can be called as part of his rebuttal to our defense.

We have an option, however. If we decide to present no defense case at all, White will have no opportunity to call witnesses on rebuttal, and, perhaps even more important, we will get to make the last closing arguments to the jury before they retire to deliberate. Adam Stein first suggested that this might be a good time for this unusual courtroom stratagem. We huddle conspiratorially at lunch and discuss the pros and cons of this high-risk possibility. It would mean we would call no character witnesses for me, none of the expert sex therapists and psychologists who could testify that the videos have scientific value for sexual dysfunction, no testimony that the material does not appeal to a prurient interest in sex, none of our key defense evidence. Among other things, choosing such a strategy seems terribly unfair to our witnesses, who have disrupted their lives and schedules to appear on our behalf. My colleague and friend Tim Black has flown over from England to testify about my overseas work with family planning; one of our psychiatrists has made substantial changes in her teaching and lecturing schedule in order to be available; and several others have gone to great trouble to support our case. How can we just turn around now and say "never mind"?

On the other hand the lawyers agree that the state has not yet carried its burden of proof. They have presented no testimony about community standards, an essential element in an obscenity prosecution. And White has put on no experts of his own to prove that the material *did* appeal to prurient interests, a burden that is his. No witness has even asserted that the material has no scientific, literary, artistic, or political value. In a trial where the literal proof of fact is the dominant form of evidence, it would be clear that the state had failed to meet its burden at this stage. But in an obscenity trial the jury has wide latitude. Obscenity is, after all, a matter of jurors' opinion, which means that resting our case on the technical failure of the state to carry its full legal burden carried a very high degree of risk.

If the jury itself was sufficiently offended by the material they had seen, we knew there was a very real chance that they might overlook the technicalities inherent in the presumption-of-innocence and burden-of-proof arguments and find us guilty because they found the material offensive. On the other hand, our going last in the closing statements might be very important. There are two big advantages to getting the last word. First, we think our courtroom defense attorneys, Cheshire and Smith, can leave a deep emotional impact on the jury, and we don't want White to have the chance to dissect their arguments and give them his slant on their arguments. Contrariwise, we will have a chance to pull apart his closing; in case he comes up with anything especially damaging, we will have the opportunity to rebut. Finally, there is the element of surprise. White is expecting at least another week of trial and will be completely unprepared to make a closing argument now. He is likely to have no more than overnight—maybe less—to get it together.

This is one of those moments when we can significantly guide our rickety craft as it hurtles down the river. Do we follow the conventional path, or roll the dice?

We decide to take the risk. It is 10:00 A.M. on the twenty-fifth when Octavis says "No further evidence by the state." The judge, expecting our trial to last many days longer, turns the floor over to us to present the case for the defense. We present a few legal motions, to strengthen our grounds for appeal should that be necessary. The motions are denied. We have one last huddle in the hallway. We decide "All systems go" for Plan B: no defense.

As soon as the court is back in session, Dave Rudolf, on behalf of the company, and then Wade Smith on my behalf announce "the defense will present no evidence, Your Honor."

The judge, I suspect, was delighted. He hardly missed a beat in rear-ranging the schedule for the afternoon.

The first order of business is to arrange a charge conference concerning the judge's instructions to the jury, which will be extremely important. We have drafted the instructions we would like to have included, and they must now be debated and resolved. Octavis White complains that he has had the draft instructions only since the previous evening and asks for a three-hour recess; the judge grants a break for only twenty-five minutes. He also sets time limits for closing arguments and makes it clear that these final arguments should be completed today! We had expected that White would nearly panic at these developments, as he surely knew that his case had not yet been fully made, but to give credit where due, he takes it pretty well in stride. He is, however, twenty minutes late returning from the break, providing us a chance to re-review our draft instructions.

No one would have the luxury of an overnight for preparation of closing arguments. We were now on a fast track to the end of the trial.

CLOSING STATEMENT OF MR. CHESHIRE:

Ladies and Gentlemen, I want to tell you a real story about a little girl who grew up in southern Russia. Her name was Lila Vahovitcz. She married a man and together in the early 1900s they ran the YMCA in that part of Russia. Late eighteen–early nineteen hundreds, they taught Christianity. They distributed Bibles and they read those Bibles in the privacy of their home. And their friends read those Bibles in the privacy of their home. And they tried to see to it that other people read those Bibles. And one day, as you know, there was a revolution in Russia, and a bunch of people came to their home, to where their family lived, where their friends lived, and they killed a lot of them. And the ones that remained were told they couldn't read that Bible. They couldn't give it to anybody. But they kept reading the Bible and they kept giving it to people. And more people were hurt. And, finally, that little girl, who had grown into a woman, barely escaped with her life and her husband, through Poland, to a land that was free, to a land that permitted citizens to read what they wished, think what they wished. And that little girl who grew to be that woman had a little girl. And that little girl was my mother. If they want to tell you that this case is not about freedom, you let them tell you. And if they want to tell you that this issue is not important to America, not just Alamance County, let them tell you. And if they want to tell you that there's not real passion around the core and the guts of the belief in this issue, let them tell you. I'm not talking, Ladies and Gentlemen, about people having sex. Whether you like it; whether you don't like it; whether it grossed you out; whether it didn't offend you, or you; or did offend you, or you, or you; I'm talking about freedom and I'm talking about the law. And I'm talking about where it says that this average citizen would conclude that the material should not permitted to be sold or delivered in Alamance County for viewing by consenting adults. If that's not a freedom issue, Ladies and Gentlemen, then there has never ever been one.

In the ensuing months and years we would tease Joe endlessly about bringing his grandmother into the trial, asking him, as future indictments were threatened in eastern North Carolina, in Utah, and elsewhere, if we could "get his grandmother for this one." But on March 25, 1987, I was deeply grateful for Joe's grandmother and for his passionate defense of freedom.

Then it was Wade's turn. He wanted our jurors to understand just how important "scientific value" might be to people. He also wanted to cast doubt, in a personal and memorable way, on the matter of community standards, and to show how difficult it would be for anyone to understand or even to know the content of community standards when it comes to sexual matters.

Our defense team outside the Alamance Courthouse. Left to right: Dave Rudolf, Adam Stein, Randell Roden, Wade Smith, Joe Cheshire.

CLOSING STATEMENT, MR. SMITH:

I commend Mr. White, Mr. Haislip, on trying this case honorably and well. They have a very, very heavy burden, and the burden is that they are to go out into this community and gather the very finest and best case that they can put together and bring it before [you] fellow citizens and present it. And I know that they have done that, and I know that if there were any evidence that they could produce to place before you, they would have done it. . . .

At times during this week, I have felt that . . . this can't be real. This is such an unusual proceeding. So strange that we're looking at these materials our fellow citizens might enjoy but we're looking at them in this context. If you had gone to a fortune-teller or someone, say, last year at the state fair and that person sat down and looked at your palm and said, "Well, here's a very interesting thing I see. This spring—now you're going to laugh about this— but this spring here's what's going to happen to you. You're going to watch five hours of X-rated movies in a row in a room with people in robes, police officers with guns, men and women you have never seen in your life, court reporters, clerks, television people, newspaper people, a whole room full of people—you're going to have to watch them with the lights [glaring] down on you so that you can look at each other and you won't want to see each other because you'll be embarrassed." If someone had told you that at the state fair last year, you wouldn't have believed it. You would never have believed it. . . .

[When we asked you], almost all of you said "I never in my life have had a conversation with my neighbors about sexually oriented materials." So not to be funny about it, but . . . you don't get out in your yard washing your car and your neighbor who is out planting some tomato plants walks over to the fence, and you don't say, "Incidentally, what do you think about sexually oriented materials?" Or . . . "how do you feel about oral sex?" You don't talk about that. That's very understandable. People just don't discuss those things. And what you said to us in jury selection, I believe is this, I really don't have any idea how my neighbors feel about these materials. I really don't know. When I think about my own neighborhood, there's Mr. Jackson up the hill from me. I bought my lot from him. I built my house on the lot I bought some twenty years ago. I have known him—I have known him so well. I don't have the faintest idea how he feels about these things. I never will. I will live my life out and die and I will never have a conversation with Mr. Jackson about oral sex. I just won't have a conversation with him about that. I won't. If he came over to the fence and asked me how I felt about it, I would make up something. I would try to figure out what he wanted me to say. I wouldn't tell him the truth. I wouldn't be interested in talking with him about it. I'd be embarrassed. I wouldn't want to discuss it. I would think something was wrong with him if he wanted to talk about that. I'd scratch my head and walk away, and that's the truth. That's the way we all are. . . .

And . . . I don't want to be dramatic about [the importance of the issue of scientific value]. I'm not a sociologist or a psychologist but I would assume that there are people who do not get chosen, that is, who have no sex partner. I assume that's true. I assume there are people who never have a sex partner, that must be the truth. They don't get chosen. I don't know why. . . . Like when you were young and you were choosing up to play softball and you tossed the bat and the other person grabs the bat and that person chooses someone and then the other captain chooses someone and there's always—and you remember—you remember him, there's Wheatie, Wheatie Richardson, he's standing there with his cap down over his ears, his ears sticking out and his pants pulled up way too high and he didn't get chosen, and he is wondering why he never gets chosen. Well, there must be people like that. Do we say to those people, you can't have these materials to look at, to enjoy? Is there some scientific value in the materials for those people? Do they receive some therapeutic, some benefit from them? I don't know the answer but I do know that you have to find that that is not possible. And as Mr. Cheshire said, if you believe that these materials can help one person like that, if these materials have scientific value for one person in your community, then you have found the defendants not guilty. . . .

Did Reverend Barkman speak for the Methodists, for the Presbyterians, for the Catholics? Did he speak for all 103,000 people who live in this county? And by what authority would he write a letter to a company which wanted to come here and say, "You can't come here; you are not welcome"? And how does that make you feel as a citizen of the county and how does it make me feel? Would Reverend Barkman be willing to impose his views on you about drinking? About smoking? Would he be willing to make up your reading list for you? Would he be willing to go down by the public library and select those books which he felt are not edifying for you and wholesome and good for you? I submit that he would. I submit that Reverend Barkman would be willing to do that.

I have thought so much of a sort of a freeze frame ending to this drama that we have had before us in the last three weeks. And I can see the pictures frozen on the screen. Mr. White—I can see his picture frozen on the screen. And I can hear a voice saying Mr. White went on and served his state with distinction and honorably. I can see Mr. Harvey's image on the screen and the words would say, "Mr. Harvey was found not guilty that day. And Mr. Harvey went on to do many great works and many good things." And the jury all walked out the door that day; they were never ever together again, had no reunions. They bumped into each other from time to time in the grocery store but that when the case was concluded, and they all walked out of the courthouse, there was a nice, sweet smell of freedom and a feeling of freedom. And I think that a verdict of not guilty in this case for all people, for all of the defendants in this case, would send a signal . . . out of this courthouse to North Carolinians everywhere that this is a free society in which we live. That jurors do have the courage of their convictions. That this is the land of the free and the home of the brave. I don't want to wave the flag too much. I know that that's not good. But there is a Walt Whitman quote that I think of so often and what it says is this, "There is no day nor week nor hour when tyranny may not enter upon this land if the people lose this robustness and spirit of defiance; there is no charm, no bar against it. The only bar against it is a robust, rough, and tough breed of men and women." And I think that is true. And I hope that you will be a robust, rough and tough breed of men and women. I hope that your vote will speak [for] freedom. If you vote not guilty, you will be saying to Mr. White, "Mr. White, you did a fine job, you're an honorable gentleman. You did everything that you could do, but in our county we believe that individual men and women have a right to receive materials in plain, brown wrappers in their post office boxes and to enjoy those materials in the privacy of their homes."

I thank you very much.

Wade's argument closed the day. The next morning, Thursday, the jury would be charged by Judge Stephens and begin deliberations.

Thursday A.M., March 26. A strange feeling at the office this morning: There is nothing more I can do! Nothing. Not even thinking about the issues or the trial can help. All I can do is silently greet the jurors when they come in, if they will meet my eyes, which, as usual, they don't, and not look overconfident in front of them.

All observers, including Tim, feel we have a good shot. Tim feels our case was very well made and he, perhaps more than the others we are close to, has the perspective to step back a little, so let's hope he's right.

The judge finishes his instructions to the jury. The jury retires for deliberation.

It is now 11:20. The jury has been out almost an hour. Now they're coming back . . . one hour! Good sign!!

Clerk says into phone, "Please tell Octavis to come over, we have a verdict."

11:29 A.M. White and Haislip return and take their seats.

11:30 A.M. Judge instructs bailiff to bring in the jury.

Judge says that no one may say anything or react emotionally when verdict is announced. Must leave if they can't handle their reactions.

Here they come.

Jury sits.

N.O.T. G.U.I.L.T.Y.

NOTES

1. *Voir(e)* is an old French word meaning "truth."
2. "Prospective Jurors Recall Defunct Drive-In," *Durham Herald*, March 18, 1987.
3. "Arguments Begin in Porn Trial," *Raleigh News and Observer*, March 22, 1987.
4. Ibid.
5. *Beacon Baptist BEAM*, August 15, 1985.

Adam & Eve employees celebrating our victory in March 1987.

CHAPTER FOUR

WAITING FOR THE
OTHER SHOE(S) TO DROP

T he federal government gave us little time to savor our victory in Alamance County. On the day of the verdict, the U.S. attorney for the Eastern District of North Carolina, Sam Currin, announced to the press that "[i]t's still full steam ahead as far as our federal investigation of Adam & Eve is concerned."[1] In the following day's papers, Currin and his deputy Bill Delahoyde were reported as "still weighing whether to file federal charges against PHE."[2] Currin was deeply angry about the verdict and, as we learned later, he was prepared to go to unusual lengths to make up for our Alamance victory and see that we got what he thought we deserved. In a memo to his staff of March 30, four days after the jury had pronounced us not guilty, Currin suggested some tactics to "get" PHE and me:

> We must regain momentum after the Adam & Eve verdict and come with as many indictments as possible. . . . [3]

To me, the idea that we should now have to face indictments from the federal government was quite preposterous. We had just gone through a grueling trial and been found not guilty. That ought to have been the end of it.

Dave and Wade patiently explained that, while our victory in Alamance was of great psychological and legal importance as a first-round victory, it in no way inhibited the federal government from prosecuting us in as many different places as they chose. Each mailing of sexually explicit materials—"obscene" mailings, as the federal authorities would no doubt argue—constituted a separate indictable offense as far as the government was concerned. It was clear by now that the Eastern District of North Carolina and the District of Utah were both planning to press forward with their own indictments, presumably for materials we had mailed to those places. Currin was trying to get others to indict as well. His staff memo continued:

I want you to subpoena [Orange County district attorney] Carl Fox to the federal grand jury as soon as possible. His role vis-à-vis Adam & Eve is going to continue to haunt every single prosecution of that company. Therefore, we need to bring him on in and question him about his entire role in this matter, including campaign contributions, etc. I don't want any delay on this. I personally believe he is in league with Phil Harvey on this matter and you might as well proceed with that assumption in mind. I want you to be tough as nails in questioning him in the grand jury.

We also need to locate some other district attorneys who will prosecute Adam & Eve in their districts. Bob Thomas in Hickory is one who I believe will do so. Perhaps Peter Gilchrist will also prosecute. We need to get state indictments of Adam & Eve in some other districts.

Contact Utah and urge them to proceed with their indictments as soon as possible. Also discuss with [Washington National Obscenity Enforcement Unit head] Rob [Showers] whether he wants the Middle District [of North Carolina] to do a RICO on Adam & Eve. If so, he needs to work the RICO case out of Washington. I doubt anyone in the Middle District has the sense to do it. . . .[4]

District attorney Carl Fox and I were hardly "in league." As noted earlier, I had consulted him on two occasions concerning his interpretation on the new North Carolina obscenity laws; he had shared his views with me, and I had taken his advice. Such preventive steps are in the best tradition of law enforcement, the kinds of consultation that should be taken more often by law enforcement authorities and those who wish to avoid violating ambiguous laws. But Currin just couldn't seem to believe that we had won our case fair and square, so he invented an impropriety to attribute to someone else.

Currin's request that his staff urge other district attorneys in North Carolina to prosecute our company was completely out of line with proper law enforcement procedure, but it was entirely in keeping with his earlier strategies to suppress sexual speech. When the North Carolina obscenity law had been broadened in October 1985, video stores, uncertain as to the new law's precise meaning, had begun removing sexually oriented materials from their shelves. At the time, Currin's attitude betrayed his contempt for the constitutional niceties of prior restraint: "Some of these stores will voluntarily close down rather than face prosecution. Either way we win."[5]

For Mr. Currin to send his deputies about "creating" new prosecutorial initiatives to punish a company he didn't like is a troubling abuse of police power. Perhaps mindful of such matters, Currin at one point gave an antipornography talk to a church group in the community and created his own "complaints" by suggesting that parishioners request an Adam & Eve catalog and then object to his office about receiving unsolicited "pornography" from Adam & Eve. It was this kind of piling-on in North Carolina, in combination with threats from Utah, that several federal judges would subsequently find improper.

The pressure continued. Sam Currin's office had conducted "voluntary" interviews with our employees, presumably to gather evidence to present to a grand jury in Raleigh. Those interviews, and demands for corporate documents, had been ongoing since well before our Alamance trial. Currin's staff seemed determined not just to deprive us of our employees' time and efforts, but to undermine their morale and their loyalty to our firm. At an interview following the raid, one employee was asked "what my parents and boyfriend thought about my working at the company."[6] Another was asked by Rob Showers if she was aware that "the company made millions of dollars and [he] asked me, 'Doesn't that bother you?' He also told me, when I explained that we deleted the name of anyone who objected to receiving our catalogue from our mailing list, 'That's what you think.' . . . Mr. Showers told me that he had prosecuted rape cases and child pornography cases and said that he 'knew' that rapists looked at stuff like what we had in our catalogue and that this urged them on. When I disputed this he said that the material was like marijuana—some people needed to get more and more of the high after smoking marijuana and other people needed to get more than what we had in our catalogue after seeing it."[7] Another inspector told an employee "that mailing any kind of pornography was like mailing a snake or a gun."[8]

Our employees had consented to undergo the interviews only because they had been assured by these same authorities that their taking part in the interview process would be a substitute for their appearing before the grand jury, as demanded by the subpoenas. For prosecutors to use the threat of a grand jury appearance to coerce "informal" interviews with our employees, with no attorney present, was a cavalier abuse of the prosecutorial process. In a hearing on this subject later the same year, North Carolina federal judge Earl Britt announced that he might consider prohibiting the government from using information garnered from these interviews. (The issue ultimately became moot.)

THE WILL TO WIN

Throughout what would become an eight-year saga, we were able to sustain the strong underlying assumption that we had to win, and that we would. Yes, there were despondent days as we were hurtled down our rough river, particularly before our victory in Alamance. But for most of our journey, most of us believed that we would prevail. Peggy Oettinger describes how she felt about this.

> After we were indicted in Utah [in 1990], I remember my dad called. He called to express concern that they had indicted me. I told him not to worry. I had never worried or felt like we weren't going to win. That may have been partly a subconscious mechanism to help me deal with the stress and the pressure, but it was more my sense that we were right and, by God, some-where down the line we would be able to prove we were right. He was a little taken aback by my confidence in this. If I had thought more about what was ahead of me, I might have worried more. Anyway, you want to spend your time on positive, constructive things, working towards winning as opposed to moaning, "Oh, my God, we're going to lose, I'm going to be in jail." That's not going to get you anywhere.

A. C. Bushnell agrees. "With a good defense team, you can win. I have a lawyer friend, Richard Pertz. He reminded me that motivation matters. You can out-work the other side. They go home at five o'clock. Your team can work all night if necessary."

There were several defining moments for this will-to-win theme. One of them occurred in the conference room of Tharrington, Smith, and Hargrove, Wade Smith's firm, in 1989. It was two years after the trial and there had been no new indictments so far, just threats, harassment, and negotiating. Our lawyers had discussed possible conditions for a settlement, a deal that would remove the sword of Damocles that hung continuously over us. Did they want me in jail? Would there be fines? Were they demanding that we go out of business? At this stage it was impossible to tell just what the other side would be willing to accept as a condition for leaving us alone.

We were speculating about whether new indictments might be immi-nent, as had been repeatedly threatened. How might we head them off? Wade, Joe Cheshire, Dave Rudolf, Adam Stein, Peggy Oettinger, A. C. Bushnell, and I were seated at the conference table. Tharrington Smith's conference room is designed to give clients a sense of reassurance. Portraits of distinguished-looking men in three-piece suits look down from the walls. The coffee ser-vice is silver, the cups good china. The chairs were covered with leather, the lights subdued, and the decor conservative. The only compromise with for-mality was the powdered Cremora that occasionally took the place of fresh milk in the little silver pitcher.

That day we were discussing plea bargains and the possibility of paying fines as part of a "global agreement" to settle all this. Wade and Joe had been in touch with Doug McCullough in Sam Currin's office; Dave and Wade had talked with Richard Lambert in Utah. We had not been able to get any response whatever from Washington, and the government's demands for guilty pleas and fines had kept escalating. We were now discussing whether or not the corporation should consider accepting a fine of $750,000, a huge figure which had recently, and with no stated justification, been increased from $500,000.

Faced with a $750,000 demand on the table, should we keep talking or should we say no and accept the consequences? Issues of principle were weighed against the certain costs of litigation. We arrived at a kind of informal polling process. Should we talk and thus imply tacit acceptance of the new demand, or say "no deal" and prepare to be indicted? A. C. believed that we should fight, that the principle was too important to finesse. But he also knew that doing so would carry real risk to him personally and to his young family. He said he wanted to consult his wife before casting his vote. He left the room to phone her. While we ruminated, Dave Rudolf suddenly stood up and said, "Goddammit, we're talking about the First Amendment here!" He looked at me. "If you don't stop the government, who will? Every time we agree to a fine, they raise the ante. If we agree to these guilty pleas and escalating fines, there'll be no end to it." He was addressing everyone now. "Someone's got to take a stand. If not PHE, who will?"

For me, it was a defining moment. I had always felt this way; still do. It was becoming more and more clear that a guilty plea on our part would lead to the annihilation of one company after another. Even now, five or six of our competitors were going down like pins. But lawyers are paid to give prudent advice. The good ones work very hard to avoid unnecessary litigation or any other form of conflict with prosecutors when they believe that negotiation is in their client's best interests. The Alamance trial, after all, had cost us nearly $500,000 and had entailed massive risks. The idea that we should be willing to make compromises to avoid such litigation had therefore always been accepted in our group. But on this day Dave had reached his limit. There was just too much at stake. All the other mail-order companies were folding their tents, signing their own death warrants.

By the time A. C. returned, the consensus had been reached to reject the $750,000 demand. A. C. recalls:

> I had told Mary I wanted to fight this, and she knew the risks, but she said if that's what you want to do, OK. When I went back into the conference room everyone had come up with other strategic reasons why we didn't want to take that offer anyway, and it never really mattered whether I agreed. But I felt better that, when the chips were down, I was willing to stand up

for the First Amendment because I did feel very strongly about that and I was willing to do it at some personal peril. And I felt good about that.

The will to win requires self-confidence. With Wade especially, this quality often manifests itself in humor in the face of enemy fire. When the defense team can relish a joke at the other side's expense, it may sometimes be false bravado. But in our case I think it represented a form of confidence that made our winning much more likely.

On one occasion during the Alamance trial the prosecutors had left the by-then famous "foot-long double dong" in one of the attorney's recess rooms, quite possibly on purpose, to remind the defense team just what pernicious products their client sold. It was now an officially marked piece of evidence for the other side, Prosecution Exhibit #123. When our lawyers assembled during a recess, Wade stuck this exhibit in the front of his pants, waved it at his colleagues, and made a pointed lewd remark. Joe recalls, "I was just blown away at the fact that the distinguished Wade Smith would show that kind of public expression of off-color frivolity. That made it ten times funnier than it would have been otherwise. If I had done it, it just wouldn't have been a surprise, but Wade. . . ."

During the trial Wade also had spearheaded a little ceremony he describes:

It was so tense, we were all working so hard, and we wanted to win so badly and we were so worried that we wouldn't. We needed anything possible to lighten this up. I had memorized the words to a song from Monty Python's *The Meaning of Life.* It goes,

Every sperm is sacred.
Every sperm is great.
If a sperm is wasted,
God gets quite irate!

It comes from the section in the movie where a Catholic family has 100 or 150 children and the father's going to have to sell some of them because they don't have food. And he explains to the children that the church won't let him use one of those little rubber things and if the church would simply permit him to use "one of these little rubber things on my dingie," he says, "we wouldn't have so many of you. But we can't do that and for that reason, we're going to have to sell some of you." And then they go into the song "Every Sperm is Sacred."

And it's a very catchy little tune. So every day during the trial, at the end of the day when the evidence would be all in and the people were gone, as we were getting our briefcases together, I'd put my arms around Joe [Cheshire] and Joe put his arms around Dave [Rudolf] and Dave would put his arms around Adam [Stein], and we would dance in a chorus line like the can-can and sing "Every Sperm is Sacred." It was sort of a tension breaker. So even now, if I get together with Rudolf and Cheshire, we'll sing this song. And it is a spoof at the government, of course, because it's like the God forces would take the position that each sperm *is* sacred and must be used in the holiest kind of way.

Wade's sense of humor also paved the way for the initiation of a new member of our legal team. Once we realized that our case was getting close attention at the highest levels of the Justice Department, we had contacted the law firm of Gibson, Dunn, & Crutcher in Washington. The firm had a reputation for conservatism and for being well-connected to the Reagan administration.

My first visit to Gibson, Dunn's lavish lobby made me fear for our budget, but we found there an attorney who made a valuable contribution to our defense. John Mintz's background and personality seemed to suit our case especially well. John had been an agent of the Federal Bureau of Investigation for twenty-five years and had served as the FBI's general counsel for thirteen. His demeanor was conservative, his style methodical and thorough. We felt that having John available to negotiate with Justice Department officials would lend considerable credibility to our position and, as he became acquainted with the facts and issues of our case, he aggressively defended our constitutional rights. He quickly recognized the unfairness of the government's tactic of threatening to indict us in several jurisdictions at once, for example, and told them so on more than one occasion. His lawyering style also complemented our other team members; he kept meticulous notes of all his meetings with Department of Justice officials, which added greatly to the accuracy and depth of the record of our case. And his credibility on the witness stand was virtually unassailable.

In the early months of this relationship, John and Wade Smith worked closely together during trips to Salt Lake City, where they negotiated with U.S. Attorney Brent Ward. John and Wade quickly developed mutual respect and trust, and when a meeting with several members of Sam Currin's staff was scheduled in October 1986 in Raleigh, they worked together again in trying to negotiate an agreement. After a long day of discussions and negotiations, Wade invited John to join him and his wife at home for dinner.

It happened that Wade had celebrated his birthday a few days before, and the members of the music group he participated in, Bloomsbury, had brought presents to their regularly scheduled practice at the Smith home that evening. A friend of Wade's joined them bearing gifts collected on a recent trip to Australia, including an outback hat and coat. The merriment that followed was climaxed by Wade dunking himself in a bathtub to test the waterproof qualities of the garments while the guests cheered him on. Wade assumed that the conservative John Mintz would be horrified by all this, but he was wrong. As John Mintz describes it,

> I think this incident was just a little spark that Wade needed to give everybody a great laugh at his expense. . . . It was a moment of hilarity based on an opportunity provided by a friend showing up with the hat. I thought it was great.

I pressed John as to how this might have impressed him about the stability of our legal staff. "It showed me good things about your lawyer," he said. "Not only was Wade a very serious man, with a wide range of interests, but a guy who had a terrific sense of humor." Thus did the FBI's former general counsel become a solid member of our defense team and the "bathtub story" a permanent addition to the lore of our case.

The fact that we were fighting for a cause as well as for our own survival was important too. Defense attorneys tend to care deeply about obscenity cases because there is an important constitutional principle involved, one that has special meaning for most members of the defense bar. Freedom is their business, after all; their work is to retain freedom for their clients. The basic idea that we must protect the freedom to speak, the freedom to create and disseminate literary and other artistic expression, is a fiercely held assumption for most lawyers whose careers are spent fighting the heavy hand of government. And how refreshing it must be to defend an obscenity case, where one has the opportunity to prove that no crime has even occurred. In this way an obscenity defense can turn into something of a crusade, as ours did almost from the beginning. Dave Rudolf says,

> After we'd agreed we'd have to fight, that conciliation with the government just wasn't going to work, then I think we all viewed it as a cause, a case that needed to be won. We realized the importance of the principle involved, which had gotten lost in the early negotiations and machinations. After we got over that point, everyone felt we *needed* to win this case. It was like, OK, if we're not going to settle this because of principle, then we'd better win.

"It's like fist fighting," says Joe Cheshire:

The person who generally wins the fist fight is not the person who's the strongest, but the person who believes he's going to win and is willing to suffer the pain it takes. And I think the prosecutors we dealt with knew, with our defense team, they were not going to beat us. After Alamance, I think we believed we would win, and when we met with them I think they knew that we believed we were going to win, and that we would fight like hell to do it.

For Dave, the will to win also had been manifested clearly during the Alamance trial.

There's a momentum in any trial. There's a feel to it. And that gets communicated to the jury in various ways. I think what got communicated to the jury here was that we all really, really cared about this. This wasn't just another case to us. It was something more personal. And in an obscenity case where the facts are not really in dispute, that's important.

EMPLOYEES UNDER FIRE

With the grand jury subpoenas issued to more than one hundred of our employees in the spring of 1987, we needed yet another good attorney to represent them. These employees were not likely to be indicted, but they needed legal representation if they were going to be interrogated by prosecutors at a grand jury proceeding or otherwise. At the recommendation of our defense team, we retained Fred Harwell, a seasoned criminal defense attorney from Winston-Salem, a nearby town that gave its bifurcated name to two brands of cigarettes. Over the course of the next few years Fred would make repeated trips with his clients to the courthouse in Raleigh; to Durham, North Carolina, where federal inspectors from Alabama conducted interviews; and, in the company of one or more of our employees, to Montgomery, Alabama, and Louisville, Kentucky. Meanwhile, numerous other trips had to be made by our other lawyers—to Salt Lake City and to Montgomery, Louisville, and Raleigh. The effort to bleed us financially was unremitting.

The strategy behind the interviews and the grand jury proceedings in Raleigh appeared to have at least two objectives. The first, noted earlier, was to demoralize our employees by intimidating and frightening them, and by persuading them of the illegality (or at least impropriety) of their employer's activities. The second, addressed explicitly in the grand jury questioning, was to elicit from our employees a detailed portrait of an organization that (so the prosecutors were convinced) was engaged in a variety of nefarious activities. They failed on both counts. Fred Harwell later described the growing frustration of the prosecutors during these grand jury proceedings. Clearly they were expecting our employees to reveal some dark secrets about company management that could be used against us. After several employees had testified without stating anything useful to the government, Fred recounts, the prosecutors expressed "great skepticism" about the truthfulness of the employees' testimony, skepticism based on the fact that no one had said anything incriminating about higher-ups at the company.

> I had to have a long conversation with the prosecutors and tell them that these PHE employees are ordinary, good people. They are not engaged in some huge pornography conspiracy. They come to work in the morning, they do their job, they go home at night. They have high personal standards, a great deal of loyalty. They understand that they need to tell the truth when they're asked to, and that's what they're trying to do. And [I said,] you need to tell me, as their attorney, if you ever have any reason to believe that any of these of my clients has said anything to the grand jury that is not true, because I'll sit down and talk to them and take care of it right away. And I can tell you over this entire time, for perhaps two or three years, not a single prosecutor or agent ever came to me and suggested that they had anything other than a *generalized* skepticism about my clients' testimony. They seemed to think that the testimony was just too good to be true, that the company could not be as well managed as the employees were saying. And I said "Well, you're the ones who put the names on the subpoenas—I didn't pick them out!"

Here is another illustration of how imaginatively (and inaccurately) we paint portraits of people and organizations we don't know. When the inspectors had first raided our premises in May, they were sure that they would find adult film production, and, I expect, evidence of tax fraud, "money laundering," drug use, and probably a number of other crimes. This is what happens when you spend a couple of years inventing a portrait of a "target" as a demon. So it seemed impossible to federal inspectors that our employees were telling the entire truth to the grand jury when they expressed loyalty to the company and reported on an honestly managed organization, one that carefully screened the sexual materials it sold and that treated its employees well. "There was an acute disappointment on the part of prosecutors that people they wanted to make out to be devils were not," Fred says. He goes on:

I believe that disappointment radiated right up the chain of command; there was an increasing sense of frustration on the part of the government that they couldn't really seem to break through to the reality that they thought existed. They kept bringing people in and just never could find anybody that fit the profile that they had in their minds, the profile of people who worked at PHE who would be "the key" to the inside. By then, of course, I knew that there was no key because I saw how the corporation was run. There wasn't a back door that you went through to a sweatshop operation.

Fred had demanded immunity from prosecution for his clients, a normal part of the quid pro quo in legal contests. Prosecutors frequently grant immunity to witnesses on the assumption that, in exchange, they will get damaging information which they can use against their primary targets. In this case they were frustrated and very, very angry. "They sprinkled immunity agreements all over the landscape and got nothing in return except bad news for the prosecution," Fred says.

Fred himself had been at least mildly surprised about the nature and character of the PHE employees he represented.

I think the thing that surprised me at the beginning was how ordinary all my clients were, ordinary in the richest tradition of rural North Carolina. I didn't know what to expect the first time I went into the office. I didn't expect to find porn production and all of that, but as you can imagine one wonders, well, this is an environment that I'm not used to. What am I going to find? I found it to be just an ordinary, open environment, and I found the people to be just ordinary sorts of people, thoughtful people by and large, artistic people. I can't think of anyone I represented who didn't seem to have a good quality of life, a richness in the way they carried on their private lives. Almost everyone had some sort of special thing, whether it was an interest in cooking or whether they were involved in some special activity. I was surprised to find a number of them to be devout churchgoers. On more than one occasion when I was at the PHE offices interviewing or counseling, the interview would be cut short because someone had to leave to go to church that evening. I think one of them played the organ in church.

Fred also notes that the prosecution was determined throughout this period to make our defense as expensive for PHE as they could. At one point Bill Delahoyde insisted that Fred tell him who was paying his bills (the company was) and tried to tell him that he was only "allowed" one client in the PHE case, that he was not legally permitted to represent several employees during the proceedings. Fred is a seasoned attorney and made it clear that who was compensating him and who he could represent was not the government's business. Had we relied on a less experienced lawyer who could be intimidated by such prosecutorial browbeating, the proliferation of lawyers might have undermined us financially even more than it did.

While Fred and our subpoenaed employees were holding back the government's juggernaut in Raleigh, the team of defense lawyers for the corporation and for me was focusing on our direct lines of defense. Some of this took the form of "sounding out the enemy," exploring possible plea bargains that might avoid another trial. Communications were frequent, and speculation was rife. Our attorneys would, from time to time, "drop by" the U.S. attorney's office in Raleigh on other business and try to see which way the wind was blowing—whether an indictment in Raleigh was likely, what mood "Utah" was in, whether we might get blindsided by North Carolina's Middle District, and, always, what agreement might be reached to avoid a costly and all-consuming trial.

This period, especially the time between the raid and the Alamance trial, produced some of our lowest and most discouraged moments. One of these was our lawyers' retreat when they all took two days off to discuss tactics and to immerse themselves in the videos and the magazines at Wade Smith's vacation house on the Pamlico River near Beaufort City, North Carolina. This weekend (for the lawyers only, I was not invited) was also meant for some very creative soul searching about our defense strategy at the trial. But morale was low. After watching all the videos, they just didn't believe that a jury drawn from the conservative, generally rural citizens of Alamance County would be open to information about freedom and tolerance. The images of Vanessa del Rio, writhing with her multiple partners, wantonly begging for sexual actions our team feared that Alamance citizens might not even have heard of, seemed just too much. Despite careful instructions from the judge (which we were confident we would get) about the precise legal definition of obscenity, they had little confidence that a jury of Alamance County citizens could be expected to "acquit" Vanessa del Rio.

Other low points came during plea bargain negotiations. Almost from the day after the raid, both parties (with the possible exception of District Attorney George Hunt in Alamance County) began probing the other to see if we might find a basis for a plea agreement. What did the government really want? Would they settle for a substantial fine? Or, as Wade put it, did they have four horses waiting to draw and quarter me, to raze our business to the ground, and to scorch and salt the earth behind us?

There was no clear answer. At times we got the message that some of the prosecutors, presumably Showers, Currin, and Delahoyde, wanted the business "out of North Carolina." At other times, the importance of Utah getting some kind of guilty plea from me personally seemed to be ascendant. At still other times, whether we were negotiating with Richard Lambert in Utah or with Doug McCullough (of Currin's office) in North Carolina, the message seemed to be that we would be required to essentially abandon our business altogether. We considered all these possibilities in the context of Wade's reminder that "if your government wants you badly enough, it will have you." Wade catalogued some of our reasons for pessimism in April 1988, two years into our saga.

> The assistant United States attorney [in Raleigh] assigned to the task of prosecuting [us] . . . is on the board of trustees of Southeastern Theological Seminary. . . . These are dogmatic people. They will not ultimately inherit the earth. But for now they are in positions to make freedom a far more scarce commodity.
>
> The second place which is a worry for us is Utah. We see them actively prosecuting people in cases similar to ours. When we met with them a year ago they expressed outrage at us and promised that Mormons would not feel kindly toward us. You will recall that they wanted you out of the business of mailing sexually explicit material. That would include Playboy-type formats. They didn't want you out of the business just in Utah. They wanted you out worldwide. They think on a large scale out there. I advised you then to get out of the business. I told you I could see no reason to stay in the business to simply prove a point. I told you I felt you should let someone else make the First Amendment points you sought to make. I believed that the cost to you was too dear in terms of time, energy, and money. I think I was right then, in spite of our victory in Alamance County.

A year later, Wade, who by then was well established as the pessimist of our team, reported further gloomy developments from a conversation with Richard Lambert, assistant U.S. attorney in Utah. "In effect," Wade reported, "this is what Lambert said."

> Other jurisdictions are after Phil. Their trigger fingers are twitching and if we had hoped that this was not war; if we had felt that the silence of the United States government meant that there was no will to come after us; if we had believed we had succeeded in beating them back in Alamance County and sapping their resolve; we were wrong on all counts.
>
> [Lambert] said he could not tell us what other states are interested in prosecution. But in effect, he said, "Read my lips. You will be prosecuted. Thornburg [Richard Thornburg was the United States Attorney General who succeeded Edwin Meese] has made obscenity one of his top priorities. You are the biggest and the most successful. The complaints against you nationwide are the loudest. You will be hearing from other places."

THE SPECTER OF RICO

Another reason for our pessimism during these dark days was RICO. The Racketeer-Influenced and Corrupt Organizations Act was originally passed by the U.S. Congress in 1970 to provide federal prosecutors with strong ammunition to use against organized crime. Since then the RICO statutes have been used with some effectiveness against organized crime and also in a whole variety of civil litigation. This has included everything from aggrieved parties suing stock brokers they believe were inadequately forthcoming about market information to family planning/abortion clinic suits against would-be dangerous demonstrators. In 1989, one man, Benson Selzer, who was in debt for $710,000 to the First New York Bank for Business, used RICO to sue the bank's chairman for having sex with his (Selzer's) wife; Selzer figured that he could collect more than he owed.[9]

An especially chilling aspect of RICO in the context of a criminal prosecution is its provisions for forfeiture of property. The RICO statutes have been used to confiscate automobiles, airplanes, homes, and boats used in the commission of a crime or believed to have been used in the commission of a crime (usually the transportation of illegal drugs) even when their owners were uninvolved in the crime itself. RICO can also be used to freeze and control, immediately upon indictment, any assets that may have been derived from illegal activity. The law thus allows the government to quickly tie up a defendant's assets—as the *Wall Street Journal* pointed out, "to hold as security for the assets to which the government would be entitled if it won a conviction at trial."[10] This raises the specter of a crippled company without access to its own assets, curtailed in its ability to do business, and, perhaps even more important in these circumstances, potentially unable to pay lawyers' fees. "The horrors of RICO are so fearsome and threatening that a company will abandon what otherwise might be a valid defense," noted Stanley Arkin, a New York defense attorney, about one high-profile securities case.[11]

While the constitutionality of RICO is on very shaky ground in the case of First Amendment–protected materials, the seizure of assets *after* a trial has been upheld by the Supreme Court at least once.[12] The confiscation of inventory and buildings following an obscenity prosecution is particularly chilling (and particularly constitutionally questionable) because the forfeiture of completely legal films and magazines and newspapers results if just two or three films or magazines or newspapers sold from or stored on the same premises are found obscene. As the RICO statutes are presently construed, for example, a mainstream bookstore that sold two copies of a single book (sale of at least two copies is needed to constitute a "pattern" of "racketeering" activity) found to be obscene somewhere in the United States could theoretically have all of its assets confiscated and forfeited to the government, including its entire inventory of books, the building in which the books were stored and from which the offending books were shipped, and also including the private homes and automobiles of the principal officers of the bookstore if those homes or automobiles (or boats or aircraft) were used in such a way that those items provided a "source of influence over" the allegedly illegal activity.

By the mid-1990s there had been two obscenity RICO trials resulting in convictions. In the first, *Pryba* v. *the United States* (1987), Pryba's business vehicles and warehouse, as well as his entire inventory of tapes, films, and magazines were forfeited. In the second, *Alexander* v. *United States*, similar confiscations (worth $9 million) took place. In both cases, the businesses were obliterated. The *Pryba* jury stopped short of confiscating Mrs. Pryba's house, in spite of the fact that the law would have permitted this because some business activities (e.g., the counting of coins from vending machines) had been conducted there. This jury apparently recognized that a private residence should receive at least a modicum of protection.

It was in this context that our plea negotiations with federal prosecutors took place. We have already seen that Sam Currin understood the power of RICO, and was hoping to get his colleagues in the Middle District[13] of North Carolina (where our business is located) to bring such a case against us even though he thought they lacked "the sense to do it."

The RICO threat cast a pall over all our other discussions. I wondered if I should put all my personal property in Harriet's name, which I naively assumed would put it beyond the government's reach. I have learned subsequently that this is one of those areas in the law where intentions are of critical importance. It is unlawful for someone threatened with a criminal prosecution to dispose of assets in anticipation of such a prosecution. On the other hand, transferring assets from husband to wife is a common practice, and if I chose to make such a transfer for reasons independent of the prosecutorial activity, there would be nothing wrong with that. So the lawyers were in a bind. Clearly, they could not advise me to do something unlawful. On the other hand, they did not want to advise me against doing something which would be legal if it were properly motivated.

In these despondent days I had a long talk with my good friend Bob Ciszewski. We sat on a park bench in Stuyvesant Town in New York City, and I asked for his assurances that if worse came to worst he would do his best to carry on those of my activities—particularly our work in international family planning—that he could manage to do.

My American Express card seemed very precious to me in those days;

because it was backed by several thousand dollars worth of credit, I knew I could at least get a room in a good hotel and a meal, no matter what else happened.

While RICO provides enormous and often inappropriate power to prosecutors, the threat of its use—even the possibility of its use—can cut the other way when it comes to plea negotiations. In part because prosecutors were so blunt about their intentions for RICO ("We wanted to do RICOs to wipe out the business," asserted the Department of Justice's Cynthia Christfield in the *Pryba* case),[14] we became determined not to step into the RICO swamp voluntarily. After our Alamance victory, for example, we were no longer prepared to risk a plea by the corporation to an offense that constituted a RICO "predicate." This is because, under RICO, an indictment for any crime for which a company has pleaded guilty in the past makes the prior conviction automatically admissible as evidence in the new trial. The earlier offense can be presented by the prosecution to the jury as part of the "pattern of racketeering." In otherwise similar non-RICO cases, prior convictions are often ruled inadmissible because knowledge of a prior conviction is very likely to prejudice a jury. Thus, if we had agreed to plead PHE (the corporation) guilty to a charge of obscenity, the risks of a second conviction (which can conceivably occur even through the accidental sale of a book or film) would have increased dramatically, risking corporate fines of such magnitude as to sink our business and/or subjecting me and probably other officers of the corporation to such a high level of risk as to likely make our continued conduct of the business impossible. We therefore felt it was untenable to continue offering the corporate plea to obscenity, and we very soon drew the line based clearly on the standard of "no plea to a RICO predicate offense," i.e., we would not plead guilty to an obscenity charge.[15]

On one occasion we were told that we would have to give up selling everything that was "sexually oriented," including magazines like *Playboy* containing "mere nudity" (a prosecutor's phrase) and mainstream books like *The Joy of Sex*. At still other times the government indicated that we could stay in business with movies and videos that had received an R rating but could not carry anything unrated or X-rated. When asked if, under those circumstances, we would still be permitted to sell lubricants, vibrators, and other sex toys, the government balked. Clearly they did not wish to condone any merchandise that was designed for the enhancement of sexual pleasure. Sex toys are not illegal in most states.[16] But we were dealing with people for whom sexual pleasure, unless specifically linked in some way to procreation, was wrong, and the sale of sexually stimulating items could therefore not be permitted to survive a negotiated agreement to which they were a party.

In these post-Alamance acquittal days, continuously threatened with federal indictments and faced with the prospect of future trials, we were prepared to plead the corporation guilty to nearly any non-RICO charge. The corporation would pay a reasonable fine. We suggested that we would be willing to submit our products to a neutral screening committee. We would "curtail our marketing of products to assure that what we sell is lawfully offered to the public and . . . to turn this determination over to an impartial committee of individuals and abide by their collective views as to what is acceptable." We further indicated a willingness to discuss a non-RICO misdemeanor plea for me.

Had the government accepted the review committee offer, made in August 1986, it would probably have spelled the death of our business. Fortunately, the acceptance of such a committee would have put the government in a constitutionally untenable position, and this part of the offer had little life; the First Amendment, as construed by the Supreme Court, makes it improper for the government to be in the "review" business even through a third party.

The determination on the part of the prosecutors to include jail time for me was also clear from the outset. Though the fear of jail time was not foremost on my mind, the implications of a felony plea were a different matter. Convicted felons (if one agrees to be "convicted" as part of a plea, there is little difference between that and conviction at trial as far as subsequent status is concerned) lose many of their civil rights, including the precious right to vote and, sometimes, a good many other fundamental rights, like free travel, that I cherish very deeply. This I was not prepared to accept. Since finding some nonfelony offense for which I could do time was a bit transparently fraudulent, this part of the process never got very far either.

TAKING THE OFFENSIVE

Our strategy during this period gradually became more aggressive. First, we determined that we would not be easy game. Prosecutors would have to fight for every foot of ground; we would file motions forcing legal confrontations at every reasonable opportunity and the government would not be able to make an easy meal of us, as it had of a few of our competitors. Secondly, we believed it appropriate to be assertive with the Department of Justice in Washington ("Main Justice") on the broad issue of obscenity and the enforcement of obscenity laws by the federal government.

Our assertiveness took the form of correspondence and requests for meetings with senior Justice Department staff in an effort to ascertain just what their standards were and how the Reagan/Meese Justice Department was interpreting *Miller*. Most of these contacts were made for us by Bruce Ennis, an experienced First Amendment attorney with the law firm of Jenner & Block in Washington. Bruce had argued First Amendment cases before the U.S. Supreme Court on more than one occasion. He was highly respected by his peers, and appeared to me to be the perfect person to move our confrontation to the national scene, to get things to the top of the Justice Department power structure, and to help us see to it that if we succeeded in our struggle, we would make good nationwide law.

Accordingly, Bruce wrote to Attorney General Edwin Meese in December 1986, and, having had no reply, again in February 1988. We made two requests. First we asked that Main Justice compile a list of magazines, books, and videos that were either indicted for obscenity or convicted of obscenity in communities throughout the United States. This is publicly available information but very difficult for a private party to compile, while it would be relatively easy for the government to do so. We asked for this information on the grounds that it would help us comply with the law. Ennis wrote,

> The availability of such a listing would greatly assist my clients in their efforts to ensure that their nationwide distribution is in conformity with the standards of the many localities into which sexually explicit videotapes are shipped. Obviously, if a particular community found a videotape obscene, my clients would refrain from distributing that videotape in that community. . . . I therefore renew my previous request that you direct your subordinates to compile such a list of prosecutions as promptly as is reasonably possible, and to make that list available to my clients and other interested members of the public. Compilation and distribution of such a list would be consistent with the highest tradition of the Department of Justice, because it would facilitate and ensure compliance with the law before a criminal act occurs, instead of waiting until the Department believes that a criminal act has occurred and then prosecuting the persons who may have unwittingly failed to comply with a particular community's standards.

We didn't have a high level of confidence that the Justice Department would compile and make this "list" available but we thought it was a reasonable request; at least no constitutional impediments prevented their doing so. But we found that we were dealing with people who were disinclined to be in any way cooperative with putative criminal defendants dealing in a line of merchandise they so clearly found repugnant. Nevertheless, it seemed to us both useful and creative to address the Justice Department on these matters and to force them to address, among other things, our clear desire to abide by a very vague law. We were not asking Main Justice to define obscenity but to tell us, as Carl Fox had done, what materials they considered appropriate for prosecution.

The very fact that we could take this position is evidence of the bizarre nature and the extra-ordinary vagueness of the *Miller* standard for obscenity.

Bruce's letter continued.

Bruce Ennis   (© Patrice Gilbert/*Legal Times*)

PHE, Inc. and Philip Harvey will continue to make every reasonable effort to stay within the law. As you know, how-ever, the test of obscenity set forth in *Miller* v. *California*, 413 U.S. 15 (1973), makes this effort extremely difficult. *Miller* incorporates vague and variable standards that at best mark a dim and uncertain line between protected and unprotected expression.

Despite the intractability of this problem, my clients have assiduously tried to ensure that none of the videotapes they distribute violates the law. In my prior letter to you, I mentioned that my clients have consulted closely with the principal law enforcement officials in the county where PHE, Inc.'s offices and warehouse are located, and have accepted their recommendations respecting the distribution of specific materials. This is only one of the policies my clients have been following in order to stay within the law.

Bruce continued with another important request which was analogous to the consultative relationship we had had with Carl Fox in Orange County, North Carolina.

I also request that the Department of Justice provide my clients with what-ever guidelines and standards the Federal Bureau of Investigation or other Justice Department officials use in investigating whether particular sexually explicit materials violate federal obscenity laws. Upon receiving this information, my clients will follow their longstanding practice with respect to standards received from local authorities, and incorporate the federal standards into our internal and external review procedures.

I would like to stress that this letter is a genuine effort to establish a cooperative relationship between my clients and the Department of Justice in order to ensure my clients' continued compliance with the vague and difficult law. I await your reply.

There had been considerable reluctance among our criminal defense attorneys to take even this posture.[17] But we decided it was worth it. We wanted to emphasize the vagueness of *Miller* and to remind the Justice Department in Washington that they were making their own judgments about what was obscene through their prosecutorial actions. They were not neutral about what *Miller* meant. We also wanted to underline the fact that the government would not roll over us easily, that we were eager to sit down and talk, but that we were not afraid. We also felt that it would be useful to have these reasonable requests in the record.

Miller v. California, the United States obscenity law, is indeed troublingly vague. Any other law as vague, if it dealt with matters other than sex, would be likely to be declared unconstitutional by our Supreme Court. (See appendix C for a fuller analysis of this matter.) In fact, the Supreme Court apparently doesn't know what to do about obscenity. Outlawing speech that does no one demonstrable harm is a clear violation of both the letter and the intent of the First Amendment (as is the outlawing of most speech which *does* or may do harm), but the Court continued to recognize throughout the twentieth century that public opinion favors some limits on sexually oriented expression and, as Mr. Dooley observed, "the Supreme Court follows the 'liction returns" very closely. The *Miller* decision's provision requiring the application of "community standards" for offensiveness and prurience permitted the Court itself to avoid reviewing films by mandating that local or statewide communities apply their own standards; the Court would no longer try to maintain one for the entire country. But this didn't quite work. Only a year after *Miller*, a Georgia jury found the movie *Carnal Knowledge*, directed by Mike Nichols and starring Jack Nicholson and Candace Bergen, obscene under the *Miller* test. The Court simply reversed the jury out of hand, much to the relief of Hollywood movie makers and to all who value free artistic expression. Since that day the Supreme Court, much to its undoubted relief, has not found it necessary to review films or books.

Despite the vagueness of *Miller*, we knew that the federal government must have its own guidelines in this area. U.S. Customs, for example, could not facilitate the work of its agents by publishing a *Miller* handbook for them to consult at ports of entry because the law's language is far too vague to provide guidance for U.S. Customs officials acting in the real world. Something more specific was obviously required. Since we could not get any information about this from Main Justice, we filed a Freedom of Information Act (FOIA) suit and received the following U.S. Customs Department guidelines.

Pornography and U.S. Customs

"Certain parameters . . . [establish] . . . broad categorization of the different types of pornographic materials (both in film and magazine form) which are currently produced and distributed. Three general themes are portrayed in pornographic literature. These are:

(1) Adult material which depicts any sexual behavior between adults. This material may be described as soft core or hard core, and will include such themes as heterosexual relations, homosexual relations, group sex, and simple nude photography. This material is, by and large, within the community standards in most areas and is produced in large quantity in the United States and Europe.
(2) Adult deviant material which depicts such acts as sadomasochism, urination, defecation, bestiality, and other "unnatural" sex acts. This type of literature is produced to some extent in the United States, but is produced in its more explicit and deviant forms in Europe.
(3) Child material depicting explicit sexual conduct or sexual acts between children and adults."[18]

The Customs Department's observation that category 1 material is "within the community standards in most areas" makes it clear that such material is not normally to be seized, while categories 2 and 3 are subject to seizure.

Similarly we sought under FOIA and received (after considerable effort and negotiation) written guidelines from the FBI.

FBI headquarters had established an "obscene matter file" in the FBI Laboratory, which included exhibits consisting "only of commercially produced pornography relating to the sexual exploitation of children and commercial adult pornography dealing with sadomasochism, bestiality, and coprophilia [feces related] behavior."[19]

Despite the Justice Department's unwillingness to provide us with any of its own prosecutorial guidelines, the pattern was now reasonably clear. The federal government, as well as our own local prosecutor, considered obscene, or at least potentially prosecutable, sexual depictions involving the "darker" themes of deviant sexual behavior. The sort of cheerful consensual adult activity depicted in PHE's materials was not a target for most federal law enforcement officials, other than those National Obscenity Enforcement Unit (NOEU) prosecutors who were now bearing down on us.

Bruce Ennis's letters to Attorney General Meese had been sent in late 1986 and early 1988. In November of 1988 he finally got a reply from Patrick Trueman, the acting director of the NOEU, who had succeeded Rob Showers in this position. Mr. Trueman refused our request for guidelines or information on the ground that providing such guidelines "would be unconstitutional" under Supreme Court rulings in *Bantam Books, Inc.* v. *Sullivan* (1963). Bruce quickly responded, pointing out that the Bantam Books case not only did not preclude a consultation between the Justice Department and parties like PHE but indeed, in some of its language, suggested such collaboration. The Supreme Court had stated in this opinion, for example, that "we do not hold that law enforcement officers must renounce all informal contacts with persons suspected of violating valid laws prohibiting obscenity. Where such consultation is genuinely undertaken with the purpose of aiding the distributor to comply with such laws and avoid prosecution under them, it need not retard the full enjoyment of First Amendment freedoms."

Having cited this and other portions of the Bantam Books decision, Bruce wrote,

> If you maintain your position that the Department of Justice cannot, or will not, respond to good faith requests for information in order to facilitate compliance with federal laws, that position will be of concern not only to my clients, but also to the public at large. It is certainly appropriate for the Department of Justice to do whatever it can reasonably do to prevent crime before it occurs by assisting citizens to conform their conduct to the law. My client, and the public, are entitled to know whether this Department of Justice will do what it can reasonably do to facilitate compliance with the law, or will, instead, lie in wait like a spider waiting to trap inadvertent violations of the law.

This was January 1989. We were sounding more confident, but we knew that there was much more to come.

NOTES

1. "Mail Order Firm Found Not Guilty of Obscenity," *Raleigh News and Observer*, March 27, 1987.

2. "No Changes Seen in Obscenity Law Enforcement," *Durham Morning Herald*, March 28, 1987.

3. Samuel Currin, Memo to Staff, March 30, 1987. This memo (and many others) were made available to us as part of what is called the discovery process in the civil suit we brought against the Justice Department, initiated in March 1990.

4. Ibid.

5. "FBI Launches Porn Crackdown, Raids 29 Retailers," *Raleigh News and Observer*, October 1, 1985.

6. Affidavit of Connie Faucett, June 13, 1986.

7. Affidavit of Cathy Long, June 16, 1986.

8. Affidavit of Rachel C. Hackler, June 13, 1986.

9. *Forbes*, January 22, 1990, p. 14.

10. "Dread of RICO Likely to Grow, May Bring Push for Mob-Only Use," *Wall Street Journal*, December 22, 1988.

11. Ibid.

12. *Alexander v. United States* 509 U.S. 540 (1993).

13. The United States is divided into ninety-four federal districts. North Carolina has three: the Eastern District where Sam Currin held sway in 1986, the Middle District, where our offices were located, and the Western District.

14. *The American Lawyer*, March 1988, p. 98.

15. Congress had added obscenity to the list of crimes that could be prosecuted under RICO in 1984.

16. The exceptions are Georgia, Kansas, Alabama, Mississippi, and Texas, which outlaw the sale of any device "designed or marketed as useful primarily for the stimulation of human genital organs." A wholesale seller of such devices commits a jailable felony offense in Texas (up to two years imprisonment). Maximum punishments for first offenses in the other four states vary from six months to one year, with second offense penalties as high as ten years. For selling a vibrator!

17. Dave Rudolf, Joe Chesire, and Wade Smith make their living defending persons accused of criminal offenses. Bruce Ennis is a civil litigator. There is a huge difference. Criminal defense attorneys instinctively try to avoid confronting the government and they especially try to avoid "jerking their beards," as Wade puts it. Civil litigators, on the other hand, are perfectly comfortable confronting the government even before the government confronts them because that is a natural part of what they do.

18. U.S. Customs Service, Staff Memo from Assistant Commissioner (Commercial Operations) and Assistant Commissioner (Enforcement), October 19, 1984.

19. FBI Manual of Investigative Operations and Guidelines, August 12, 1986.

CHAPTER FIVE

OBEYING THE LAW, IGNORING THE LAW, FLOUTING THE LAW,

People everywhere just want to be free.
—1960s pop song

Somewhere during all this, our company had started making some pretty good profits. We had good years and bad years like every other company, but overall we were doing well. Despite our massive legal bills, and possibly because the government was so efficiently decimating our competitors, we prospered to the point where I, as majority shareholder, became what most people would consider wealthy.

I have always had mixed feelings about this, especially when it moves on to the word "rich," a term that makes me very uncomfortable. I am the youngest of five children, and by the time I was born my parents were in their forties and my father's business had prospered. He had pulled himself up from poverty pretty much in the great American tradition, but by becoming prosperous, he deprived me of the opportunity to do the same thing. I'm not complaining about that. But when I was a child, we always lived in one of the largest houses in Macomb, Illinois, and because there is such a strong American tradition that respects the virtues of surviving strict financial limitations, I was often embarrassed about living in that big house. Working hard to become rich is both acceptable and nearly universal; actually being rich seems to be a different matter.

In Macomb, this sometimes became a taunt. Popular movies about "poor little rich kids" generally assumed them to be spoiled and unworthy. Certainly it felt to me, in the small-town Midwest, that being a child from a wealthy family was a severe social stigma. I vividly remember my girlfriend in sixth grade (or the girl I hoped would be my girlfriend) telling me that she didn't want to keep going to the movies with me on Fridays because she was afraid her friends would think she was just interested in me for my money. It is hard not to smile over that incident now, but at the time it was devastating. I lost Judy Lircey by being "rich"!

105

This and related incidents have always made me feel a bit ambivalent about inherited wealth, even much later in life. As Adam & Eve succeeded over the years, I remember thinking with real satisfaction that I had, at a point I took the trouble to define, made more money from my own efforts than I had inherited from my parents. Somehow the money I had made on my own seemed more honorable.

Perhaps in part for these reasons, I have never understood extravagance. The idea of showing off one's wealth strikes me as childish and meretricious. I understand the urge, the sort of nobody's-gonna-kick-sand-in-my-face-anymore Charles Atlas syndrome, but it has no appeal for me. Neither do I respect wealth's value as a yardstick in the marketplace to measure how well you are doing. According to this measure, if you don't continue to make more money this year than you made last year, you are somehow failing, as your success meter is not showing appropriate progress. Measurements taken, meter read, how does one assess the wealth remaining in his or her hands, and what do we do with it?

The two categories of personal wealth, it seems to me, consist of (a) that money which one may reasonably need for one's personal needs and for one's family, and (b) everything else. Absent an extreme and uninsured medical emergency or an unusually large number of children in college at the same time, it seems to me that a family's personal needs can be adequately met with $100,000 after taxes no matter who you are. Very few families have this much, of course, but it always surprises me that a substantial percentage of the families that do seem to feel they're short of money. I can understand why some people might find it *pleasurable* to spend more than that, but I can't understand why anyone would profess to need more than that. After all, $2,000 per month each for food, housing, clothing, and entertainment is a very generous budget. Unless you include capital purchases, like a vacation home, I've never spent that much, and can't see any reason to.

The other category of personal wealth is what you may use for things beyond your own needs, and in this category I am very acquisitive and greedy. As I have described, I came to the business world from the nonprofit world, falling into a profitable enterprise almost by accident. During my years with CARE and subsequently with Population Services International and DKT International, a great deal of my time and energy was spent in fund-raising, meaning getting others to donate money so we could do what we (and the donor) thought should be done. The idea of generating one's own funds for this purpose was, and is, altogether delightful. Indeed, when Tim Black and I first started Adam & Eve and had stars in our eyes, the thought of a Robin Hood business selling contraceptives and sexual accoutrements to the relatively wealthy citizens of the United States in order to generate funds to subsidize the sale of contraceptives in poor countries struck us as marvelous. And it has been. Federal tax regulations permit one to deduct from taxable income all contributions to qualifying charitable organizations, up to one-half of taxable income, and for most of the past twenty-five years I have taken full advantage of that deduction. The result has been a big boost for the overseas family planning and AIDS-prevention programs, indeed the life's blood of DKT's early program years, when it was possible to start a half dozen contraceptive social marketing programs in places like Ethiopia and Vietnam pretty much on our own hook, and *then* approach the donors for ongoing support of activities we had already demonstrated could work.

My colleagues in the nonprofit world are sometimes envious of this ability to get things done quickly and flexibly with discretionary funds, and I don't blame them. It is especially pleasurable to be able to make a quick decision in an important situation when I know that most other nonprofit managers would have to go through a cumbersome decision-making process requiring committees, board members, or donors. We just do it, and move on.

Much of the money I've been describing I only get to fondle on its way through my otherwise heavily taxed financial corpus, but it's fun moving money around, even if you don't keep it. I remember the first time that Adam & Eve made enough to distribute, on a single occasion, a little more than $200,000 to me personally. I walked from one savings bank to a second one in order not to leave more than $100,000 in any one bank. The FDIC insurance limit was $100,000 and I wasn't taking any chances.

That first six-figure deposit in the Orange Savings and Loan in Chapel Hill, North Carolina, is a very sweet memory. That was money I had made, money I had earned on my own through the free enterprise system, and it was a pleasure to get the little passbook with six digits in the balance.

The first time I wrote a check for seven figures also gave me a rush. Then the money was gone, contributed, as I intended, to DKT International. I make such contributions with only occasional hesitation, always with some enthusiasm. I have no sense of loss or regret at parting with money under these circumstances (well, maybe an occasional twinge), because I cannot think of any better possible use for it. So there is a taste of real pleasure in giving it away and continuing to supervise the programs that those funds make possible.

Having plenty of money also broadens the prospects for spontaneous generosity. If one of my stepchildren needs financial assistance, and it makes sense, I can help. I think I enjoy this especially because it was the way my father often expressed his affection to us. During one period when he and my mother visited each of their five children, spread across the United States, Dad would leave a new refrigerator in every home. "Hmmm," he'd say, sauntering into the kitchen of one of our places, "This refrigerator is a little bulky. No automatic defroster. You could use a new one." This meant that you would get a new fridge, even if you didn't much want one. For my father, equipment was love.

My experience has taught me that paying taxes, very large amounts of taxes, sharpens one's passion for limited government. The first time I paid Uncle Sam $1 million of my own money, the shortcomings of the bloated federal bureaucracy came into very sharp focus. That money could have been used to run a major program in Calcutta to benefit some of the world's most desperately poor people. Instead, it was going to the government to help subsidize raisin advertisements in Japan, pay benefits to millionaire farmers, seize another automobile in the futile and immoral war on drugs, make life even worse for America's poor through dysfunctional subsidization, or pay part of the salaries of the few hundred thousand employees of the Department of Agriculture, who now vastly outnumber the number of farmers in the United States. These and a whole lot of other things the federal government throws money at inappropriately come to mind when you write a big check to pay for it. And the process of doing so sharpens one's interest in limiting the size and scope of a government that now consumes nearly a third of our national wealth.

In this context, the withholding tax, it now appears to me, since I no longer operate on that basis, is doing democratic society a great disservice. When taxes are withheld at their source, and employees never get to see the money, never have it in their own possession, the payment of income taxes is relatively remote and painless. If everyone had to sit down four times a year, as I do, and write a check to the federal (and state) government, the act of paying taxes would be brought home to all of us and government expenditures would be much more closely scrutinized than they are now. I think that that would be very good for our society.

When the subject of bad laws—laws that should not or at least may not be obeyed—comes up, Harriet reminds me that citizens of this or any society cannot simply decide which laws they will obey and which they will ignore. On one level, this is absolutely right. If we all decided which traffic lights we were going to stop at public safety would be imperiled.

On the other hand, there are laws that virtually all of us ignore. Many of these laws are violated by Americans without their even knowing it; others are deliberately violated or even flouted.

Overall, those laws that we feel an obligation to obey are the laws that control our behavior in ways that affect the well-being of others. Shopkeepers must be paid. If we take a taxi ride, we have made a contract and we must keep it, as must the driver. We cannot park our cars on our neighbors' lawns. There is a consensus in our society, and in all civilized societies, that we must obey the laws that prohibit violence by one citizen against another, prohibit the theft of others' property or the defrauding of our fellow citizens (a form of theft), and similar laws that protect citizens from the depredations of others. And we recognize that such rules must be enforced. As Lenny Bruce, who understood the difference between necessary laws and bad laws, put it, "You can't crap where I sleep."

It is another kind of law that is bad, and which most of us feel comfortable ignoring: those laws that attempt to govern our private behavior even when such behavior has no impact on the lives of others, or when the impact is welcomed by those whom the behavior affects. For example, I doubt that even the members of the Supreme Court, whose respect for the law can reasonably be assumed, have ever paid the slightest attention to the sodomy laws in Virginia in the conduct of their sexual lives. Those laws make it a felony for anyone—including husbands and wives—to practice oral sex or anal sex, and nobody honors such proscriptions. Yet the state of Virginia demands one to five years in prison for this act, Idaho insists on a minimum five-year punishment, and sixteen other states similarly outlaw these "crimes against nature."[1]

Another category of laws that are almost universally ignored are the laws prohibiting gambling. Anyone who puts up even trivial amounts of money to join the office pool to bet on football games or an NCAA tournament is guilty of a misdemeanor. The person who keeps the office pool records is probably violating *two* laws, and the penalties for "possession of gambling records" can be severe—up to a year in jail in Maryland, for example.[2] Some states penalize you for possessing a lottery ticket even from a state where the lottery is legal. Despite this, it is estimated that Americans place several billion dollars in illegal bets every week on pro and college football games during the fall. More than $5 billion, virtually all of it illegal, is bet on the Super Bowl alone.[3]

The argument that laws governing private consensual behavior are bad laws was put best by John Stuart Mill more than a century ago.

> [T]he sole end for which mankind are warranted, individually or collectively, in interfering with the liberty of action of any of their number is self-protection. That the only purpose for which power can be rightfully exercised over any member of a civilized community, against his will, is to prevent

harm to others. His own good, either physical or moral, is not a sufficient warrant. He cannot rightfully be compelled to do or forbear because it will be better for him to do so, because it will make him happier, because in the opinions of others, to do so would be wise or even right. These are good reasons for remonstrating with him or reasoning with him, or persuading him, or entreating him, but not for compelling him or visiting him with any evil in case he do otherwise. To justify that, the conduct from which it is desired to deter him must be calculated to produce evil to someone else. The only part of the conduct of anyone for which he is amenable to society is that which concerns others. In the part which merely concerns himself, his independence is, of right, absolute. Over himself, over his own body and mind, the individual is sovereign.[4]

If we humans are free, independent, autonomous beings, a coercive government should not dictate how we conduct our private lives, except when that conduct impinges on the equal rights of others. An ACLU board member summed it up thus: "Every adult human being has the right to inhale, imbibe, ingest, or insert anything he/she chooses into his or her own body."

But despite an American tendency to accept these libertarian principles, we continue to pass and preserve laws designed to control private consensual behavior, in the name of "morality." Where we should, in Mill's words, be remonstrating, reasoning, and persuading, we instead bring in the full power of the government to fine and imprison those whose private behavior does not conform to cultural norms or, more often, to what some among us would like those norms to be. Such laws are capriciously and differentially enforced; most are more frequently ignored than obeyed; they are usually hypocritical attempts to create an ideal behavior rather than reflections of what humans are actually like. To focus on only one of many such subjects, they reflect little or none of our scientific knowledge about sexuality.

An interesting case in point is our cultural hang-up over masturbation. Masturbation is not a criminal offense, but our societal concern about this nearly universal and utterly harmless practice reveals rather starkly our inability to accept our own sexual nature. Our fears about it are starkly revealed in the following advice from a contemporary Mormon church handout.

> Masturbation is a sinful habit that robs one of the Spirit and creates guilt and emotional stress. . . .
>
> Never touch the intimate parts of your body except during normal toilet processes. . . .
>
> Dress yourself for the night so securely that you cannot easily touch your vital parts. . . .

Put wholesome thoughts into your mind at all times. Read good books—Church books—Scriptures—Sermons of the Brethren.

Pray. But when you pray, don't pray about this problem[!].

[I]f you are tempted to masturbate, think of having to bathe in a tub of worms, and eat several of them as you do the act. . . .

In very severe cases it may be necessary to tie a hand to the bed frame with a tie. . . .[5]

American public figures, authors, and others approach this subject at their peril. The distinguished physician Dr. Joycelyn Elders lost her job as surgeon general after a firestorm of publicity following her suggestion that masturbation might be a subject worthy of attention in our public schools.

Reactionary populist (and perennial presidential candidate) Patrick Buchanan has helped maintain America's preoccupation with masturbation. On one CNN *Crossfire* segment with Judy Blume, Buchanan brought the subject up repeatedly. Blume is an author of popular books for adolescent and preadolescent girls, and her books have become highly controversial because they occasionally deal with the subject of masturbation in a forthright and nonjudgmental way. (A Judy Blume protagonist sometimes discovers, and enjoys, "my secret place.") On the *Crossfire* episode, Buchanan produced copies of Blume's books with these passages highlighted. "Finally," said Blume, "I just turned to him and said, 'Mr. Buchanan, are you hung up on masturbation or what?' "[6]

Perhaps this concern is part of the slippery slope argument—that if youngsters masturbate they will soon be on their way to frenzied and unprincipled sexual preoccupations incompatible with getting good grades and graduating from high school. If that really is the concern—that masturbation may be a risk factor for an unproductive and undisciplined life—why don't we study the matter? We know already

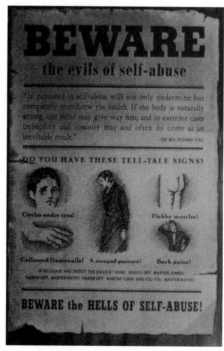

This early twentieth-century poster warned observers of the hellish consequences of masturbation.

that a substantial majority of Americans of all ages masturbate and a substantial majority of Americans are productive.

The fear of uncontrolled sexuality (as perhaps exemplified by the freedom to masturbate) is reflected in the pronouncements and actions of our policy makers and legislators. It appears to be based on the conviction that we all must be "controlled" to some degree in our private as well as our public conduct in order that the glue that holds civilized society together not disintegrate. Many such people feel that, if Americans are permitted to revel in "excess," even in the privacy of their own bedrooms, society will somehow suffer. President Richard M. Nixon expressed this view when he commented in 1970 that "an attitude of [sexual] permissiveness [could] contribute to an atmosphere condoning anarchy in every other field—and would increase the threat to our social order as well as to our moral principles."[7]

Too, there is the matter of pleasure for its own sake. In the Christian religion particularly, major currents suggest that anything that is pleasurable is, ipso facto, sinful. Self-denial is seen as a virtue in various manifestations of the Christian church, from the celibacy of priests to the asceticism of nuns and monks to various dietary restrictions. The assumption seems to be that if it feels good for its own sake, it must be wrong. This formula seems to apply especially to sex. When it comes to other sinful pleasures we are inclined at least to assess the potential harmful repercussions, but with sex, pleasure automatically equals sin. In other areas of life we do not normally consider pleasure, even for its own sake, to be sinful. I've never heard anyone suggest that we should deny ourselves the pleasure of a trip to the top of a beautiful mountain on a lovely summer's day or the pleasure to be had from beautiful music. Even the more sensual pleasures we get from sports are OK. But sex gets us all tied up in knots about the pleasure principle.

Our cultural preoccupation with masturbation and related matters provides an important clue to the psychology of those who feel impelled to control everyone's sexuality. Most such sexual "abnormalities" can be subjected to legal penalties, some of them severe.

SEX LAWS

In the United States we still have laws that variously prohibit prostitution, fornication, adultery, and virtually all forms of sexual intercourse or sexual contact other than procreative coupling (penis-vagina intercourse) by married heterosexual couples.

Here are a few examples of these laws in practice.

The Crime of Adultery: Old Laws Dusted Off [1990]

A 28-year old woman will be arraigned next month in Northern Wisconsin, where she is to stand trial on one of the rarest of criminal accusations: adultery.

No one in Wisconsin can recall the last time a county prosecutor sought to enforce the state's 19th-century law that requires sexual fidelity inside marriage. A felony punishable by up to two years in the state penitentiary and a fine of $10,000, adultery has not been an issue in Wisconsin courts since the early part of the century, lawyers say.

But the state's case against Donna E. Carroll has focused new attention on these relatively obscure statutes.[8]

Here is an example of the trap governments fall into when they attempt to regulate private consensual behavior. Donna Carroll and her husband were undergoing a contentious divorce and custody battle. Both had been seeing other romantic partners. The man with whom Mrs. Carroll had an affair was not charged and neither was her husband (who had the perspicacity to commit his indiscretions in another state). The adultery charge was brought against Mrs. Carroll (who, by the time all this was in the news, had moved out of her home and set up housekeeping with her new lover), at least partly because her husband was a friend of the district attorney and used that friendship in a vindictive move against his wife, who had made the mistake of admitting her affair during testimony in a family court hearing.

In Connecticut, legislators have now addressed that state's nineteenth-century statute proscribing extramarital sexuality. After four spouses—a husband and three wives who were drawn into the legal adultery net in connection with acrimonious divorces—were indicted on adultery charges in 1990, the legislature voted to scrap the law.[9] This decision continued a civilizing trend. Connecticut's first adultery law had called for both participants to be whipped "about the naked body" and branded with a hot iron on the forehead with the letter *A*.[10]

Our armed services have always prescribed rules about private behavior that go beyond that demanded in civilian life, sometimes for good reason. But the inanity of laws about particular sexual acts was made manifest in the witch hunts that ensued following the 1997 prosecution for adultery of Lt. Kelly Flinn, an unmarried Air Force lieutenant who was an outstanding pilot and the first woman ever to fly a B-52. (In many jurisdictions, Lieutenant Flinn, being single, could not be charged with committing adultery. In Georgia, for example, only married people can commit adultery; in Minnesota a single *man* can commit adultery with a married woman, but not the other way around [(609.36) 1996].) In the military, Lt. Flinn, charged with adultery for having an affair with a married man, avoided a court martial by accepting a less-than-honorable discharge from the Air Force.[11] Thus did we American taxpayers waste more than a million dollars in training for this top-gun pilot whose private sexual behavior would almost certainly not have affected her flying ability one whit.

Hard on the heels of the Flinn debacle, Air Force Gen. Joseph Ralston was similarly maltreated. General Ralston, who was the deputy chief of the Joint Chiefs of Staff in 1997, would almost certainly have been promoted to the chairmanship of the Joint Chiefs had not a guardian of the public morality phoned the military sex offense hotline (which by this time had become a source for witch-hunting) about an affair he had had with a civilian many years before while separated from his wife. Since Lieutenant Flinn, a woman, had been officially accused of the same offense, it became necessary as a matter of "fairness" that the general also be treated in this way. General Ralston withdrew his name from nomination.

Such foolish destructiveness is the inevitable outcome of laws attempting to govern our private sex lives. The absurdity of it all (though not the pain and suffering caused to the many persons directly concerned) was summed up in a cartoon by Jeff MacNelly for the *Chicago Tribune*. Second World War Gen. George S. Patton, pistols on both hips, stands before a huge flag addressing his troops, "But I can't go with you, men . . . I had this fling with a dancer in Morocco" (Fig. 5-1). Commentator Charles Krauthammer similarly observed on PBS's *Washington Week* that, had we fired all the adulterers in the military chain of command in the Second World War, "we'd all be speaking German."

FORNICATION

Fornication is normally defined as sexual intercourse between two people of the opposite sex, neither of whom is married. If a single person (especially a male) has sex with someone who is married, he may be guilty of adultery as well as fornication in some jurisdictions, and could theoretically be prosecuted on both counts for a single act. But the fornication laws, still on the books in the late 1990s in seventeen states and the District of Columbia, are meant to address those of us who, while single, have had sexual relations with other single people. This occurs frequently in mainstream American culture between two people who intend to marry or who may wish to try out a relationship of cohabitation before marriage. As a middle-class phenomenon, this

Figure 5-1

practice is increasingly accepted as normal and legitimate, even desirable. But it is also, in the jurisdictions noted above, a crime.

This "crime" provides a particularly good example of selective and differential enforcement. Perhaps the least enforced of all American sex laws, fornication laws are used to discriminate against people prosecutors don't like, usually poor people. In an Idaho case in 1996, a prosecutor decided to prosecute mothers of illegitimate children who applied for welfare benefits. Seventeen-year-old Amanda Smisek was charged with (and admitted to) the crime of fornication, difficult to deny as she was pregnant at the time and had never been married. She was given a one-month jail sentence and ordered to take "parenting" classes. Her sixteen-year-old boyfriend was also convicted of fornication, put on probation, and sentenced to community service. Their real crime was not cohabiting or having sexual intercourse, but applying for welfare benefits for a child born out of wedlock.[12]

The Crime That Dare Not Speak Its Name

February 1990. (The first letter from James David Moseley had arrived [at *Playboy*] almost a year earlier.)

Dear Sir:

The purpose of this letter is to ask for your help. I am being held in a Georgia prison for the crime of sodomy (*per linguam* in vagina). I committed this act in private with my own wife. She is over the age of 21. I was convicted under the Georgia sodomy statute for simple consensual sodomy—a law that penalizes nonaggravated, nonviolent sodomy between consenting adults with a sentence of up to 20 years.

Although she was an accomplice, my wife was neither charged nor tried. I was sentenced to a total of five years. I'm to serve two years in prison and three more on probation. Probation in Georgia can be revoked for as little as a traffic violation, a DUI or an arrest without conviction.

My life has been virtually destroyed. I have lost everything, including my family.

Playboy took Moseley's letter seriously, followed up, and obtained more details. Here is the magazine's description of subsequent events:

His estranged wife had asked him to tie her up and have sex. He tied her feet and had oral sex with her but felt that something was wrong.

"My wife brought the initial charges. Her reasons? To get custody of our two boys. She is a vengeful, spiteful person."

His wife accused her husband of two counts of rape, two counts of aggravated oral sodomy and two counts of aggravated anal sodomy for allegedly violating her on two separate occasions in February 1988. The jury did not buy her story (in part because her own sister testified in Moseley's defense that she had an ulterior motive in asking to be tied up: She had learned that he had spoken with an attorney and wanted to stage a pre-emptive strike).

"The prosecutor [a woman] made it seem like I had committed a capital crime—'Your mouth touched her vagina!' she screamed. I didn't even know what was going on. And I still can't believe all this. It was presented to the jury as though I were the lowest, most degraded piece of scum on earth because my mouth touched her vagina. I felt like some sort of human sacrifice to appease Georgia's tribal gods. What hypocrisy! As though the prosecutor's mouth had never touched a sexual organ!"[13]

It is difficult to state more dramatically the necessity for liberty in our homes than in the cases of David Moseley in Georgia and Donna Carroll in Wisconsin. Both were unfortunate to be married to vindictive spouses, whom they are no doubt better rid of. But such intrusion by the government cannot be reasonably justified, whether or not it is being used to punish, humiliate, or extract concessions.

MAN CAUGHT BY SODOMY LAW
Judge Gives Ten-Year Sentence for 'Crime Against Nature'

William C. L. "Lee" Fry, 23, had been in prison for 19 months when the Greensboro *News and Record* published this report on November 12, 1989:

> "I couldn't believe it," the former Marine Corporal recalled recently during an interview at his new home, the state prison in Lincolnton. "I held my composure until I went back to jail and called my family. Bitter? Yeah, I'm bitter."
>
> Fry . . . [was] in prison . . . for a crime that an estimated 80 to 90% of American adults have engaged in—an irony that draws outrage from civil liberty lawyers and disbelief from other prison inmates.
>
> "If they lock me up for this," Fry says, "they should lock everyone else up for it, and if they do that, they won't have room for the bank robbers and rapists."
>
> Fry's plight casts a shadow on every North Carolina couple—homosexual and heterosexual, unmarried and married—who engages in oral sex, said William Simpson, legal director for the North Carolina Civil Liberties Union.
>
> "This is the first time I have ever heard the law applied to what was, according to the jury's findings, consensual activity," he said. "It would literally apply equally to married couples acting in the privacy of their own bedrooms, and that's truly offensive.
>
> "I think it's outrageous."

Fry had been accused of breaking and entering his former girlfriend's mobile home and having sex with her against her will. The jury had found him not guilty on all of those counts, believing Fry's testimony that their sex had been consensual. But Lee Fry had made a fatal error during the trial. He admitted that the woman, Diane Sanders, had performed oral sex on him at her own initiative. In 1988, this was a felony punishable by ten years in prison in the state of North Carolina (the penalty has subsequently been reduced). "We had to go with that one because he admitted it on the stand," the jury foreman later reported. And the prosecutor, Greg Butler, stated, "We always add it in [the sodomy indictment]. In this case, I'm glad we did. Without it, he would have walked."

"We always add it in." This means that, for example, lazy prosecutors who do not wish to take the time to build a solid case against someone accused of a real crime, a depredation of one human by another, can just "add in" an easier felony and then see if the defendant can be tricked into admitting guilt because it is something that no one thinks of as a crime, or even as wrongdoing. It means that prosecutors who can "add it in" do not need the same level of proof, beyond a reasonable doubt, when they bring more serious charges against people they don't like. They are thus empowered to bring an indictment and go to trial with a weak case because maybe they can get a conviction on the basis of a sodomy charge alone.

Our system of jurisprudence and our concept of justice under law is built on the premise that the accused can confront his/her accuser, be fully informed of the crimes with which he/she is charged, and be able to offer a full defense. When we have bad laws, laws that can just be "added in," we undermine the very basis of our jurisprudential system.

William Fry was released from prison in 1990, having served nearly two and a half years on the sodomy charge.

SEX IN THE PEACH STATE

Michael Bowers, the attorney general of Georgia, seems to personify what can happen when discriminatory and archaic sex laws are used as weapons.

In his best-known case, Bowers brought charges against Michael Hardwick, who was discovered enjoying consensual sexual relations with another man in the privacy of his home by police who were there investigating an unrelated matter.

In upholding the right of the state of Georgia in *Bowers* v. *Hardwick* to punish such conduct, the Supreme Court, in a five to four decision in 1986, referred to the long history of societal prohibitions against homosexual conduct. This argument, ignoring Mr. Hardwick's privacy rights, was based on very shaky intellectual foundations. Because mankind has always looked down on (and often punished) homosexuality, it must be constitutional to do so. One of the five justices in the majority, Lewis Powell, asserted after his subsequent retirement that "I think I probably made a mistake,"[14] in voting to uphold the conviction in the *Bowers* case.

For Georgia Attorney General Bowers, this was just the first in a series of sex-related legal matters. In 1996, Mr. Bowers withdrew an offer of employment to Robin Joy Shahar, who had been offered a position in the Georgia Department of Law, when he found out that Shahar was a lesbian and was planning to openly marry another woman. Shahar sued, claiming that Bowers had violated her First Amendment rights of intimate and expressive association as well as her freedom of religion. Bowers asserted that Shahar's open lesbianism cast doubt on her ability to uphold Georgia's sodomy statutes. Shahar lost her case on appeal. As Anthony Lewis wrote in the *New York Times*, the majority of the Court of Appeals "assumed that Ms. Shahar had a protected interest in her lesbian relationship. But it was outweighed, [the court] found, by Attorney General Bower's claim that keeping her on the staff might lead the public to question his office's credibility and its commitment to enforce the law against homosexual sodomy."[15]

But the game wasn't over. Soon after the Shahar episode, Attorney General Bowers admitted to a decade-long adulterous (therefore illegal) affair with a married employee.[16] What a soap opera! Adultery! Sodomy! Homosexuality! Michael Bowers is a one-man legislative sex circus. It remains only to note that Georgia law also prohibits the sale of objects "designed or marketed primarily for the stimulation of human sexual organs."[17] The purchase of such a stimulator constitutes an illegal transaction punishable (for the seller) by a maximum one year in prison.

BIG-GOVERNMENT CONSERVATIVES; BIG-GOVERNMENT LIBERALS

The urges of both the political Left and the political Right to control our lives has been nicely summed up by David Boaz, vice president of the Cato Institute:

> Conservatives want to be your daddy, telling you what to do and what not to do. Liberals want to be your mommy, feeding you, tucking you in, and wiping your nose.[18]

Sex laws, of course, are primarily associated with the conservative side of the aisle. But in the we-know-what-is-best-for-you department of government "benevolence," today's modern-day American conservatism and liberalism merge. Both ideologies favor large-scale government intervention in the private lives and activities of citizens, but only in those areas that they, for their own often special reasons, believe to be appropriate. American "conservatives," daddy-like, want government intervention to prevent us from reading entertaining sex books, from engaging in homosexual relationships, to prevent women from having abortions, to forbid anyone from smoking marijuana (though not the much more dangerous ordinary tobacco). "Liberals" want the government to interfere by taxing us strenuously, taking income from some to give it to others (who are by no means necessarily poor), regulating businesses in ways that drive up consumers' costs, and guiding our behavior through the tax code.

Neither set of beliefs has much intellectual substance. No ideological framework can reconcile a belief in laissez-faire economics and the state control of private sexual behavior. Equally, there is no ideological or intellectual consistency in proposing "benevolent" government interference in private business and health-care activity, and, at the same time, a hands-off policy to sexual and reproductive matters.

A conservative in India is opposed to the slaughter of cows (because traditional conservative Hindus hold cattle to be sacred), and a Russian conservative in 1990 was a Communist. Conservatives in Sierra Leone drum up support for female genital mutilation, a traditional practice of cutting off the clitoris (and often more of the genitals) of young girls.[19] These conservatives have little in common with each other or with an American conservative, except, possibly, a resistance to change. This lack of ideological coherence was well summed up by Nobel laureate economist Friederich Hayek in a classic 1960 essay. Today's conservatives, Hayek pointed out, are fully prepared, despite protestations about "getting government off our backs," to use the power and authority of government for their own purposes. They even fear any weakening of governmental authority. This position, Hayek observed, is difficult to reconcile with the preservation of liberty.

> In general, it can probably be said that the conservative does not object to coercion or arbitrary power so long as it is used for what he regards as the right purposes. He believes that if the government is in the hands of decent men, it ought not be too much restricted by rigid rules. Since he is essentially opportunist and lacks principles, his main hope must be that the wise and the good will rule—not merely by example, as we all must wish, but by authority given to them and enforced by them. Like the socialist, he is less concerned with the problem of how the powers of government should be limited than with that of who wields them; and, like the socialist, he regards himself as entitled to force the values he holds on other people.
>
> When I say the conservative lacks principles, I do not mean to suggest that he lacks moral conviction. A typical conservative is indeed usually a man of very strong moral convictions. What I mean is that he has no political prin-

ciples which enable him to work with people whose moral values differ from his own for a political order in which both can obey their convictions.[20]

When Hayek refers to socialists, of course, he is referring to those proponents of left-wing politics who advocate large government, including government that plays an active and intrusive role in the economic affairs of a nation. Most American liberals would deny the socialist label, instead paying at least lip service to the virtues of free-market capitalism. Indeed this is the classic definition of a liberal: a belief in democratic principles, a free and open society, and free markets.

This brings us to libertarianism, a set of principles based on the classical liberal tradition.

Libertarians do not want to function as either mommy or daddy; libertarians assume that we are adults.

A libertarian holds that government should be strictly limited and its powers confined to those enumerated in the Constitution. Such a government serves primarily to protect the liberties of its citizens, including the right to pursue happiness, each of us in our own way, provided only that we do not interfere with the equal rights of others. Government does not exist to patronize us (the government is *our* servant), or to tell us how to conduct our sex lives, when to fasten our seat belts, or with whom we should trade or otherwise do business. Libertarianism trusts all adult citizens to be the autonomous and responsible beings that they by nature are, fully capable of cooperating, free of government direction, with other citizens in an environment of enforceable laws that are designed solely to prevent depredations of some citizens by others and to maintain a reasonable framework of contract law so that agreements can be enforced. A libertarian government would have no basis for, and no interest in, protecting citizens from obscene writings or marijuana because all adult humans, being autonomous and responsible individuals, are entitled to make decisions about such things for themselves. They may choose their own paths to happiness (or, if they so choose, misery) as long as they don't interfere with the rights of others. Equally, all persons are expected to deal with the consequences of their actions and not expect government to ameliorate their errors.

As long as we continue to pass laws that criminalize private consensual behavior, prosecutors will try to enforce them. As long as we imbue legislators and other leaders with the authority to dictate other people's private behavior, no matter how pleasurable and fulfilling that behavior may be, we will be authorizing an unjustified role for government as despot.

Many of these convictions on my part were forged and illuminated by what would unfold in *PHE, Inc.* v. *U.S. Department of Justice.*

NOTES

1. Virginia code, sec. 18.2-361; Idaho Code, sec. 18-6605.

2. Md. Ann. Code art. 27, sec. 362.

3. Danny Sheridan, "Playboy's Pro Football Forecast," *Playboy*, September 1997.

4. J. S. Mill, *On Liberty* (New York: Penguin Classics, 1985), p. 68.

5. Mark Peterson, "Steps in Overcoming Masturbation," Council of the 12 Apostles, circa 1989.

6. Marianne Macy, *Working Sex* (New York: Carroll & Graf, 1996), p. 77.

7. Nadine Strossen, *Defending Pornography: Free Speech, Sex, and the Fight for Women's Rights* (New York: Scribner, 1995), p. 177.

8. "The Crime of Adultery: Old Laws Are Dusted Off," *New York Times*, April 30, 1990.

9. "Four Arrests for Adultery Raise Legal, Privacy Issues in Connecticut," *Boston Globe*, September 9, 1990.

10. "Bill to Void Adultery Laws Go to Weicker," *New York Times*, April 4, 1991.

11. "Air Force Averts Trial of Female B-52 Pilot," *Washington Post*, May 23, 1997.

12. "Pregnant Teenagers Thou Shalt Not," *Economist*, August 3, 1996.

13. *Playboy*, February 1990, p. 44. Mercifully, in 1999, the Georgia Supreme Court struck down that state's sodomy law as in violation of Georgia's own state constitution.

14. "Lewis Powell, Gentleman: A Justice Who Achieved Greatness Quietly," *Greensboro News and Record*, August 27, 1998.

15. A. Lewis, "Homage to Virtue," *New York Times*, June 13, 1997.

16. F. Rich, "Straight Bashing Season," *New York Times*, June 15, 1997.

17. O.C.G.A., Sec. 16-12-80.

18. David Boaz, *Libertarianism: A Primer* (New York: Free Press, 1997), p. 104.

19. "Africa's Culture War: Old Customs, New Values," *New York Times*, February 2, 1997. The roots of this vicious practice reflect the same antisex bias so often evident in traditional (conservative) policies. By destroying the center of woman's sexual pleasure, clitoridectomy is thought to make women more faithful.

20. Friederich Hayek, "Why I Am Not A Conservative," in *The Constitution of Liberty* (Chicago: University of Chicago Press, 1960), p. 397.

CHAPTER SIX

"ZEAL AND VENGEANCE"
We Strike Back

The words of his mouth were smoother than butter but war was in his heart. His words were softer than oil yet were they drawn swords.

—Ps. 55:21

"We get it with our mother's milk," Wade is saying. He tiptoes across his office, raising his knees as high as he can, moving silently and with great care toward the door. "This is how we want to appear to the prosecution." He takes two more careful steps. "This is the way we want to appear on their radar, and this is how we want them to see us." He is at the door now. He opens it silently, slides out, and disappears.

He comes back into the room, walking normally. "We want to be off their radar. We want to slip away so they don't notice us, so they don't even know we are here."

Wade has good reason for living by this philosophy. Not many years back, for example, he defended Jeffrey McDonald, a Green Beret physician accused of murdering his wife and two children. McDonald had been investigated by the military, which did not find serious cause to believe that he was involved in the murders, and he had been given an honorable discharge. But he then went on the *Dick Cavett Show* and complained bitterly about the government's behavior in his case. "He called the government a bunch of incompetents for failing to find the killer of his family," recalls Wade.

So the government said "OK, if you want a trial, we'll give you a trial." And they indicted him. And the prosecutors all said to me had he not done that nothing would have happened. But he woke up the government, and the government is a dangerous, very dangerous, commodity to deal with, and it has enormous power. It has an endless supply of money. And if it wants you, if your government truly wants you, your government will have you. That is the philosophy, that is what we get as criminal lawyers from our mother's milk.

123

I learned that a corollary to the low-radar strategy is not to motivate the other side. Most of our defense attorneys shared this philosophy—that the enemy should never feel they were facing a powerful army, that we were pretty much just bumbling along, defending ourselves only as necessary, and that the assumption was that the prosecution was much stronger and more powerful than we could ever be. This meant always treating the other side with respect, even deference, and never challenging them belligerently.

Wade had learned this lesson early in his career as an assistant football coach and he enjoyed telling the story on himself. He had, so he believed, single-handedly motivated an opposing football team to give his own North Carolina Tarheels a severe pounding.

> I had a job on Saturdays working as an assistant to the coaching staff of the football team. . . . On this occasion the coach, Coach Jim Hickey, was in the team room, and the stadium was filled with people. We were playing Maryland. We were getting ready to go out on the field, and Coach Bob Thalman, one of the assistant coaches, came in and Coach Hickey left the room. Coach Thalman then gave a great inspirational speech in which he said that the team was letting Coach Hickey down, that the team had not done well despite Coach Hickey, that it was horrible what was happening, that we had great material and so on. Then the team just erupted en masse, they just charged the door and got stuck in the door trying to get out, and then just went roaring out onto the field. I was in the middle of that mob, never feeling such a powerful emotion in my life, and as I went up into the press box, I passed a promontory over which I could look and see the Maryland team having their team prayer. They were all down with their hands clasped. I said, "You sons of bitches are going to get your asses kicked." They were all down kneeling, and they all looked up to see me, and they [were] just furious! And then they went out onto the field and Carolina lost thirty-four to nothing. Carolina didn't have a chance—Maryland just went out and beat the daylights out of us. And all the years after that, I knew it was my fault that Carolina lost. I never told anybody, but years later I finally confessed. It was a great lesson in life, and I concluded that I should always do the opposite. That I should cause my enemy to think that I wasn't angry.

During the first two years following our Alamance trial, this remained a guiding principle in our strategy. "Don't wake the sleeping giant," was a watchword, along with its corollary, "Don't let the giant know we are getting ready for war." Even though the giant was awake and stirring, we did not wish to do anything that might provoke additional governmental ire, or otherwise give them reason to pursue us with any more vigor than they already were.

But events were brewing that would eventually convince us that a more confrontational strategy was required. Bruce Ennis, our civil litigator, had encouraged us almost from the beginning to be aggressive; as the government's "Project Postporn," an undertaking subsequently ballyhooed in the press by DOJ, began to unfold in 1987 and 1988 and its prosecutions began to succeed, Bruce's recommendations for a counteroffensive began to seem more and more reasonable.

POSTPORN

Department of Justice
Washington, DC

Office of the Assistant Attorney General

MEMORANDUM [undated except as to presentation date]

TO: H. Robert Showers
Executive Director [National Obscenity Enforcement Unit]

FROM: Cynthia Christfield [NOEU]

RE: Project PostPorn

Presentation to the Task Force meeting on April 22, 1987

PROJECT POSTPORN

Project Postporn is a national project consisting of multi-district, simultaneous prosecutions of major mail order obscenity distributors. . . .

Objectives
    1. To have a significant impact on the mail order distribution market.
    2. To put major mail order obscenity distributors out of business.

Agencies
    1. US Department of Justice, Federal Obscenity Task Force
    2. US Postal Inspection Service . . .

Where to prosecute:

1. Districts of receipt/46 have been selected.

2. Districts where predisposition can be shown. Where prohibitory orders or complaints are on file.

3. Districts where AUSAs [Assistant US Attorneys] have expressed an interest in this project or have agreed to participate.

How:

1. Three to four USA districts are assigned to each target company to prosecute.

2. One of those assigned districts is appointed the primary, or lead, district.

3. All districts will:
— make test purchases from the assigned target company
— conduct grand jury investigation
— indict
— plea or take to trial

4. Primary districts [*sic*] additional responsibilities include:
— coordination of all stages of the investigation and prosecution and of information sharing;
— search warrant preparation and execution in the district of mailing;
— grand jury investigation on the corporation identity and principals.

When:

1. Current stage: Targets selected, strategy developed, getting AUSAs on board, and getting materials to AUSAs for their review.

2. Test purchases made by June 1st.

3. Indictments by September 1st. . . .

We were, of course, completely unaware of the existence of this memo and dozens of others like it at the time. That Edwin Meese's National Obscenity Enforcement Unit, the group headed by Rob Showers from North Carolina (who had helped supervise the 1986 raid on Adam & Eve) was organizing a nationwide campaign to destroy as many businesses as it could in pursuit of the private agendas of its most conservative members was a well-kept secret. (We would learn these details later in the discovery process in the suit we brought against the Department of Justice.) Less well hidden, because the government truly saw nothing wrong with it, was the strategy of simultaneous, multidistrict prosecutions that the government was engaging in, and this is where it erred most egregiously. DOJ's Cynthia Christfield, who had bragged at an earlier federal obscenity trial in Alexandria, Virginia, that the government wanted to bring RICO prosecutions to put "out of business" those companies whose products the DOJ found objectionable, further amplified the Postporn strategy in another memo.

> Operation Postporn is a joint national project between the Department of Justice, specifically the Federal Obscenity Task Force, and the US Postal Inspection Service which targets 14 major mail order distributors of sexually explicit material for investigation and prosecution.
>
> A total of forty-six US Attorney districts [out of a total of ninety-four] have been selected to conduct simultaneous, multi-district prosecutions against these targets. For each of the 14 targets, a USA [United States attorney] district has been selected to be the primary, or lead district with two or three districts designated as secondary districts. . . .
>
> Similar, simultaneous prosecutions are going to be conducted in three to four districts of receipt of each mail-order target. . . . [1]

Here was the central feature of the antipornography strategy of the U.S. Department of Justice. The idea was that, by bringing simultaneous prosecutions against a mail-order company in several different parts of the United States, the company would be forced to defend itself on several fronts at once and, whether an obscenity conviction was ever obtained or not, the target company would likely be destroyed through the simple expedient of financial annihilation by being forced to defend itself in so many places.

This strategy had originally been proposed by Utah U.S. Attorney Brent Ward, the stony-faced prosecutor in Salt Lake with whom Wade and John Mintz had been negotiating. In a letter to U.S. Attorney General Edwin Meese in September 1985, Ward had called for a "nationwide pornography prosecution strategy," including a task force of U.S. attorneys and local district attorneys "selected from communities having a standard of obscenity favorable toward pornography prosecutions. . . . The heart of [the] . . . strategy," Ward asserted,

> calls for multiple prosecutions (either simultaneous or successive) in all levels of government in many locations. If thirty-five prosecutors comprise the strike force, theoretically thirty-five different criminal prosecutions could be instigated simultaneously against one or more of the major pornographers.

He added that such a strategy would "test the limits" of the companies' endurance, since "there is a limit to the prison terms and fines to which the principals in these companies will subject themselves."[2]

Ward's letter reflected the single-mindedness and complete lack of subtlety characteristic of the NOEU prosecutors at the time and of the several U.S. attorneys for whom the suppression of sexual materials constituted a major priority. For Ward, the redeeming value of some sexual materials, the lack of prurient characteristics—a key component in the definition of obscenity as Ward well knew—and the thousands of gradations of sexual explicitness were all irrelevant. He and his assistant Richard Lambert had specified that if we agreed to a plea bargain with them, we would not be able to sell even material like *Playboy* and *The Joy of Sex*. It was clear that for Ward and for several of his colleagues who played key roles in this drama—Rob Showers, Bill Delahoyde, Richard Lambert, Patrick Trueman, and Sam Currin—sexual materials were, ipso facto, evil, and should be suppressed.

Attorney General Edwin Meese and his assistant in the criminal division, William F. Weld,[3] shared these views. Meese's Justice Department, particularly the National Obscenity Enforcement Unit, was dominated by antipornography activists, making it difficult for cooler heads to point out the constitutional limitations within which they were required to work. The multiple-prosecution strategy, for example, was itself constitutionally improper because of its chilling effect on First Amendment rights. But the true-believer passions of the antipornography prosecutors overwhelmed other DOJ voices. FBI Agent Robert Marinaro would later testify that Ward, Showers, and Trueman "became zealots about . . . pornography, and their religious beliefs overstepped good judgment in terms of how they should go about looking at this material."[4] FBI Agent Raymond Bernard characterized Showers's reputation among FBI agents as "a fanatic, a zealot, and you can't trust him and [North Carolina Assistant Attorney General William] Delahoyde."[5] Given such ideology, it was not difficult to understand why the use of a multiple-district prosecution strategy made perfect sense. Technically, an obscenity prosecution can be brought anywhere a transaction involving sexually oriented materials has occurred. So why not bring several prosecutions at once, and stamp out the business?

Obscenity, as defined by the Supreme Court, is not protected by the First Amendment, but all sexually oriented expression that does not meet the definition of obscenity *is* constitutionally protected. And all sexual speech is presumed innocent until proven guilty; that is, sexually oriented videos and magazines are presumed to be protected speech—legal speech—until they are found to be obscene by a jury (or, occasionally, by a judge). For the U.S. government to set about putting "out of business" companies that sold presumptively protected sexual expression (whether the prosecutors thought the materials were obscene or not) through a pattern of multiple simultaneous prosecutions that were, in some cases, not even designed to result in a conviction at trial is an egregious violation of the First Amendment protection of free speech.

"HARD-CORE" VERSUS OBSCENE

Because the Supreme Court in *Miller* had used the term "hard-core" several times in referring to what the Court would, in that decision, define as obscene, many prosecutors had begun to consider the terms to be synonymous. Though the Supreme Court did not give this or any other definition for this term in their opinion, "hard-core" in turn was taken to mean a depiction of actual sexual penetration, what is scientifically referred to as "intromission." But of course explicitness—here the explicit depiction of sexual penetration—does not define obscenity at all. As numerous juries and court decisions have made clear over the twenty-five-plus years since *Miller*, depictions can be highly explicit and still not obscene, as is the case with countless educational videos and books, for example, as well as X-rated entertainment without violence or degradation; contrariwise, graphic depictions of sadomasochism or coprophilia (feces-related sexual behavior) can be found obscene even if no sexual penetration is shown. Numerous would-be experts have been seduced by the simplicity of the "hard-core" = obscenity definition.

In one such example, one of our attorneys, John Mintz, received a phone call from Jim Reynolds of the Criminal Division of Main Justice in October 1986. Reynolds had called in response to a letter John had written to the DOJ on our behalf. He told John that it was DOJ policy that *any* depiction of explicit sexual activity was obscene and prosecutable, a position contrary to long-settled law. Similarly, Gary Bauer, an antisex crusader who briefly joined the race for the U.S. presidency in 2000, revealed his confusion on this matter in a June 1, 1991, letter to the *Washington Post*. Defending Senator Mitch McConnell's Pornography Victims Compensation Act, Bauer asserted that it covered only "sexually explicit" material that would therefore, as a practical matter, be "obscene under the test of *Miller* v. *California*."

This casual oversimplification is, I think, what led so many of the Postporn/NOEU memo writers and prosecutors to misuse the term obscenity when they referred to materials being sold by the companies they were targeting. They apparently reasoned that, if the material was hard-core, it could, ipso facto, be considered obscene. The casual comingling of these terms by government lawyers, interchanging "obscenity," "pornography," and "hard-core" material as if these were equivalent terms, reflects a distinct lack of sophistication about the law, a deficiency that would plague the DOJ throughout these proceedings.

In 1991, DOJ spokesman Doug Tillett confused the matter further. "We believe in a fairly bright line as to what is obscene," he said in an interview with the *Congressional Quarterly Researcher.* "People like Phil Harvey would have you believe it's all garden-variety hetero sex, but there's bestiality, homosexuality, child porn, and violence."[6] Tillett was swinging wildly here. Homosexual depictions are no more obscene than "garden-variety hetero" sex; they are subject to the same *Miller* tests. Child pornography has its own law, and was irrelevant to our proceedings. Bestiality did not occur in any of the materials the DOJ was indicting, and violence was extremely rare. So Tillett was blurring his "bright line" even as he asserted that such a line existed. Attorney Marjorie Heins of the ACLU put this in perspective at the time. "They want a bright line" that makes obscene a good many titles now available at local Waldenbooks stores, "including . . . the high art drawings of Aubrey Beardsley, and the Kama Sutra."[7]

The DOJ's confusion about legal terminology was matched by their naïveté over basic First Amendment issues. Just before and in the early days of Project Postporn, experienced litigators like Brent Ward and less experienced ones like Robert Showers and Cynthia Christfield bragged openly about putting "pornographers" out of business through the multiple/simultaneous-prosecution strategy and/or through the use of RICO. They should have known better, for the relevant First Amendment principles are quite clear. Showers was, as we shall see, warned by DOJ attorneys about this. The deliberate suppression of "objectionable" nonobscene speech through a strategy designed primarily to financially decimate the speakers (in this case, companies that sell sexually oriented materials) is, as we would later show, a clear violation of fundamental constitutional principles. Ward, Showers, and their colleagues should have known this. As they learned it, they would stop talking about "shutting down" businesses and begin asserting that what they had meant was really something else all along.

FREEDBERG: THE GOVERNMENT TRIUMPHS —AT A PRICE

The first party to resist the DOJ's multiple-prosecution strategy was Avram Freedberg.

In January 1988 a search warrant was executed at Freedberg's company, Consumer Marketing Group (CMG) in Stamford, Connecticut. Gary Jones, a postal inspector from Utah who had also participated in the raid on our company in 1986, led the search. A few days later, Freedberg was served with subpoenas from the northern federal districts of Mississippi and Indiana, the District of Delaware, and the District of Utah.

In February, Freedberg's lawyer, Elkin Abramowitz, met with Utah Assistant U.S. Attorney Richard Lambert (Lambert was a party to most of these prosecutions) in Salt Lake City. As related in Mr. Abramowitz's affidavit (PHE 570),

> Mr. Lambert . . . indicated that . . . Freedberg and CMG would be prosecuted . . . [simultaneously or] consecutively in all four districts; or, if necessary . . . in additional districts, until convictions were eventually obtained. Lambert further intimated that, if multiple federal prosecutions of plaintiffs did not result in conviction, plaintiff Freedberg should be prepared to face parallel state obscenity prosecutions. Mr. Lambert added that he . . . [and other prosecutors] may also prosecute several other CMG employees, including Mr. Freedberg's wife, Rhoda Freedberg, for alleged obscenity violations.[8]

Threats to prosecute spouses and adult children of the managers of mail-order businesses were an integral part of the DOJ's strategy to intimidate and frighten these companies out of business. They would employ this again in the Karl Brussel case and in several others. Lambert apparently had reason to believe that Freedberg would be concerned about his (Freedberg's) wife in this context, because in the early plea negotiations he indicated that Mrs. Freedberg might not be prosecuted if Mr. Freedberg agreed to a felony plea on behalf of himself and his company.

Abramowitz and his colleagues made a valiant effort to persuade DOJ of the unfairness of the multidistrict strategy they were threatening to use against his clients. In March, he and attorney David E. Kendall (representing CMG) met with Rob Showers and Cynthia Christfield in Washington. At that meeting and again subsequently, Showers confirmed that the prosecutors would be proceeding against Freedberg and CMG "on a coordinated, multi-district basis."[9]

When the push came, Freedberg and his attorneys were ready. They immediately filed a lawsuit in the D.C. District Court, requesting declaratory and injunctive relief as to the multidistrict prosecution strategy.[10] With remarkable speed, on June 8, 1988, Judge Thomas Penfield Jackson* ordered that the preliminary injunction be granted in its essential part. He enjoined

---

*Jackson is the judge who later became famous for ordering the breakup of Microsoft.

the DOJ from seeking indictments against Freedberg and CMG in more than one federal district, noting that simultaneous criminal prosecutions of the same individual for the same offense in four separate federal judicial districts "cannot possibly be consistent with due process." Having found the government's strategy unconstitutional on Fourteenth Amendment (due process) grounds, Judge Jackson did not address its First Amendment implications.

Freedberg's lawsuit and Judge Jackson's decision provided immediate leverage for Freedberg and CMG. Whereas prior to the lawsuit, Richard Lambert and others had been insisting that a plea agreement must include "substantial" jail time for Freedberg, they were now prepared to swap the civil suit for much more favorable treatment of Freedberg, assuming that he was willing to go out of business. George Burgasser, then Special Attorney to the National Obscenity Enforcement Unit, summed up the terms of the final plea: "Freedberg and CMG will stipulate to the dismissal of the pending civil suit in the D.C. District Court with prejudice."[11] In return, the government would not ask for any jail time for Avram Freedberg.

From the government's point of view, the dismissal of the civil suit was the key to the settlement. They emphatically did not want the civil suit to be tried because a trial could have established permanently the unconstitutionality of their multidistrict strategy. The prospect of risking what was then the cornerstone of the DOJ's antiobscenity strategy was anathema to them, and the government was prepared to forgo any punishment of Mr. Freedberg in exchange for getting rid of the civil case.

CMG entered a corporate plea to obscenity violations in Utah, Mississippi, and Delaware. The company simultaneously agreed to cease operation by consent decree, i.e., to cease to exist. For a nonexistent corporation to have a criminal record is, of course, a matter of negligible consequence.

But Freedberg also gave up his First Amendment right to engage in any business dealing with sexually oriented materials. In his plea he agreed to the government's out-of-business demand on behalf of himself, his company, and his wife. With his signature alone, he and his wife, Rhoda J. Freedberg, agreed "not to promote, sell or distribute" anything that depicts "human genitalia" or sexual intercourse "or any other erotic subject directly related" to these things.[12] A strict reading of this language would keep both Freedbergs out of the business of selling garden statues of naked cherubs.

Despite the lifelong relinquishing of these First Amendment rights, Freedberg's lawsuit had given him the leverage to settle his case without incarceration. But in addition to "getting out of the business" and giving up his company, he gave up any chance of altering the legal landscape within which the Department of Justice could operate. Once his lawsuit was dismissed, Judge Jackson's earlier decision that the government was in violation of due process was generally ignored by the DOJ, which proceeded as before with multidistrict prosecutions.

The *Freedberg* decision, however, was a wake-up call for at least one lawyer at the DOJ. Paul C. McCommon III was a special attorney in the National Obscenity Enforcement Unit, advising Rob Showers and others on the legal implications of their strategy. He had participated actively in Project Postporn, but as the strategy became increasingly blatant, and particularly after the Justice Department manual was changed to explicitly encourage multiple prosecutions in obscenity cases,★ McCommon felt that he had to speak out. The memo excerpted here was, of course, completely unknown to us at the time; it was produced during our civil suit against the DOJ. This memo was considered so incendiary by its addressee, Robert Showers, that shortly after receiving it, he ordered all copies destroyed. It is likely that Showers lost his job as a result of this order; destroying evidence is a serious crime.[13] But Showers's reasons for suppressing this document are clear from its contents: The NOEU had slipped over the edge of constitutionally permissible behavior.

US DEPARTMENT OF JUSTICE, WASHINGTON, D.C., MEMORANDUM

"Project Postporn" and the Danger of Multiple District Prosecutions Coordinated from Washington, DC

September 14, 1988

To: H. Robert Showers   From: Paul C. McCommon III
    Executive Director   Special Attorney
    National Obscenity   National Obscenity
    Enforcement Unit   Enforcement Unit

Over the past year, I have become increasingly concerned about "Project PostPorn" and the practice of "simultaneous multiple-district prosecutions"

★ The U.S. Attorney's Manual stated prior to 1987 that multiple prosecutions "will *not* be authorized unless the materials are transmitted to a different district, the materials are different than those involved in the first [i.e., an initial] indictment, and the materials are of such an explicit nature that there can be no question as to their obscenity." In 1987, at the instigation of Assistant U.S. Attorney William Weld, this language was essentially reversed to encourage multiple prosecutions "where the size of the [defendant's] organizational structure suggests that a multiple district prosecution approach . . . will be most effective." United States Attorney's Manual § 9-75.310 (October 1, 1988).

generally, but particularly where such a project is controlled according to DOJ policy guidelines from Washington. On several occasions, I have advised you of my concerns, but I don't feel you have taken my warnings seriously.

. . . Much of what I state herein relates to your conduct during the previous 18 months. The reason for this is that it will always be your conduct which will form the factual basis of a lawsuit, motion to transfer, or motion to dismiss (i.e., *Freedberg*).

It . . . became known to me for the first time last Fall that we had a policy regarding multiple district prosecution, stated in USAM [U.S. Attorneys Manual] S9-75.320. This policy, that we sent to the USAs in our correspondence, stated in part: (1) The NOEU must be "consulted" prior to initiating a case; (2) the NOEU must "coordinate" the investigations; (3) a law enforcement agency "must consult" with the NOEU prior to referring the case to a USA; and (4) indictments must be "approved" by the NOEU prior to filing. . . .

Also, since at least March, 1987, you have given speeches heard by many AUSAs and others, where you have stated your purpose for multiple-district cases which is to keep the defense attorneys busy and running around the country. You have also used the "bat and ball" analogy, that we want them playing in our ballparks with our bat and our ball. I think a judge could easily find improper forum shopping, based on this expression of prosecutorial motivation and based on your degree of control as provided by DOJ policy. . . .

The above facts, considered together, indicate a serious problem. Because the vast majority of USAs on your subcommittee do not have extensive First Amendment experience, they should be made aware of this problem before the decision is made by Ed Dennis to send out the "go ahead" letter to USAs. I believe we are derelict in our duty if we do not warn them that, considering the above facts, additional Freedberg-type lawsuits and/or granted motions to transfer are foreseeable.

In the present matter, the facts raise an "appearance" of an improper motivation. Moreover, I am concerned about your "bat and ball" speech, and whether that information would come out in a Freedberg deposition, whether it has appeared in newsclippings from your speeches, or whether an AUSA somewhere might admit having heard you say that.

Conclusion

. . . [The] districts should be authorized to proceed independently and at their own pace, to minimize the appearance of Washington control.[14]

It should be noted that McCommon was no renegade liberal in the DOJ. Indeed, he had come to Main Justice with impeccable antipornography credentials, directly from Citizens for Decency Through Law. The CDL had been founded by antipornography crusader Charles H. Keating Jr., and provided many ideas and two of its lawyers to the NOEU. McCommon was one of those lawyers. He had sent an Adam & Eve catalog to Rob Showers while he was still with the CDL, suggesting that sufficient evidence to prosecute us was now available. He added, "If I can do anything further to assist you [in prosecuting Adam & Eve], please let me know."[15]

But now McCommon was clearly worried, and he had put his boss on notice. What happened next would be spelled out in D.C. District Judge Joyce Hens Green's memorandum opinion and order in our lawsuit (September 1993).

> Soon after he distributed his memorandum, McCommon was strongly criticized for issuing the memoranda [*sic*]. McCommon relates that Showers told him that
>
>> if this memorandum ever got out, it could cause tremendous problems for the cases, not to mention him [Showers] personally. He handed me the original memorandum and said here is the original, I want you to gather up the copies and I want you to get the diskette from the secretary who typed it and I want you to shred it.
>
> McCommon Dep., at 422. A short time later, Showers was placed on administrative leave . . . and left the office later in 1988.[16]

The NOEU campaign had stumbled badly; Showers was gone for good.

SHOULD WE STRIKE BACK?

McCommon's memo set out several of the arguments that would provide the basis for our suing the Department of Justice two years later. Indeed, had we known of this memo at the time it was written in 1988, we would not have waited two more years to file our lawsuit; with this proof of concern from the government's own attorney, we would have launched an attack to settle this issue once and for all.

But we knew neither of this nor of any other reservations within the DOJ about its strategy. What we saw was the DOJ on the roll, indicting mailorder companies in multiple districts and putting them literally, finally, and truly out of business through plea bargains, thus fulfilling the NOEU's stated objectives.

Very few trials were conducted in this process. By the government's own count, seven companies, including Avram Freedberg's and others from Wisconsin to California, were simply eliminated from the American landscape by threats of multiple prosecutions and consequent plea bargains.

Despite the dangers posed by the growing success of the Postporn strategy, including their success in getting rid of Freedberg and his lawsuit, our attorneys were still extremely reluctant to sue. One reason was some very good news from the Eastern District of North Carolina. As early as June of 1987, one of our attorneys had spoken with Douglas McCullough in that office, and McCullough had called the Adam & Eve case "moribund." Since that time, we had come increasingly to believe that the Eastern District would drop its case. Then, in the spring of 1989, the Eastern District office returned to us twenty-seven cartons of materials they had subpoenaed for their grand jury and, when queried by the press, stated that they would proceed no further against us. This was three years after the raid in which the Eastern District had been conspicuous participants, and two years after our trial in Alamance County. The Raleigh *News and Observer*, in an editorial on May 11, 1989, made its opinion of the whole process very clear.

END OF A FOOLISH CRUSADE

In March of 1987, an Alamance County jury acquitted the Adam & Eve mail-order company of Carrboro of state obscenity charges. But a crusade by the US attorney's office in Raleigh to nail the firm on federal charges continued—and continued, and continued.

Finally, Assistant US Attorney William Delahoyde says that documents seized in a May 1986 raid on the firm, 27 boxes of them, have been returned, and that the government will not pursue its case. But it's hard to say how much money has been wasted in blind pursuit of Adam & Eve, which distributes contraceptives and sexually oriented films and reading material. And Mr. Delahoyde offered little explanation of why the investigation had dragged on for so long.

On the 1987 jury was a cross-section of average citizens. The state law leaves the definition of obscene to "contemporary community standards." In about one hour, that jury—its members consisting of, among others, a textile worker, an insurance salesman, a housewife, a minister's son and a church choir member—decided that Adam & Eve had not violated those standards.

Alamance County is not exactly the Vegas of the Piedmont, and the verdict should have sent a message to federal prosecutors. But then-US Attorney Samuel T. Currin Jr. and Mr. Delahoyde continued to spend the public's money and waste the time of the public's servants. After the verdict, Mr. Currin said the federal investigation was "full steam ahead." His engine was stoked with tax dollars.

Mr. Delahoyde now has run out of track. And in closing his investigation, he said the Alamance verdict was a factor in the decision. It takes him a long time to ponder factors—in this case, more than two years. That is an outrageous delay.

Not all investigations pan out or result in indictment. But those motivated by zeal and vengeance ought to come with a money-back guarantee.

By the time the Eastern District of North Carolina had decided to drop out, it was increasingly clear that the Utah case, too, was becoming stale. There was still a year to run on the five-year statute of limitations, but four-year-old cases—especially cases that depend on community standards—become increasingly difficult to prosecute. So we were beginning to believe that the Utah case, too, might be postponed until it simply collapsed. To our defense attorneys this seemed solid evidence that our strategy was working. That strategy had been tough, but defensive. We had made the government fight for every inch of ground, filing motions to suppress their subpoenas, negotiating hard and often, demanding return of improperly seized evidence. This was our "we're-not-a-tasty-morsel" strategy, in Dave Rudolf's phrase. "We wanted to be a morsel that would be very unpleasant to chew on," he says. "Let someone else be the tasty morsel." This we had done, and it seemed to be working—up to a point.

But there were danger signals, too. We hadn't forgotten Richard Lambert's statement to Wade that other jurisdictions' "trigger fingers were itching"—that attacks from unknown quarters were clearly in the cards.

Then, as if to prove the veracity of Lambert's threats, in December 1989, when Utah still had plenty of time to indict us if they chose, we received a subpoena from the Middle District of Kentucky indicating that they, too, were opening an investigation. A new front had been opened in the war against us.

Our team believed that we could fight off Kentucky with the same tactics we had used with Eastern North Carolina: stall, fight, negotiate, hang tough. But with this new proof of the government's continuing intent to use the multiple-prosecution strategy against us, talk of a counterattack became more urgent. Kentucky made the fourth jurisdiction to come at us, and it was clear that the Meese Justice Department was not going to be deterred by defensive tactics. The Kentucky prosecution raised the stakes because, while the other jurisdictions had all participated in the raid and had all been among those crusading against us since 1986, Kentucky represented new blood, a fresh horse for the government cavalry. We were not pleased by this obvious sign that the DOJ was broadening its attack.

Should we strike back? A lawsuit based on the constitutional issues raised by the government's obvious bad faith and its multiple-prosecution strategy seemed increasingly feasible. Yet we knew that suing the government in these circumstances would be like declaring nuclear war.

Bruce and I had been hawks about suing all along. Civil litigators like Bruce are generally more comfortable with confrontation, with going on the offensive, than criminal attorneys, whose job it is to defend. On top of that, Bruce had been, for five years, the chief counsel to the American Civil Liberties Union. In that position, one of his primary responsibilities was suing the government over issues of individual civil liberties. He had become accustomed to "taking on the eight-hundred-pound gorilla," as he described it.

I, too, had gotten comfortable with suing the government, and for reasons largely unrelated to the present litigation. In 1977 I and the nonprofit family planning organization I had founded, Population Services International, together with PHE had sued the State of New York over the constitutionality of its laws inhibiting access to contraceptives.[17] New York's laws had confined the sale of nonprescription contraceptives to pharmacies; forbade the sale of all contraceptives to minors, whether married or single; and prohibited all display or advertising of contraceptives. Our suit asserted that these restrictions represented an unconstitutional barrier to people's right to contraceptives and to PHE's right to sell them. We won at the state level, and our case was appealed to the U.S. Supreme Court, which ruled seven to two in our favor.[18] Contraceptives have been far more widely available in the state of New York ever since. In addition I had initiated a lawsuit against the federal government in 1981 over its restrictive abortion policies in the funding of family planning programs overseas. We had won this case at the district level, but lost on appeal.

Neither of these lawsuits, which involved very aggressive stances against major governmental entities, had resulted, so far as I could tell, in any repercussions against me or our organizations. We had won one case and lost the other and that was that. In the process I had come to feel that suing the government, especially when it interfered with private constitutional rights, was a good, patriotic thing to do. That is still what I believe.

So Bruce and I, supported by our marketing manager Peggy Oettinger, wanted to fire our biggest guns. We saw no reason to wait.

But our defense attorneys were wary. Declaring war openly on the Department of Justice was contrary to all their instincts. There were other reasons, too. In a letter to me on February 27, 1990, Joe Cheshire summed up some of these concerns.

> Dear Phil:
>
> . . . . In the past several years, we have been successful in keeping you from being indicted [again] by threatening to defend you vigorously wherever you have come under attack. . . . When push comes to shove, the Government has either backed down (North Carolina) or not proceeded (Utah) with prosecution. This has been done without striking out at the Government in an affirmative way. . . .
>
> The grand jury action in Kentucky may be no more an indication of prosecution than it was in North Carolina or Utah. The prior strategy (i.e., contest the subpoenas, vigorously negotiate with no quarter given, be in a position to win, if necessary, while letting the Government know that our success and their failure is inevitable, without striking an affirmative blow that might force indictment) seems to have been successful. Thus, we believe that serious consideration should be given to holding off the filing of the civil suit until we are sure it is necessary. . . .
>
> Serious consideration needs to be given to the possibility that filing the civil suit may ultimately result in one or more of us being unable to represent you in a criminal context. . . .

This last point was of deep concern to all of us. We could envision circumstances under which the proceedings of the civil suit might lead to the disqualification of one or more of our criminal defense attorneys on the basis of a conflict. It was clear, for example, that, if we sued, Joe and Wade and Dave, as well as John Mintz, would have to provide testimony about the repeated threats we had received from the federal government—particularly in Utah—during the many discussions that had taken place. These threats were a critical part of the government's tactic to put us out of business, and they would have to be documented. Because the threats had been made at those meetings with our lawyers, they, our lawyers, would have to provide testimony, either in the form of affidavits or deposition testimony, as part of the civil case. This meant that our defense attorneys in providing such evidence, would have to serve as impartial witnesses, establishing the facts, rather than as advocates. The prospect disturbed them on several levels. First, many lawyers simply don't like being witnesses in any litigation in which they have an advocacy role. The extent of this concern varies a great deal from lawyer to lawyer, and it is a deeply emotional issue for some of them. An extreme case was described by Jonathan Harr in his book *A Civil Action*. Lawyer Jan Schlictman, whose case against the W. R. Grace and Beatrice companies is described in the book, could simply not bear the idea of serving as a witness in his own case, and he very nearly lost an important round as a result. "When I take the witness stand, I cease being an attorney for my clients. I become a witness in this case subject to all the rules of examination. I can no longer be a professional, objective advocate for my clients," Schlictman told Judge Walter J. Skinner at a hearing in January 1983. "I cannot take the stand without withdrawing as counsel in this case."[19]

Judge Skinner argued with Schlictman, clearly believing that Schlictman was inventing, or at least greatly exaggerating this conflict, and he ordered Schlictman to take the stand. "I respectfully refuse to take the stand," said Schlictman. "I ask the court's forbearance and [to] allow me to argue why it is unnecessary." At this point Schlictman was risking his entire case, many would say unnecessarily, on this issue of principle. It was obviously of tremendous importance to him.

In our case, Joe Cheshire had at first seemed almost equally adamant. Joe was most concerned, as indicated in his letter above, about having our key defense attorneys disqualified. But the thought of being a witness in the same proceeding in which he served as advocate made him intensely uneasy. "There's something professionally uncomfortable about moving from the realm of advocate to the realm of witness in the same proceeding," he told me. "I don't know how to explain the discomfort, it's just there."

Wade, on the other hand, was not really troubled by this dual role. "I had to testify and I didn't have any choice," he told me later. "I thought it was a perfectly good experience." Wade's only discomfort apparently was about billing. "It seemed unethical that I should bill you for time in which I was being a witness, because witnesses are not supposed to charge."

Dave Rudolf explains his position this way: "I think lawyers are generally control freaks, and it's much easier to be a control freak when you're a lawyer than it is when you're a witness. You lose control, or at least the illusion of control, when you're a witness. Maybe we kid ourselves into believing we really have all that much control as lawyers. But as a witness you have no control at all."

Discomfort aside, the major concern on everyone's minds was the possibility that having our lawyers function as witnesses might disqualify them from defending us. By now the team had worked together for four years; they were working very well with one another and were convinced they could lead PHE and me through this tortuous river journey successfully. The prospect of having any of them disqualified was deeply disturbing to us all.

And we knew that the government would try to knock out our defense team if they possibly could. For example, if we were to be indicted in Kentucky or Utah subsequent to filing the civil suit, we would likely file a motion to dismiss the indictment based on the bad-faith motives of the prosecutors. Indeed, given the arguments we would raise in our civil case, it would be illogical *not* to file such a motion. If our defense attorneys had to appear before a judge to support such a motion, testifying about conversations they had had one-on-one with prosecutors—conversations that would help establish the improper motives of government officials and therefore the unlawfulness of the entire prosecutorial process against us—then their role as witnesses in establishing such facts could come into direct conflict with their advocacy roles. A judge would not likely countenance a situation in which a defense attorney cross-examines a prosecutor on the stand, confronting him or her about what was said between them at a private meeting some months before. The odds of this happening were not great, particularly if evidence provided by our lawyers was confined exclusively to the civil case and not to any subsequent criminal proceedings. But it was a cause of very considerable concern all the same and made our decision about filing the lawsuit much more difficult.

We remained on a knife edge. Joe was convinced that a lawsuit would trigger an indictment; Bruce and, to some extent, Dave believed that filing a suit after an indictment—in other words, waiting too long—would greatly weaken our posture with the lawsuit because it would look defensive and retaliatory, whereas if the government indicted us after our filing of the suit, it would make *them* look retaliatory (as indeed it did).

We had many a long debate around the attorneys' conference tables. Should we sue? I remember staring down at the traffic on West Franklin Street outside Dave's Chapel Hill office on several occasions, pondering the odds while the debate went on in the room behind me. Failing to arrive at a decision about the proper course of action, I mindlessly counted the cars going in and out of the McDonald's across the way.

BRUSSEL TIPS THE BALANCE

It was the Karl Brussel/PAK Ventures case that finally tipped the balance. PAK was another mail-order retailer of sexual materials and the government's behavior in this case, in late 1989 and the first half of 1990, was so egregious and so successful in decimating Brussel's family and his business that we finally came to the conclusion that the juggernaut would crush us next if we did not move to prevent it.

The scorched-earth strategy that DOJ brought against Brussel and his company was total. Its prosecution is described with lawyerly restraint and devastating detail by Brussel's attorney, Edward H. Rosenthal, in a sworn statement.

Declaration of Edward H. Rosenthal
1. I am an attorney practicing with Frankfurt, Garbus, Klein & Selz, P.C., at 488 Madison Avenue, New York, New York 10022.
2. We represented Karl Brussel in connection with obscenity prosecutions brought by the federal government against Mr. Brussel, his son Matthew Brussel, his wife Jill Brussel, and PAK Ventures, Inc. ("PAK") in the Eastern District of Virginia, the Eastern District of North Carolina, and two federal districts in Alabama. . . .
5. PAK, Karl Brussel, Jill Brussel, and Matthew Brussel were targets of at least five interrelated grand jury investigations focusing on alleged violations of federal obscenity statutes in North Carolina, Alabama, and Virginia.
6. In about August, 1989, Karl Brussel, Jill Brussel, Matthew Brussel and PAK were indicted for violations of federal obscenity statutes in the Eastern District of North Carolina. . . .
7. In about December, 1989, Karl Brussel, Jill Brussel, Matthew Brussel, and PAK were indicted for violations of federal obscenity statutes in the Eastern District of Virginia.
8. In about February, 1990, Karl Brussel, Jill Brussel, Matthew Brussel, and PAK were indicted for violations of federal obscenity statutes in the Southern District of Alabama.
9. In addition, more indictments were threatened, including indictments in the Western District of North Carolina.
10. Upon information and belief, Representatives of the National Obscenity Enforcement Unit, including Patrick Trueman, were coordinating all the prosecutions. They consistently made clear to defendants that they would be prosecuted consecutively in multiple jurisdictions unless they agreed to a guilty plea which would include their ceasing involvement with sexually explicit expressive material and forfeiting certain business assets including expressive materials and the means of producing expressive materials. . . .
12. The National Obscenity Enforcement Unit made clear that the condition that defendants go out of the business of distributing sexually-oriented materials was a requirement of any plea, and that this demand was not negotiable.
13. In March 1990 . . . Karl Brussel, Jill Brussel, Matthew Brussel and

PAK were indicted on obscenity charges in the Middle District of Alabama.

14. The trial was scheduled in the Eastern District of Virginia to begin on March 27, 1990. The trial in the Eastern District of North Carolina was scheduled to begin on April 23, 1990. The trial in the Middle District of Alabama was scheduled to begin on May 14, 1990. The trial in the Southern District of Alabama was scheduled to begin on May 21, 1990.

15. I believed that the defendants had a chance of acquittal in the Eastern District of Virginia trial. Nevertheless, the federal prosecutors made clear to us that regardless of the outcome of that case, within a few days of the verdict defendants would be prosecuted in another jurisdiction, and that this process would be repeated until convictions were obtained or defendants agreed to plead guilty.[20]

After Brussel's indictment in the Eastern District of North Carolina, Dave Rudolf had been asked to join the Brussel defense team. This meant that Dave was aware in complete detail of what the government was doing in the Brussel case. Those events changed Dave's mind and convinced him that we should go ahead with our lawsuit. "It was now clear," he recalls, "that the DOJ recognized no limits on its multidistrict prosecution strategy."

The DOJ demanded that "Karl Brussel . . . plead guilty personally and his exposure will be a three year maximum; Matthew Brussel must also plead personally, and his exposure will be a three year maximum; Jill Brussel would receive pre-trial diversion; the Corporation would plead guilty and pay a fine of $750,000, agree to cease business activities in sexually explicit matter, and forfeit all business assets including but not limited to, video recording equipment, all sexually explicit masters and video cassettes, all blank video cassettes, and any other business equipment including personal computers which are owned by the business."[21]

It is worth pausing to note here that the government, in its majesty, is demanding that father and son give up their liberty, perhaps for as much as three years, under conditions where their physical safety might well be in question. The wife is spared. The business pays a huge fine and gives up its assets and disappears from the face of the earth forever. And all this is not because the Brussels had harmed anyone in any way or cheated anyone—Karl Brussel was not accused of shortchanging his customers, or failing to return their money when requested, or misleading anyone with false advertising. Rather, Brussel faced the prospect of four trials in three months—an intolerable burden—because a handful of people who held positions of power in the federal government believed that the sexual content of the material the Brussels sold was obnoxious. While they may also have believed that the material the Brussels sold was illegal, that was a matter of opinion. It is not exaggerating to state that the mighty engines of the law were used to destroy Brussel and his business because the expressed sexual tastes and preferences of certain law enforcement officials were different from those of the Brussels' customers.

So the Brussels, father and son, entered guilty pleas to disseminating obscenity in the Eastern District of North Carolina, the Western District of North Carolina, the Southern District of Alabama, and the Middle District of Alabama. Karl Brussel agreed to serve one year in jail, and PAK Ventures disappeared from existence.

> The Justice Department crowed about the plea agreement.★ "This latest in an unbroken string of successful mail-order obscenity prosecutions has eliminated what is believed to have been the nation's largest mail-order distributor of obscene materials," said Edward S. G. Dennis Jr., an assistant attorney general. . . . The department contends that it has won 19 anti-pornography convictions in 17 districts since mid-1988.[22]

That did it. While Joe Cheshire was still reluctant, and suing the government still represented something antithetical to everything Wade Smith's instincts told him, we decided to risk it. With Dave Rudolf's conversion, Wade and Joe went along. We would sue the U.S. Department of Justice, including Richard Lambert and Patrick Trueman by name.

We were all convinced of the basic soundness of our constitutional claim. Furthermore, our defense attorneys had great respect for Bruce Ennis and his team. Had Dave and Wade and Joe not felt that Bruce was the best possible attorney to lead our countercharge, they would probably not have agreed to it. "I had a lot of confidence in Bruce," notes Dave. "I had always been impressed with his work, and that was a big part of the reason I was confident about the civil suit."

Bruce had presented his strategy to us in considerable detail. The egregiousness of the government's behavior was clear. Furthermore, Judge Jackson in the Freedberg case had given us a very encouraging precedent; at least one federal judge in the D.C. circuit was clearly disturbed by the constitutional implications of the multiple-prosecution strategy. We concluded, in Dave's words, that the government dog "was not going to stay asleep, and we might as well go ahead and bite first."

★A violation of Smith's Law: Never rub your opponent's nose in the dirt. In this case it helped hasten our decision to sue.

On March 26, 1990, three years to the day from the date of our "not guilty" verdict in Alamance County—and this really was a coincidence—*PHE, Inc.* v. *United States Department of Justice* was filed with the U.S. District Federal Court in Washington, D.C.[23] Our complaint, the basic document of most lawsuits, named the Department of Justice, Attorney General Richard Thornburg, the NOEU, Patrick Trueman, Richard Lambert, and Joseph Whittle (U.S. attorney for the Middle District of Kentucky) as defendants and stated that these parties

> and their predecessors and agents, including Samuel T. Currin (Currin), formerly US Attorney for the Eastern District of North Carolina, and Brent D. Ward (Ward), formerly US Attorney for Utah, all of whom will be referred to collectively herein as "defendants," [at last; how good it felt to have the shoe on the other foot] have been acting in concert, in their official capacities, with the knowledge of each other, to implement a common plan, conspiracy or scheme, and under color of law. To this end, defendants . . . have engaged in a deliberate, systematic, and long-standing effort to coerce plaintiffs [us; that sounded good, too] to cease distribution of sexually oriented materials, including materials defendants have conceded are not obscene and are protected by the First Amendment from governmental suppression. . . . During the course of this four year effort, defendants' objective . . . has been to use or threaten to use prosecutorial powers to coerce plaintiffs to cease distribution of non-obscene expressive materials. In short, defendants have abused their prosecutorial powers in a deliberate effort to coerce plaintiffs to cease distribution of expressive materials defendants could not, and would not, prosecute as obscene, and they have varied the threat and pressures they have brought to bear on plaintiffs in order to coerce the self-censorship of as broad a range of non-obscene expressive materials as plaintiffs can be coerced to forego. . . .
>
> In particular, defendants have threatened to institute simultaneous multiple prosecutions, and/or multiple consecutive prosecutions, against plaintiffs and their officers and employees unless and until plaintiffs cease distribution, nationwide, of all sexually oriented expression to which defendants object, whether or not obscene. . . .
>
> At various times, defendants have explicitly threatened to prosecute plaintiffs for distribution of allegedly obscene expressive materials unless plaintiffs cease distribution of *all* sexually oriented expressive materials, including materials defendants have acknowledged would not be found obscene, such as *The Joy of Sex* and *Playboy Magazine.*

This matter of *Playboy* and *The Joy of Sex* became an issue of considerable argumentation and publicity, and it caught the attention of federal judges both in Washington and later at the appeals court in Denver. The Justice Department contended over and over again that we had misrepresented their position, and that they never asserted that *Playboy* and *The Joy of Sex* were obscene. This is perfectly true. But at no time in any of our pleadings, including this complaint, did we assert that the DOJ had declared these publications to be obscene. Our point was that, in extensive conversations about conditions for a settlement of our case, Richard Lambert and Brent Ward had insisted that we would have to cease selling even such clearly *nonobscene* publications as *Playboy* and *The Joy of Sex* if we wished to reach an agreement and stay in business. Thus they were using the prosecutorial process to try to suppress speech that they themselves did not believe to be obscene.

Our complaint went on to make clear our opinion that these prosecutors were employing these tactics in pursuit of their own personal agendas.

> Defendants have invoked and threatened to invoke the prosecutorial powers entrusted to them unless plaintiffs cease distribution of even nonobscene sexually oriented expressive material because defendants personally favor suppression of a much broader range of sexually oriented materials than would be found obscene under the standards set forth in *Miller v. California*, 413 US 15 (1973), and because of their belief, as they have told plaintiffs, that the world would be much improved if they could force plaintiffs to shut down their business and cease distribution of such nonobscene but sexually oriented materials. . . .
>
> Defendants have taken and threatened the actions complained of herein to punish plaintiffs for distributing lawful expressive materials defendants find personally offensive.

It was also important to establish "bad-faith" motivation on the part of the government. Bad faith in this context did not mean personal animus or outright chicanery, but that the government was engaged in something other than what it claimed to be doing: it was abusing the prosecutorial process and the authority of the prosecutor's office to threaten trial activity, much of which it had no intention of carrying out.

> Defendants have acted in bad faith, have abused their powers as federal officials, and have engaged in a systematic and purposeful effort to convince plaintiffs that they would be subjected to multiple prosecutions for obscenity offenses, and would be proceeded against in forfeiture proceedings, even though defendants did not at that time actually intend to institute such multiple prosecutions or forfeiture proceedings, and defendants did all this for the

purpose and with the expected and foreseeable effect of coercing plaintiffs to cease distribution of constitutionally protected expressive materials defendants knew they could not directly suppress through obscenity prosecutions or forfeiture proceedings.

Our complaint went on to detail the sequence of events from May 1986 until early 1990 when the lawsuit was filed. We reminded the court that the government had refused to provide information and assistance we had requested in Bruce's several letters "for the improper and bad faith reason that defendants do not want plaintiffs to distribute even entirely lawful sexually oriented materials. Defendants have no interest in assisting plaintiffs to avoid any violation of law. Defendants would prefer to trap plaintiffs with even one inadvertent violation of law, which defendants could then use as leverage to coerce plaintiffs to cease distribution of lawful sexually oriented materials."

As a constitutional basis for our plea for injunctive relief, we cited both the First and the Fifth Amendments. The government's efforts to silence us "before there is an adjudicated finding that the suppressed speech is obscene is an unconstitutional prior restraint in violation of the First Amendment." Further, "Defendants' plan to seek indictments against plaintiffs simultaneously in multiple jurisdictions is a violation of the due process clause of the Fifth Amendment," as well as the double jeopardy clause of the Fifth Amendment.

We asked the court to "preliminarily and permanently restrain defendants" from undertaking simultaneous multiple prosecutions of us, from using threats to force us to curtail our constitutional rights, and from threatening actions against us—including searches, seizures, and subpoenas—if we refused to substantially curtail the distribution of constitutionally protected sexually oriented speech. We also asked for injunctive relief against any proceedings against us in Utah or the Western District of Kentucky based on any action prior to the filing of the lawsuit. (This was a long shot, since the courts seldom interfere with executive branch determination of what they choose to prosecute, but we believed there was at least a chance that we would be able to demonstrate sufficient bad faith on the part of the government in Utah and Kentucky to justify an injunction against prosecutions arising from investigations already underway in those two jurisdictions.)

Finally, we asked for an injunction from the court forbidding the gov-ernment from taking or threatening any action against us in retaliation for filing the suit itself, and we asked for reimbursement of our legal fees (another long shot, but certainly worth the try).

★ ★ ★

The fat was in the fire. Our case was assigned to Federal Judge Joyce Hens Green. Bruce and his colleagues quickly researched Judge Green's background and her decisions in related cases. Their conclusion was that she would likely be fair and reasonably sympathetic to our side. She would take seriously Judge Jackson's earlier decision on a nearly identical matter, though that would not likely be decisive. Bruce was concerned however that the government might have better success with a female judge when they raised arguments about the perniciousness of pornography, especially because of the "exploitation of women" argument.

On April 19, the judge conducted a hearing at which we presented oral argument to support our plea for relief. The government attorneys countered. Bruce was relieved that Judge Green focused straight on the constitutional issues at hand and did not appear to be distracted by emotional arguments concerning the sexual nature of the materials. She appeared to be fair and thoroughly businesslike. Our optimism inched upward.

While we were waiting for Judge Green's decision, a few discussions between Wade, John Mintz, and Richard Lambert in Salt Lake City continued desultorily. But our discussions now were heavily colored by speculation over the outcome of the lawsuit.

On July 23, after three months of nail biting, the decision came down. Our injunction was granted! The government would not be permitted, while the lawsuit was pending, to use its multiple-prosecution strategy against PHE, Inc., or me. The other requests were, for the time being, ignored, but our central request—forbidding the use of the multiple-prosecution strategy until we could try this civil case "on the merits"—was granted.

Judge Green's opinion:

> ORDERED that plaintiff's motion for a preliminary injunction is granted and defendants United States Department of Justice, United States Attorney General Richard Thornburg, the National Obscenity Enforcement Unit ("NOEU") and its Acting Director Patrick Trueman, Assistant United States Attorney for the District of Utah Richard N. W. Lambert, and United States Attorney for the Western District of Kentucky Joseph M. Whittle are preliminarily restrained and enjoined from causing or permitting indictments to be returned against plaintiffs, or either of them, in more than one federal judicial district within the United States, pending determination of this case on the merits or further order of this Court.[24]

In addition, Judge Green, who had obviously reviewed the entire case with great care, had included a good deal of language very supportive of our cause—language that would turn out to be useful when we went to war in Utah and argued our case before the Tenth Circuit Appeals Court in Denver (the Tenth Circuit includes Utah). She pointed out, for example,

> the disparity between the resources of any criminal defendant and the federal government may mean that plaintiffs [PHE and Harvey] may be forced out of business before they ever have their day, or in this instance, days, in court. Like the plaintiffs in *Freedberg*, the instant plaintiffs face "annihilation, by attrition if not conviction."
>
> . . . [I]t must be presumed, as plaintiffs allege, that defendants [the government] are acting in a coordinated effort to cause plaintiffs to face criminal prosecutions in multiple federal district courts for the purpose of coercing plaintiffs to refrain from distributing materials which defendants acknowledge are constitutionally protected. It must also be presumed that defendants are pursuing the strategy of multiple prosecutions in order to win a war of economic attrition and drive plaintiffs out of their chosen profession.

In other words, the very strategy outlined by Ward in 1986, reiterated by Cynthia Christfield in 1987, successfully conducted by the DOJ against a dozen companies, and described in a strong warning memorandum by the government's own lawyer in 1988, was now held to be unconstitutional on its face. How sweet it was. The injunction meant that the government could bring us to trial in only one location while the civil lawsuit was conducted, a process that everyone recognized might take a year or possibly two. This meant that we would be able to defend ourselves vigorously at one trial (if it came to that) and at the same time pursue our civil claims against the government and its bad-faith prosecution of our company. Judge Green's opinion had spoken directly to this point.

> [I]t is clear that . . . [PHE and Harvey's] First Amendment rights cannot be adequately protected by defending themselves simultaneously or *seriatim* in each separate district in which they may be indicted. The enormous disparity between plaintiff's resources and the resources of the government means, as a practical matter, that plaintiffs could be swiftly driven out of business before they ever set foot inside a courtroom.

We were still bouncing down the river, and the currents were strong. But now we had a life raft.

NOTES

1. Memorandum "To Janis Kockritz, From Cindy Christfield, RE: Operation Post-porn Legal Issues," Department of Justice, 1987. This memorandum appears to be undated. Date stamp may be illegible on the copy produced in evidence. Probable date is between May and December 1987.

2. Brent Ward, letter to Edwin Meese III, Attorney General, September 6, 1985.

3. Weld was subsequently elected governor of Massachusetts, where he claimed libertarian credentials. He was no libertarian in 1988.

4. Robert Marinaro deposition, May 24, 1991.

5. Raymond Bernard deposition, March 20, 1991.

6. *CQ Researcher* 1, no. 31, December 20, 1991, p. 976.

7. Ibid., p. 977.

8. Affidavit of Elkin Abramowitz, May 17, 1988.

9. Ibid.

10. A request for declaratory and injunctive relief normally includes a request to the court to enjoin the government from taking certain actions, usually with immediate effect.

11. Memorandum from George C. Burgasser, NOEU, to Ronald Noble, Special Counsel to Assistant Attorney General, Washington, D.C., October 14, 1988. The dismissal of the lawsuit "with prejudice" means that the plaintiffs are precluded forever from suing again over the same matter.

12. Plea Agreement: Avram C. Freedberg/Consumer's Marketing Group, Ltd., November 22, 1988. The inclusion of the unusual spousal commitment in this agreement may not even be legally binding on Mrs. Freedberg. That the government permitted, even in 1988, the anachronistic practice of a husband's signature binding his spouse on matters unrelated to their marriage is startling. I recall asking Avram Freedberg about this at the time. He said he had been quite surprised that the government did not demand his wife's signature on the agreement as well as his.

13. Showers's departure from the DOJ in 1988 may also have been influenced by alleged improprieties in his use of government travel funds. As the *Washington Post* reported in November of that year,

> The Justice Department is conducting a criminal investigation of its top pornography prosecutor for possible misuse of travel funds in connection with trips he made to religious meetings, government sources said yesterday.
>
> The Office of Professional Responsibility (OPR) . . . is carrying out the probe of H. Robert Showers with the assistance of FBI agents, said the sources, who asked not to be identified.
>
> Investigators are trying to determine whether Showers scheduled official trips at taxpayer expense that permitted him to attend meetings of Christian religious groups in his hometown of Raleigh, NC, and other cities, said the sources. *Washington Post*, November 2, 1988.

14. The full text of McCommon's memorandum is given in appendix D. This memo was obtained as part of the discovery process in our civil suit.

15. Letter from Paul C. McCommon III to H. Robert Showers Jr., May 18, 1984.

16. Memorandum Opinion and Order, *PHE, Inc., et al.* v. *U.S. Department of Justice, et al.*, Joyce Hens Green, September 30, 1993.

17. *Carey* v. *Population Services International* 431 U.S. 678 (1977).

18. In one of the more colorful dissenting opinions from our highest court in recent decades, Justice William H. Rehnquist (he was not then Chief Justice) asserted, "[If] [t]hose who valiantly but vainly defended the heights of Bunker Hill in 1775 . . . , [those whose blood] was shed at Shiloh, Gettysburg, and Cold Harbor . . . could have lived to know that their efforts had enshrined in the Constitution the right of commercial vendors of contraceptives to peddle them to unmarried minors through such means as window displays and vending machines located in the men's room of truck stops, notwithstanding the considered judgment of the New York Legislature to the contrary, it is not difficult to imagine their reaction."

19. Jonathan Harr, *A Civil Action* (New York: Vintage Books, 1995), p. 116.

20. Declaration of Edward H. Rosenthal, Civil Action No. 90-0693, June 21, 1991.

21. Ibid.

22. "N.C. Mail-Order Firm Sues to Bar Federal Prosecutions," *Raleigh News and Observer*, March 28, 1990.

23. Complaint For Declaratory and Injunctive Relief, *PHE, Inc. et al.* v. *U.S. Department of Justice*, No. 90-0693 (D.D.C. filed March 26, 1990).

24. Memorandum Opinion and Order, *PHE, Inc., et al.* v. *U.S. Department of Justice, et al.*, Joyce Hens Green, September 30, 1993.

CHAPTER SEVEN

PORNOGRAPHY AND CLASS

Would you let your servant read this book?
—Crown prosecutor at the trial of *Lady Chatterly's Lover*

Class.
Whatever happened to "please, may I?"
and, "yes, thank you"?
and, "how charming"?
Now, every son of a bitch is a snake in the grass.
Whatever happened to class?

—*Chicago*

As one indication of my own occasional blindness to the nuances of class, I have changed my mind about trailer parks. In the past, when Harriet and I drove by some of the more forlorn of these congregations of mobile homes, treeless and metallic, we would agree that they were ugly and change the subject. Now I understand that the propensity of many Americans to live or vacation in mobile homes and to pull them together into little communities with spinning plastic whirligigs, plastic deer, and sometimes flamingos out front is at least to some extent a matter of preference and taste.

My epiphany, if that's not overstating it, occurred at a particularly rustic and lovely development in Pennsylvania near Prince Rupert Lake. Large lots of one or more acres were being sold for single-family dwellings—the more expensive homes; some smaller lots were being sold for more modest vacation homes. All were carefully screened by trees for the maximum sense of privacy and closeness to nature. The lots, reasonably priced, were selling slowly, and the developer, a friend of ours, expressed his hope for further careful, environmentally sensitive, but still profitable development of the project. He noted, however, that one particular spot was already nearly sold (or rented) out: the portion of this forested area designated for recreational vehicles and mobile homes. We paid a call. This "camp" was a source of both pride and embarrassment to our friend. The RVs were helping pay for the water, electrical, and sewage services being supplied to the development. Yet their presence and their community aesthetics seemed to fall far outside our friend's relatively pristine vision for the wilderness area he was converting.

What a sight! Here, in row upon row of designated stalls, surrounded by lovely forest on all sides, were twenty or more (truly) mobile homes, recreational vehicles lined up no more than fifteen or twenty feet apart with multiple rows of plastic propellers revolving out front, satellite dishes poking up between the trailers, barbecue paraphernalia, and aluminum and plastic folding tables and stools. People were coming and going, obviously enjoying themselves and each other's company, taking pleasure in this community, including their proximity to each other.

To me, the thrill of the outdoors lies in solitude and closeness to nature. But here were people who clearly enjoyed being close to other people even while they were enjoying the natural beauty of the place. Privacy was of little importance and their sense of aesthetics seemed completely unconnected to the immediate surrounding environment. Clearly, that people would deliberately go to considerable lengths and expense to enjoy the out-of-doors in this way was a fact it was time for me to accept.

The experience reminded me again that we must be very careful about whose expression we condemn—particularly when it comes to coercively muzzling others—because in large part our preferences come down to taste. I am no admirer of rapper Snoop Doggy-Dogg. I think the sounds and rhythms of most rap music are obnoxious. The advocacy of violence against women, against the police, against *anyone*, is advocacy of what runs counter to my most deeply held beliefs. But I struggle to remember that such preferences are also to some degree a matter of taste.

Outspoken critics of the "coarsening" of American culture include columnist George Will, Judge Robert H. Bork, the late Professor Allan Bloom, and former education secretary William Bennett. Will has written numerous columns deploring the graphic sexual and violent depictions in, among other things, rap music and other popular forms of entertainment. Judge Bork's book *Slouching Towards Gomorrah*[1] echoes these views and also affirms Will's policy of reprinting some of the more vulgar and controversial lyrics from these songs in order to display the details of their content. I have no objection to this practice. There is no reason why those of us who defend the First Amendment should be unaware of the exact language and images we are helping to protect. One noteworthy example is the description of a man who is in jail with hardened criminals and, repeatedly raped, has his teeth knocked out by an assailant who smashes his mouth against the corners of a metal bed so that, toothless, he will be more accommodating to the sexual demands of his tormentors. He is reduced gradually to the stature of a weeping, pathetic vegetable.

Compare this with Nine Inch Nails's song "Big Man with a Gun," quoted in Judge Bork's book, which contains numerous expletives, describes forced fellatio, asserts "Maybe I'll put a hole in your head," and suggests that the "big man" will ejaculate on (probably) a woman, and ends "Me and my fuckin' gun."

Most of us would consider both of these descriptions/depictions to be repugnant, coarse, and objectionable. But while George Will and Judge Bork deplore and, in Bork's case at least, are prepared to ban and censor the second depiction through government action, Will lavished some praise on the first depiction/description as being a valuable (if graphic) part of an outstanding piece of literature. That is because the story of the man whose teeth were smashed out to make him a more accommodating fellator is a scene from Scott Turow's first novel, *Presumed Innocent*, a book that Will particularly liked.

So even conservative arbiters of the "coarseness" of American culture are highly selective about what they consider to be coarse. The most vile descriptions of the most dreadful sexual and violent acts are acceptable to many cultural conservatives if they are presented through a medium or format which they consider to be artistic, or at least worthy. Will himself noted that, in *The Sopranos*, a graphic television series whose language can be "numbingly ugly," the sex and violence "derive integrity from the artistic context."[2]

Another example: the gang raping (consent is not clear, but it is doubtful) of Fanny, the circus Fat Lady, in E. L. Doctorow's *Loon Lake*. A hundred men stand in a circle inside a circus tent, drinking, cursing, laughing, and betting on the staying power of Fanny's sexual assailants as she lies, naked and bloody, in the mud. There is "a bitter foul smell of burning nerves, and shit and scum, [as] men leap . . . on her, on each other, squatting on her head, crawling over her, falling on her, shoving bottles in her. . . ."[3]

What is the difference between this and the "torn vaginas" described in rap music and so deplored by Will, Bork, and Bennett? A big part of the answer is, I think, a matter of taste. Shakespeare's Caliban can declare "I smell horse piss" because Shakespeare is a recognized genius, but when Al Goldstein, publisher of *Screw* magazine, says the same thing, he is guilty of contributing to the coarseness of society.

In Aristophanes's classic play *Lysistrata*, the women of Athens band together and determine that they will withhold sex from their men in order to stop war. Like much of Aristophanes's work, it is a bawdy play, full of irony and sharp wit. The bawdiness is inherent in the play's artistic premise, particularly the characterization of men as both puerile and presumptuous, easily tamed and manipulated by women's sexuality. At one point Cinesias "bursts into sorrowful song":

> *Oh what, tell me what, can this woeful laddie do?*
> *And who, tell me who, can this woeful laddie screw?*
> *Philostratus, I need you, do come and help me quick:*
> *Could I please hire a nurse for my poor young orphan prick?*

And at the end of the play, Lysistrata, the heroine, facilitates a peace negotiation by having the male antagonists point out their territorial claims on the body of a naked woman who has, in the words of one character in the play, a "lovely cunt."[4]

Judge Bork would no doubt have urged Aristophanes to make his points about sex and war, about the relationship between men and women, in some less explicit manner. Aristophanes would not have agreed, I think. Nor do I.

The use of sexual terminology and symbolism is common in art and literature, as is violence. Art that teaches us, moves us, challenges us to think about the human condition in new ways, is often shocking and disturbing. It is intended to be.

Judge Bork would have us believe that today's popular culture "is more vulgar than at any time in the past." He looks back fondly on the 1930s, when performers sang about "the way you look tonight," with a warm smile, a soft cheek, "nothing for me but to love you."[5] But public lynchings were sometimes popular "entertainment" in the 1930s, too, a phenomenon that strikes me as a lot more coarse than any form of rap. Going back a bit further, popular culture also included throwing dead animals at people in pillories, nailing peoples' ears to wooden walls so they could not move their heads when spat upon or hit with rocks, animal baiting, gawking at physically deformed human beings, and similar pastimes. In England, the torture of animals for sport included cat-dropping, bear-baiting, and setting dogs upon tethered bulls.

Early in American history our forebears enjoyed watching women being drowned, or nearly drowned, in the ducking stool, the humiliating and brutalizing of people in stocks and pillories, the cutting off of ears and slicing of noses, and branding with hot irons.

The point is not to excuse the coarse excesses of the present by pointing out that we have had even more of them in the past. Rather, it is to suggest that American culture, like the culture of modern societies everywhere, has been for centuries on a gradual civilizing trend, becoming less crude and vulgar rather than more so. We discourage practices that cause pain and suffering to animals as a form of amusement; both dog fighting and cock fighting are pretty well subdued (though not eliminated). We don't execute prisoners in public, and we are substituting lethal injection for more brutal forms of execution. Preventable violent death, though still very high in the United States, is on a downward trend, not an upward one. In many areas, vicarious violence, from televised "wrestling" to the verbal food fights on political commentary programs such as *McLaughlin & Co.*, is being substituted for true violence, and that is a very good thing.

Our culture is not only less violent, it is becoming healthier in many other ways. Researcher Everett Carl Ladd notes that the number of Americans volunteering for charities doubled between 1977 and 1995. We are spending more and more time, and more of our own money on community groups and charitable causes.[6]

Perhaps most tellingly, American culture, even in its most traditional forms, is expanding and becoming accessible to more and more people. "From 1965 to 1990, America grew from having 58 symphony orchestras to having nearly 300, from 27 opera companies to more than 150, and from 22 nonprofit regional theaters to 500," notes author Tyler Cowen.[7]

CLASSY VERSUS TRASHY

What are the fundamental differences between "classy" literary passages and "trash"? Sexual explicitness is common to both types. The sexually explicit passages from the work of Henry Miller, from James Joyce's *Ulysses*, from D. H. Lawrence's *Lady Chatterly's Lover*, as well as much Japanese and Indian erotic art and temple sculpture are all as candid and imaginatively sexual as anything in today's down-and-dirty adult videos or *Hustler* magazine.

Is it the passage of time that makes earlier images acceptable? Do we automatically retain some respect for the pornography of antiquity? Does homosexual intercourse depicted on a Greek vase represent something of greater value than the same activity depicted in a 1990s video?

Some would argue that the difference lies in the work's inherent artistic merit, and this may be linked to the passage of time in a kind of Darwinian way. Some drawings and sculptures are crude and bumbling; others are executed with beauty, or at least artistic flair. Some sexually explicit passages in literature, including awful descriptions of torture and mutilation in a sexual context, are rendered powerfully and memorably; some are just angry, shouted words. "It takes decades, and sometimes even centuries, to separate the cultural wheat from the chaff," notes Cowen.[8] Because emotions about contemporary matters so often run very deep, it is difficult to know how gangsta rap will be perceived fifty years from now. While I think much of it is crude and unlikely to survive, the same was said of the work of D. H. Lawrence and Henry Miller. And certainly the same was said repeatedly of Lenny Bruce, one of the most remarkable social commentators of any age—and, I have no doubt, of Aristophanes. "Each new medium or genre has been accused of corrupting youth and promoting excess sensuality, political subversion, and moral relativism," notes Cowen.[9]

There is another aspect of the "problem" of contemporary music lyrics so decried by Bork, Will, Bennett, Bloom, and their admirers. While authors like Bloom are distressed about the "masturbatory" aspects of our culture, others make the point that many of these lyrics advocate violence, and it is true that certain rap lyrics and some other modern music lyrics do advocate, if their words are taken literally, the killing of police and others. All the same, it is important to remember that advocating violence against those in authority is neither new nor unexpected. I oppose it, but I do not believe that it can be outlawed without undermining our most basic rights to speech.*

IS PORNOGRAPHY "COARSE"?

If American society, examined over the long term, is becoming less coarse and brutal rather than more so, if American culture in its rich and varied forms is expanding rather than diminishing, what role does pornography play, and where does it fit in to this landscape?

First, very little violent content appears in sexually explicit erotica in the United States. There are a variety of indicators of this. The cartoons in *Playboy* magazine have been analyzed in minute detail by people trying to prove that all sexual material tends to be violent. The review found that suggestions of violence and coercion appears in less than 5 percent of such cartoons and is decreasing. Our own company now reviews more than seven hundred new X-rated video titles every year. Of these, virtually none contain sexual violence, and only a small fraction contain any form of coercive sexual activity or sexual degradation sufficient to cause our sex therapy experts to raise a red flag.

Violence and coercion are, of course, rife in our other entertainments.

---

* The U.S. Supreme Court permits the prohibition of advocacy speech only when it "is directed to inciting or producing imminent lawless action and is likely to incite or produce such action" (*Brandenberg v. Ohio*, 1969). Also proscribable are "insulting or 'fighting' words which by their very utterance inflict injury or tend to incite an immediate breach of the peace" (*Chaplinsky v. New Hampshire*, 1982). Subsequent decisions have made clear that these standards are meant to be difficult to meet.

There is much less violence in men's sex-oriented magazines, for example, than there is in the detective or even sports magazines. X-rated videos and films contain far less violence than mainstream movies, a fact that is particularly conspicuous when X-rated stories are compared with the R-rated "slasher" films that feature titillating sexuality commingled with gruesome violence. Edward Donnerstein, a respected researcher on the impact of sexually expressive materials, and his colleagues have repeatedly pointed out that slasher films and other violent depictions show a much greater negative impact when examined in laboratory studies than do nonviolent sexual images, no matter how explicit.[10]

The absence of violence in most X-rated material may not necessarily be good, by the way. As we have noted, violence is a central theme in much classical and modern drama and literature. We tend to deplore the "excessive" violence of current entertainment while ignoring the importance of the violence in the Greek epics, in Shakespeare, and in modern masterpieces by such authors as Dostoyevsky, Tolstoy, Conrad, Mailer, Vonnegut, and Steinbeck.

On the other hand, the fact that most sexual materials are essentially free from violence and coercion is no comfort to those who would censor sexual speech. The very absence of violence tends to make X-rated material more widely acceptable, which compounds the problem of suppressing it. I am pleased that our company has played a role in this process. By insisting on the dual review of sexually explicit materials by outside reviewers, we have strongly encouraged the producers of such material to eschew violent and coercive themes. While I believe this has had the effect of nudging the industry away from violence (probably good), it also means self-censorship on the part of the producers (maybe not so good).

Mere lack of violence does not make pornography "classy," of course. Author Sallie Tisdale has pointed out that we should hardly be surprised that pornographic depictions are not particularly tasteful, since most American entertainment is not very tasteful. There is scant reason to suppose that sexually explicit entertainment is going to be any higher-toned than equivalent forms of diversion on daytime talk shows or the television tabloid program *Hard Copy*.[11]

There are distinctions, however. Taste and class have played a particularly important role in the suppression of sexual materials because of elitism. Perhaps because the "lower-body" nature of sexuality was thought to be especially dominant (and dangerous) among the "lower classes," political and intellectual elites have often been especially concerned about suppressing sexual imagery among the poor or the less educated. The censorship thus motivated was professed to be censorship on behalf of, or to "protect," more susceptible, "weaker" members of society, whose sensibilities are assumed to be not so discreet or robust as those of the more affluent and better educated. As the Commission on Obscenity and Pornography pointed out in the 1970s, "As the lower classes became more literate, the ruling classes felt more pressure to control freedom of expression in literature; while they had not been overly concerned about the effects of erotic writings upon themselves . . . the fear of pornography's effects on youth as well as on the lower classes was a concern."[12]

Such a view of the world is, of course, the very stuff of tyranny. Once people attain positions of power they are almost always inclined to think they know better than others what is good for those others. It is very easy to start thinking that "they"—usually those who are less fortunate, of lesser status, of less education, usually poorer—cannot make certain decisions for themselves. This has been going on for some time. When trains were introduced in England, the first Duke of Wellington is said to have remarked, in all seriousness and with visible trepidation, to the upper house of Parliament in London, "My Lords, these iron horses will enable the lower classes to move about!"

At the end of the twentieth century, comedian Drew Carey made a closely related point: "All the government's doing is discriminating against poor people. It thinks poor people are like cows, that poor people can't think straight: If we let them hear dirty words or see dirty pictures, there's going to be *madness*! If you're poor and all you can afford is a 12-inch black-and-white TV and can't pay for cable—you're so protected! You'd probably be happier if you could see some pornography, a pair of titties, once in a while on free TV. But a pair of titties on free TV? The government figures if you saw that, you'd just explode!"[13]

Class-based views of pornography take many forms. "Once upon a time," observes a *New York Times* writer, "obscenity was confined to expensive leather-bound editions available only to gentlemen. . . . One of the questions asked by the crown prosecutor [in the trial of the publisher of *Lady Chatterly's Lover*] . . . was: 'Would you let your servant read this book?'"[14] Indeed, one of the earliest common-law decisions involving obscenity reflected this elitist attitude. The Queen's Bench ruled in 1868 that, to be obscene, material must have the power to "deprave and corrupt those whose minds are open to such immoral influences."

The elitist component in the view that finds American culture "coarse" is supported by the "We-They" phenomenon (see chapter 11). "Elitists need to feel that they belong to a privileged minority," Tyler Cowen observes. "Contemporary culture, however, is massive in size, diverse in scope, and widely disseminated. Elitists have a hard time sustaining their self-images if they admit that our culture is wonderful and vibrant."[15] The problem for cultural elitists, in other words, is that so many Americans are now participating in the explosion of cultural entertainment that the former elites have become just better-educated members of the hoi polloi.

Supreme Court Justice David Souter has provided us with a relevant example of the class or "taste" component in the acceptability of differing forms of entertainment. While concurring in the Court's decision to uphold an Indiana ban on nude dancing, Justice Souter pointed out that he would not likely support any law banning nudity in a production of *Equus*, or *Hair*, or other forms of "higher" entertainment, i.e., the sort of entertainment that a Supreme Court justice might himself choose to enjoy.[16] In other words, nude dancing in an acclaimed opera where the audience pays $75 per seat will always be protected, while nude dancing on a platform in a bar filled with blue-shirted working men will often be outlawed. Such views by Court justices are especially dangerous because the Supreme Court represents the last bulwark against those who would censor free expression.

But the hoi polloi will not—and should not—give up such sexual rights easily. Now that the lower classes are not only moving about on trains, but have the leisure for reading and entertainment, there is in the marketplace a preference for sexualia that the elites often find obnoxious but that has a rightful place. In American culture, this phenomenon is exemplified by Larry Flynt's *Hustler* magazine. It offends practically everyone. *Hustler* has been excoriated as misogynist, racist, and just plain revolting. Those purporting to speak for particular groups have pointed out the gynecological explicitness of *Hustler's* photography, the fact that women are often portrayed in cartoons and jokes on *Hustler's* pages as objects and playthings, that black women are satirized as raunchy and unwashed, that the magazine is anti-Semitic. But in fact, *Hustler* is an equal-opportunity denigrator. This point was best expressed by writer Randy Katz. "There are, first of all, three general categories of individuals whose discomfort owing to Mr. Flynt's publication is not to be underestimated: 1) women who are demeaned and insulted by *Hustler*; 2) men who are demeaned and insulted by *Hustler*; 3) domestic farm animals who are demeaned and insulted by *Hustler*."[17] He's right. In *Hustler*, everybody gets it, including animals. Blacks, male and female, are satirized brutally. White males are portrayed as buffoons and child molesters. Presidents, paupers, Latinos, Asians, and anyone from the "upper crust" are mercilessly pilloried. Indeed the sharpest barbs and most devastating derogations in *Hustler* are reserved for hypocrites in positions of power. As writer and sociologist M. G. Lord observes, "*Hustler's* scatological fantasies have less to do with penetrating women than with rage at not having penetrated the privileged classes."[18] Laura Kipnis adds, "The catalog of social resentments *Hustler* trumpets, particularly against class privilege, makes it by far the most openly class-antagonistic mass-circulation periodical of any genre."[19]

There is nothing that gives *Hustler's* editors greater pleasure than bringing down the high and the mighty, puncturing the bloated pomposity of people in positions of power and authority which, at the present time, are usually held by white men. Indeed *Hustler's* "Asshole of the Month" column has attacked white men almost exclusively. The outrageous *Hustler* parody of white male Jerry Falwell (which suggested that his first sexual experience was in an outhouse with his mother) was only the most famous. Falwell sued Flynt, and the case went all the way to the Supreme Court. All nine justices upheld *Hustler's* right to parody, even viciously, a well-known American personality.

The animal appeal of *Hustler,* in which the lower body triumphs over the rational, intellectual upper body, stands in stark contrast to the class aspirations represented by the images in *Playboy.* In Milos Forman's film about Larry Flynt, the Flynt character remarks, in the context of yet another obscenity prosecution, "All I'm guilty of is bad taste." I think this is largely true. The outrage so many people feel over *Hustler* magazine is in no small part based on taste. The much more tasteful *Playboy* was defended even by relatively conservative members of the Meese Commission, most notably Dr. Park Dietz. Dr. Dietz also had a few good words to say about *Penthouse,* whose depictions of the inner labia of women's vulvas are every bit as explicit as *Hustler's.* But *Penthouse* and *Playboy* are classier. *Playboy's* smoking-jacketed gentlemen are the very epitome of the elite dream, and *Penthouse,* too, exudes a fantasy of wealth and upper-crust exclusiveness. *Hustler,* contrariwise, goes out of its way to harpoon the upper crust, to denigrate those Ph.D. elitists, to fart on the pretentions of the ruling class, or anyone pretending to be holier than thou. It supplies a bracing tonic for two million readers every month. But it manages to offend practically everyone else.

"[T]he journey from *Ulysses* to *Hustler* involves more than a move from literature to smut, from words to images. It involves the transition from the preoccupation of an educated minority to the everyday fantasies of the blue-collar majority . . . . *Hustler* is the servant's revenge."[20]

Legal scholar Laurence Tribe adds,

Understandably anxious to avoid the embarrassing literary censorship of earlier times, the [Supreme] Court has retreated to a posture in which the erotic tastes of the educated and well bred emerge as part of the "grand conception of the First Amendment and its high purposes in the historic struggle for freedom," while the less-fashionable eroticism of the masses becomes the mere subject of commercial exploitation of obscene material [*Miller* v. *California*, 1973]. Even if an intelligible line could be drawn between the two categories—and Justice Brennan seems correct in concluding that it cannot—it would remain the case that "grossly disparate treatment of similar offenders," to use Justice Stevens's phrase, would inhere in the Supreme Court's own "enlightened" position of selective tolerance for the tastefully salacious coupled with contempt for the coarsely vulgar.[21]

A final point about the "lower-body" appeal of pornography in the context of class structure: each of us has a "lower-class," animal-like component when it comes to sex; this is probably one of the things that scares us. Our gentle, intimate lovemaking can sometimes turn rough, guttural, animalistic, and this is often very satisfying. A report from *Redbook* magazine about the pornography preferences of some well-educated women is a case in point. A female writer invites six of her women friends over for an evening of pornography viewing; they are going to rate different kinds of sex movies and discuss what turns them on. Their intellectual assessment of pornography is that it's pretty trashy stuff. "The actresses wear cheesy blue garters and prance and mewl on frilly bedspreads. And what's with the ludicrous groans and nauseating interior decor?" asks the author in her preamble.

Still, they aren't much impressed with the high-toned *Playboy* videos. And the safe sex depictions don't appeal. "I don't want to fantasize about safe sex," Emily announces. "I have that. I want to fantasize about lots of men."

The women give passing grades to some mainstream, well-produced sex films like *The Dinner Party*, but they are surprised at their own responses to some "down and dirty" material.

> A man and a woman are in the kitchen. She's face-forward against the wall, and he has his fingers inside her. Whether or not they love each other is anybody's guess. . . . We are watching *Sodomania*, a selection from my hard-core category. It shows lots of anal sex, lots of kinky sex, some of it pretty disturbing, as well as lots of licking and probing that I won't describe. From the packaging to the lighting to the squinty stupid look on the biker guy's face in one scene, the video is colored by an overall low-budget crassness.
>
> But what's this? No one wants me to turn it off. The room is very, very quiet. Finally Denise speaks up.
>
> "I think the appeal of things like this," she says, "is that it puts the nasty

back into sex. When you get to be an adult and a mother, you explain sex to your children as something so healthy, a natural extension of love. That nasty thrill kind of goes away at a certain point in your life."[22]

Here's a very good case of the lower body dominating our "better" selves, and the propensity of our "lower-class," animal components to emerge in a sexual context. Scary? For many it clearly is.

This kind of schizophrenia is common in many parts of our lives. In the 1970s, advertising executive Jeffrey Feinman referred to it as the "pot-smoking cop" phenomenon, by which he meant that many young policemen who conscientiously upheld the law in their official lives on duty nonetheless thought nothing of taking a few drags on a marijuana cigarette at a weekend party. "Everybody's favorite book is 'Shakespeare,' " Feinman maintained. "If you ask them, practically no one reads popular books." Similarly, we are all inclined to assert that we favor tasteful erotica, but when it comes to actually selecting a video we often choose plain, hard-core sex.

It is a good sign that more people are telling it like it is these days.

Sallie Tisdale: "The surprise is how many . . . women prefer the old hard-core films," she says. And, describing herself, she notes, "Any amateur psychologist could have a field day explaining why I prefer low-brow, hard-core porn to feminine erotica."[23]

Similarly, Linda Williams, professor of film studies at the University of California at Berkeley, who has made the analysis of pornography an important part of her academic research, observes, "As a feminist . . . I admire the female empowerment of the new couples' pornography as well as the woman-centered adventurousness and play of lesbian pornography. Yet personally I find both of these pornographies boring and gay male porn exciting. I won't even begin to speculate why."[24]

Most of our time and energy is spent in the world of the mind, and of affections, achievements, and work. This is also the part of ourselves that we like to emphasize to others, the part we are proud of. But we are all animals, too, and there is nothing wrong with that. Recognizing not only that other people have different tastes but that each of us ourselves has a "tasteless" lower-body streak is an important lesson for the functioning of a civilized society. We must control and direct our animal nature, but we should not try to deny it. Suffering endless guilt over the fact that we have animal urges is pointless and destructive; channeling those urges in creative and joyful ways is productive and valuable.

NOTES

1. Robert H. Bork, *Slouching Towards Gomorrah* (New York: ReganBooks [Harper Collins], 1996.

2. George Will, "Pushing the Plain Brown Envelope," *Washington Post*, September 14, 1999.

3. E. L. Doctorow, *Loon Lake* (New York: Plume/Penguin 1996), p. 128.

4. Aristophanes, *The Acharnians, The Clouds, Lysistrata*, trans. A. H. Sommerstein (New York: Penguin Books, 1973).

5. But what should we make of the following from Judge Bork's book, which is meant to show how coarse most of us are: "One evening at a hotel in New York I flipped around the television channels. Suddenly there on the public access channel was a voluptuous young woman, naked, her body oiled, writhing on the floor while fondling herself intimately. . . . Meanwhile, a man's voice . . . informed the viewer of the telephone number . . . that would acquaint him with other young women of similar charms and proclivities. I watched for some time—riveted by the sociological significance of it all." Bork, *Slouching Towards Gomorrah*, p. 129.

6. E. C. Ladd, *The Ladd Report* (New York: Free Press, 1999).

7. Tyler Cowen, "Is Our Culture in Decline?" *Cato Policy Report*, September/October 1998, p. 10.

8. Ibid., p. 12.

9. Ibid.

10. See Edward Donnerstein, D. Linz, and S. Penrod, *The Question of Pornography* (New York: Free Press, 1987), and "Prof. Says 'X' Less Damaging than 'R,' " *Daily News*, University of California at Santa Barbara, April 23, 1991.

11. Sallie Tisdale, *Talk Dirty to Me* (New York: Anchor, 1995).

12. Commission on Obscenity and Pornography, "Technical Report," vol. 2, 1970, p. 79.

13 Interview with Drew Carey, *Reason*, November 1997, p. 34.

14. "Has the First Amendment Met Its Match?" *New York Times*, March 6, 1977. Cited in Laurence H. Tribe, *American Constitutional Law* (Mineola, N.Y.: Foundation Press, 1996), p. 918; bracketed words are Tribe's.

15. Cowen, "Is Our Culture in Decline?" p. 12.

16. *Barnes* v. *Glen Theatre, Inc.* (1990). Apparently recognizing the elitist basis for his support for the ban on nude dancing in *Barnes*, Justice Souter reversed his position in a 2000 decision in *City of Erie* v. *Paps A.M.*, voting this time with the minority. (By a 6–3 majority, the Court upheld the city of Erie, Pennsylvania's right to require dancers to wear at least pasties and G-strings.) This time Justice Souter stated that he felt the city should have to demonstrate the harmful secondary effects of nude dancing; in *Barnes*, he had averred that the harmful effects could be assumed. "A Change of Mind and a Deft Mea Culpa," *New York Times*, March 30, 2000.

17. Randy Katz, "Our View" (editorial), *Everybody's News* (Cincinnati, Ohio), undated, 1997.

18. M. G. Lord, *Lingua Franca*, April/May 1997, p. 43.

19. Laura Kipnis, *Bound and Gagged, Pornography and the Politics of Fantasy in America* (New York: Grove Press, 1996), p. 130.

20. "Has the First Amendment Met Its Match?" cited in Tribe, *American Constitutional Law*, p. 918.

21. Tribe, *American Constitutional Law*, p. 918, footnotes omitted. Tribe's book was written before the nude-dancing decision in *Barnes* v. *Glen Theatre*, but he perfectly describes Justice Souter's reasoning in that case.

22. Julie Rigby, "Oh! Oooh! Ewww! 7 Women Review the New Sex Movies," *Redbook*, October 1995, p. 73.

23. Sallie Tisdale, "Talk Dirty to Me," *Harper's*, February 1992, p. 44.

24. Linda Williams, "The Visual and Carnal Pleasures of Moving-Image Pornography," address to the Society for the Scientific Study of Sex, April 1997, p. 19.

CHAPTER EIGHT

FOCUS GROUPS AND ALL THAT JAZZ

Utah

[S]ex and obscenity are not synonymous. [To the contrary], [s]ex . . . has indisputably been a subject of absorbing interest to mankind through the ages; it is one of the vital problems of human interest and public concern.

—*Roth* v. *United States* (1957)

In 1991 the Utah Jazz basketball team had a guard whose job it was to be a wall. He was easily seven feet tall, heavily built, a pale gargantuan. He was neither fast nor graceful, but standing stolidly, arms outstretched between an opponent and the basket he was defending, he presented a formidable and immovable obstacle. Opponents tended to bounce right off him, though the agile ones could also outmaneuver him.

As I sat with my fellow indictees and our attorneys watching a Jazz home game in Salt Lake City, it seemed to me that there must be an analogy between the implacable stolidity of the Utah prosecutors, their humorless rigidity in our plea discussions, and this awkward giant on the court. Would we be agile and fast enough to outfox the Utah threat?

Attending a Utah Jazz game was like being inside a pinball machine. Lights flashed and blazed everywhere, touting beer and automobiles. Buzzers squawked, bells rang, and there was no moment during which the senses were not assaulted, mostly with sights and sounds unrelated to the sport of basketball or any other athletic endeavor; I have not attended a professional basketball game since.

We were in Salt Lake City to prepare for trial. In July 1990, just two months following Judge Green's injunction forbidding the DOJ from indicting us in more than one jurisdiction, the federal government had handed down indictments against PHE, me, and five other employees and former employees of PHE for violation of obscenity statutes in the District of Utah all the way back in 1986. Here in Utah, it appeared, was where the Department of Justice would take its best shot; this would be its trial. We could not be indicted anywhere else until the Utah drama was fully played out.

166

The Utah indictments were almost certainly motivated in major part by the government's desire for retribution against us for having brought a civil suit against them. Until our lawsuit, it seemed pretty clear that Utah was going to let things drop; the "offense" we had committed there was already more than four years old, and the saber rattling (at least about indictments) had quieted. I was convinced that additional motives for this indictment included the government's desire to have more leverage in bargaining with us to dispose of the civil suit. It also provided them with an excuse to refuse to provide deposition testimony in the civil case. They would maintain that they couldn't give testimony in the civil action without jeopardizing the new criminal proceedings.

One reason that I was so certain of the vindictive motivations behind these indictments was the fact that three of the indictees no longer worked for PHE and had left our employ several years previously. That two of these three former employees were parents of young children was not lost on us either. It was apparent that the government was trying to involve the most vulnerable of our people, irrespective of the fact that they were no longer in the business of marketing or selling sexually oriented materials. This struck me as a particularly sleazy move on the government's part, and it hardened my resolve.

Meanwhile we had to prepare to be tried in Salt Lake City. Utah had been involved from the outset; Assistant U.S. Attorney Richard Lambert seemed to be everywhere in the Postporn prosecutions, and ours as well, though we noted that he always worked very hard to reach a plea, and had not actually conducted an obscenity trial, either during this period or earlier.

We had speculated about Utah as a venue for an obscenity trial and there was a good deal of disagreement among us about how difficult it would be to win here.

On the one hand there was a whole string of arguments—and documented evidence—about the extremely conservative views of Mormons and of a Mormon-dominated culture toward sex and sexually oriented materials. This by itself constituted a serious problem. Beyond that, there was a sense among many people we talked with (especially outside Utah) who believed that Mormons are somehow "different" in their approach to life. Mormon families tended to be very large, and the church refused to condone any form of birth control. The church was also infused with an aura of secretiveness. Mormons enthusiastically ran Boy Scout troops but had nothing to do with the Girl Scouts. They officially banned smoking and caffeine as well as alcohol, yet condoned, albeit surreptitiously, polygamy. They wore mysterious temple garments under their street clothes and conducted no business on Sunday. There was the wonderful Mormon Tabernacle Choir, of course, and those first-class ski resorts. But weren't Mormons a little strange, especially on the subject of sex? Some of us felt, especially after our plea negotiation meetings, that we were entering a kind of invasion-of-the-body-snatchers syndrome, that the minds of devout Mormons (like the true believers from some other denominations) seemed to have been taken over by an outside force and that they could simply not be rational on sexual matters.

My good friend Robert Ciszewski, a perspicacious man not given to exaggeration or fear mongering, stated bluntly, "You do not want to be on trial in front of a Mormon jury on a charge of obscenity. Period."

On the other hand, those closer to the scene were not quite so intimidated. Jerry Mooney, the Salt Lake lawyer who represented us as local counsel in Utah, had already defended against numerous obscenity prosecutions in Salt Lake City. Two had gone to trial, and Jerry had won them both. Jerry pointed out that only about half of a Salt Lake City jury pool would be Mormon. He had also found that the liberty arguments resonated pretty well with Mormons—the right of individuals to enjoy the privacy of their own homes without undue interference from government. After all, the Mormons had come west to escape government domination. Freedom, religious freedom particularly, remained very important to them. Mormons also stress free agency—the principle that each individual is free to choose a right or a wrong course.

In addition, Jerry had encountered some pleasant surprises. Mormon women, he pointed out, were not so docile and accommodating as some Mormon men might lead one to think. Given an opportunity, seated on a jury and immune from at least some communal pressures, a few of these women had appeared to relish the prospect of poking their thumb in the eye of the Mormon establishment by voting for acquittal in a obscenity case.

And then there was the matter of forum shopping. Wade Smith was itching to stand in front of a Salt Lake City jury and state in his soft Carolina accent, "Ladies and gentlemen, the only reason we are here in Salt Lake City, defending a North Carolina company and citizen, is because the government believes that you will not give my client a fair trial." The fact that the federal government, with an opportunity to indict a North Carolina company in at least two North Carolina districts, had hauled us all the way to Utah for something done more than four years previously might seem quite unreasonable to a Utah jury, we hoped.

But all this—except for Jerry Mooney's experience—was pretty speculative. We decided that we should research the issue as best we could and find out just what we were up against. Accordingly, in February, accompanied by jury-selection expert Marjorie Fargo, we traveled to Salt Lake City to conduct a series of carefully structured focus groups.

We would convene three groups. One would be an all-Mormon group, the second a mixed Mormon/non-Mormon group, and the third an all non-Mormon group. Each group would be asked to discuss issues relating to personal freedom, sexually explicit materials, the influence of the Mormon Church on sexual attitudes, and related matters. Then each would examine some of the indicted materials, both magazines and video excerpts, and a discussion would follow.

The conducting of focus groups under these circumstances takes place in a kind of legal limbo, and the issues one confronts illustrate again how bizarre obscenity laws can become. If certain videos and magazines are indicted, it must be presumed that the government considers them to be obscene, and, if the materials are obscene, their dissemination is illegal. On the other hand, to properly defend oneself against such a charge—to prove that such materials are in fact not obscene—a logical piece of pretrial research is to show the material to representative members of the community and get their response. Yet the act of showing is, itself, a form of dissemination, an act which can itself be considered illegal. So we all had some reason to be nervous as the focus group participants were selected and briefed. We most emphatically did not want Richard Lambert or Brent Ward to find out that we were conducting these groups.

All participants were carefully informed about the nature of the research and the fact that it would involve looking at explicit magazines and a video. They were informed that their discussions would be videotaped. As a condition of participating, they were required to sign a confidentiality agreement, promising not to discuss the research with anyone. In turn, all participants were provided with written assurance that their names would never be revealed in connection with the project.

THE ALL-MORMON GROUP

It was clear from the outset that the participants in this group were strongly opposed to all sexually explicit materials. While they supported the concept of the right to privacy, in terms of "being allowed to do what I want in my own home," when the group was asked, "Is viewing sexually explicit materials ever appropriate?" the group unanimously said no.

When asked what the community standards are that influence their opinions, they stated that the church was the strongest. As one participant noted, "Everyone knows what LDS [Latter Day Saints; i.e., Mormon] doctrine says—it's a way of life—you know how to believe." Another woman noted

"The church doesn't have to say anything explicit—you're taught how to believe—you know what to do." And another said, "If you break church law you suffer the consequences. Sure, we have free agency to do what we want, but we know what's expected."

This group was very shocked by all the materials presented. After looking at the magazines (titles included *Gang Bang Birthday* and *Ursula's Anal Friends*), one participant noted, "That's somebody's daughter—it breaks my heart." The observations concerning the video, which contained multiple participants of mixed races engaged in sexual intercourse and oral sex, were stronger—"Disgusting," "Sick," "If I'd known it were that bad I wouldn't have come," "How could a person degrade themselves to put themselves on tape?" When the group was asked to discuss the case concerning Adam & Eve, the consensus was simply that these materials have no place in the state of Utah, and if it were up to the group they would ban it all.

Sitting in an adjacent room watching these proceedings, I was profoundly depressed. Clearly, the tolerance for sexual materials in an all-Mormon culture was near zero. Despite the fact that one or two members of this group insisted that Utah was more liberal than many other parts of the country, this clearly did not apply to the subject of sex, at least not when Mormons were dealing with Mormons. In front of this group as a jury, our attorneys would have faced a near-impossible task.

THE MIXED GROUP

When the mixed group of Mormons and non-Mormons was asked whether viewing sexually explicit material was ever normal, one participant related that her mother-in-law had wanted to see one "dirty movie" before she died, just "to see what the fuss was all about. She watched it, and that was that—never asked about it or wanted to see another. It was just natural curiosity." Other participants agreed, saying that curiosity would probably lead most people to see some form of sexually explicit material in their lifetime, especially in their younger years.

One of the Mormon participants in this group also noted, "Human beings are sexual beings, but the culture, especially the [church] subculture here in Utah, leads people to suppress sexual behavior. For example, a child touching his penis, that's a natural thing to do, but some mothers here might slap their hand . . . it leads to dysfunctional adult sexual behavior. . . . Kids have very strange beliefs [about sex] because of the secretive nature here."

One mother observed, "We send our children out of state to either California or Florida every year for one reason. I want my children to be exposed to the things [there]. There is a shock when you go outside of this culture. I wouldn't raise my kids anyplace else, but they need to see what the outside world is like so they're ready for it."

Concerning community standards: "The religious beliefs are the community standard. . . . The church teaches from the time you're a child—they don't have to come out and say it. . . . People here have been raised as puritans about sex—it's not explicit, it's pure, it's behind closed doors, it's secret."

One Mormon woman related an incident that illustrated the role of the church on a neighborhood level. She had found a bag of sexually explicit magazines on her lawn and put them in her trash. Her son had salvaged a few and passed them around among his friends. One of the boys was caught by his parents with a magazine, and when asked where he got it, replied with his friend's name. News got out among the parents, and the woman was approached as to why she had these materials and why her son had them. No amount of explanations or apologies would suffice—even the neighborhood bishop was brought in, and chastised her and refused to believe her story. "To this day there are people on my block who won't talk to me."

When this mixed group viewed the materials, however, they were almost as upset with them as the all-Mormon group. All the magazines were deemed offensive. People said they were "offended by the whole thing," and "saddened," and "depressed." One said, "A young mind viewing this may assume it's okay to do these things. . . ." After viewing the video group members said they felt "cheated," "debased," "saddened by the whole thing." One participant said she "felt very naive—I grew up in a different world. Have I been on another planet?"

I recall particularly one woman who said, referring back to an enthusiastic oral sex scene, that "I'm one of those who believes that two people shouldn't even drink out of the same glass." Clearly, for her, the idea of taking a penis in her mouth or permitting her husband's mouth to come in contact with her genitals was an utterly alien concept. She would likely vote against permitting the dissemination of such depictions if, for no other reason, because they seemed like something "from another planet." It occurred to me even then that this is also one of the many ways that sexual depictions can be useful. It is perfectly possible that this same woman, or others like her, could have thought about the subject, perhaps read that oral sex is practiced by a majority of American couples, and reconsidered her own view of the matter. If she did so, the result could very likely have been improved sexuality in her marriage, greater intimacy with her husband, and a benefit for all concerned.

THE NON-MORMON GROUP

The non-Mormon focus group tended to confirm some of that otherworldly, invasion-of-the-body-snatchers hypothesis that some of us had had about Mormonism. As the non-Mormons slowly began discovering that there were no Mormons in the room, they visibly relaxed. This discovery was not prompted; they had not been told that they were an all non-Mormon group. But it gradually became clear in the course of discussing the Mormon religion and its influence on life in Utah that the members of this group were clearly influenced by the knowledge that they would not be judged, in this discussion at least, by Mormon standards, and this quickly changed the atmosphere. The result was a veritable litany of anecdotes about how non-Mormons are victims of Mormon attitudes toward outsiders.

One participant said, "I can't feel comfortable going out in my yard working, drinking a glass of wine or a beer, because my neighbors will get upset." Another said, "You're an outsider if you are non-LDS." Another observed that Mormons at her job "were always trying to convert me." Another participant told of moving to a new house. "Some men came over to help us unload our van, but when they saw we had beer in the van that was it, they left." One woman's father had had the experience of being told by Mormons to close his service station on Sundays. When his corporation insisted he stay open seven days a week, the Mormons in his community took the issue to their wardhouse on Sunday and advised all members to stop frequenting his station. Most had obliged.

The group also discussed what they called the hypocrisy of the LDS church in relation to moral issues. "We have a neighbor who is a Mormon, and he'll talk to us outside one way, but then he'll come in our house and use all these cuss words around us because we're not Mormon . . . my husband jokes that he just has to come over and let loose sometimes." Another commented, "When Mormons go to a Las Vegas convention . . . oh, do they let their hair down. They'll even light up and drink . . ." Another woman, married to a Mormon, described a family reunion in Wyoming where her husband's Mormon relatives were sneaking over and asking her and her husband for alcoholic drinks.

As far as the government of Utah is concerned, the group unanimously agreed that "the church is the government!" Several said that whenever the church wants a law passed it is passed, and members of the church will start lobbying by phone based on what the church demands. Several participants agreed that "you wouldn't dare make comments like this [to Mormons] . . . if you wanted to live and work in this state!" Another said, "You aren't free to say what you think . . . because they run the state."

When the time came for this group to see the sexually explicit materials and judge them for use in the state, the response differed markedly from the other two groups. While this group was also offended by the materials, their attitude was more indifferent. The general mood seemed to be "Well, it's not for me, I don't need this stuff, but it doesn't bother me if someone else has it."

When they were asked whether the community standard in the state of Utah would accept such materials, there was near unanimity in deciding that none of it would be accepted in the state. Asked why the community standard was so conservative, one observed, "Because this is *Utah!*"

When asked why they continued to live in what was apparently an unfriendly environment, some mentioned the supposed lower crime rates. Many Mormon participants had referred to "the outside," meaning non-Mormon communities, with fear and anxiety, seemingly convinced that non-Mormons live in crime-ridden cities devoid of morality and meaning; the non-Mormons in this group clearly shared some of those views. (In fact, crime rates in Utah are higher than the average for the nation. In 1995, Utah was tenth highest among the fifty states in total index crimes per 100,000 population.[1] Property crimes are notably high. The state's record on murder is better than the national average, though on rape it is worse.)

While watching this group had been a pleasure compared to the other two, there remained a depressing fact. These non-Mormons, while they weren't pleased about it, clearly accepted the fact that Salt Lake City was a Mormon community, that they were living in a Mormon-dominated culture, and that Mormon rules constituted the community standard. To the extent that a decision about obscenity rested on local community standards, they would be likely to find something obscene if they thought it violated the standards of the Mormon community.

I had been on an emotional roller-coaster watching these groups. There were those heart-in-the-throat moments when so many of these representative members of the Utah community were so absolutely, positively sure that what we had done in their state must be illegal that I despaired of our winning a trial here. On top of that, I couldn't avoid the emotional turmoil that came from the apparent certainty of these (and, I knew, so many other) people that our materials were bad, that selling such material must at the very least be wrong. I knew, of course, that we had done all that was necessary to assure that the materials we sold were benign, not harmful, often useful. But, on an emotional level, brought up as most of us have been with a sense of shame and guilt about sex, it was easy to fall prey to the rigid consensus of these otherwise congenial-seeming folks that this material was evil, even though I knew that it was not. Several times that day I had to take a deep breath, review in my mind the unanimous opinions we had received from the sex therapists, and remind myself how meticulous our standards were.

Our attorneys, meanwhile, were learning a lot. Wade Smith, for example, had tried out the argument that sexually explicit magazines are "just paper," not toxic chemicals or anything that could really harm a person. The groups would have none of that. "The Declaration of Independence is 'just paper'" was a remark that settled the issue as far as these folks were concerned. The "just paper" argument would not be used in any subsequent defenses.

Joe Cheshire found these focus groups to be particularly useful.

> Of all of the things that we did in all of the prosecutions, to me the focus groups in Salt Lake City were the ones that helped the most. There were intelligent people on those focus groups who had very rigid thoughts, and I could see the rigidity of their thoughts. I could measure those thoughts against what happened when you had two groups together. You could see the difference. In the mixed group, the Mormons, although they would still express their views, wouldn't express them with the same rigidity, so I could compare how the two groups related to each other when they were mixed together, as they would be, serving on a jury.
>
> In an obscenity trial, what it all comes down to is how you're going to motivate those people, how you're going to strengthen the ones that you know don't want to have censorship and how you're going to diffuse the argument—in a nice, gentle way—of those you know would like to have this stuff banned, so that when they get back in the jury room they don't reach a consensus that banning it is the answer. That's what it's all about. You can go get all of the experts you want; it doesn't make a damn bit of difference. In the final analysis it's an emotional reaction, of jurors trying to justify—or being willing to modify—their emotional biases in a group together, to make a group decision.

THE PARADOX OF ADVERSITY

"I think he's wearing real shoes," I heard Joe Cheshire saying to Peggy Oettinger. "He must take this very seriously." Peggy and Joe were walking a few yards behind me on Main Street in Salt Lake City. It was our second visit, and this time Peggy and I and the four other indictees were all in Salt Lake City with our attorneys to be arraigned on obscenity charges. Joe's reference to my footwear harked back to one of our attorneys' standing jokes about their primary client: I had disappointed them consistently, they maintained, by not fulfilling their image of a successful sex products dealer. Where were the gold chains? Where were the fancy clothes, open-necked shirts, Gucci shoes? My five-year-old Volvo and the Hush-puppy-type shoes I normally wore presented a pretty unexciting image. The Volvo still contained some confetti from our post-trial celebrations four years before in 1987. The car, the shoes, and my propensity to drink vast quantities of Diet Coke all underlined the fact that I was a "disappointing" client.

When they weren't kidding me about this, our lawyers were, of course, delighted with this stodgy image. It gave them an opportunity to stress my lack of interest in personal wealth, my international family planning activities, my background with CARE, and a lot of other good-guy stuff that belied the stereotype many people have of businessmen dealing with sexually oriented merchandise. I am happy to represent something of a paradox in this regard. As suggested, it is useful in these legal battles to be unglamorous. Also, as a committed iconoclast and contrarian, I find it personally satisfying to be something other than what people expect.

We reached an intersection at 4th South. Salt Lake City has for some years been equipped with those beepers for blind pedestrians at intersections that indicate noisily when the pedestrian "go" light is on. In a city with remarkably little traffic and very wide streets (originally designed to accommodate wagons drawn by teams of four or six horses or oxen, and wide enough so a full team could turn around in the road) the beeping sound echoes sometimes eerily up and down the broad streets, a muted cacophony of alien-seeming noise. But Salt Lake has an immediate antidote to an outsider's feeling of physical alienation. When you glance up, from almost anywhere in the city, you can see beautiful snow-capped mountains at any time of year. Just letting your eyes rest on those vistas quickly reinstates a sense of earth, a sense of wholeness, and the knowledge that much of the physical environment is beautiful, welcoming, and nearby.

This second trip to Utah reminded me of how much executive time was being taken away from the business. I had to figure that the prosecutors wanted this; with managers forced to defend themselves all over the country, it would be increasingly difficult to keep PHE operating profitably. Our operations were being harmed in at least three ways. First, the threat of prosecution and punishment was, of itself, a palpable harm, a constant distraction for management. Second, the cost of litigation was depriving our fourteen employee-stockholders* of substantial sums of money. And of course the lit-

---

*At the time PHE had fourteen shareholders, all of them employees. By 1999 we had more than fifty employee-shareholders.

igation was taking a great deal of my own time and the time of many others in the company. The irony is that, in retrospect, I can't really say that the company suffered from the fact that I was so thoroughly distracted with these matters. I had always been a ferocious delegator. Even prior to our first raid in 1986, I had spent a great deal of time away from PHE working on international family planning, and people had come to expect, for better or worse, that I would leave much of the day-to-day running of the company to others. Most of those who did this work were grateful for the authority, and were thus prepared to pick up anything that I might leave to others as a result of spending so much time on our battle with the Feds.

There were other ironies.

The first was my discovery that there is nothing so energizing to an organization as an attack from outside, especially when the attack is perceived by those inside as being entirely unjustified. The more intense the attack, the more energized the organization.

I have stated previously that the morale and cohesiveness among PHE employees was never better than in the period before the trial in 1987. That was the time of our most frantic preparation, the greatest level of distraction among managers and many other employees who were forced to take time away from their regular duties. Yet the fact that our very existence was under threat lent astonishing cohesiveness to everyone's efforts, pushed aside the petty politicking that so often intrudes on the day-to-day functioning of organizations, and unified us all in the battle for our existence. No one needed persuading that our phones had to be answered, our catalog mailings had to go out on time, our customers' packages had to be shipped; all of these things were more important than ever because an army of prosecutors was at our gates. If we did not do our jobs better and more skillfully than we had ever done them before, we would be toast, finished, gone.

The result was that the company became more rather than less efficient, absorbing the additional duties involved in searching out and gathering tens of thousands of pages of documents, appearing before grand juries, being interrogated by federal authorities, spending many long hours with lawyers, and still accomplishing everything needed for the operation of our business. "This is a great place to work," said one of our employees, after our post-trial celebrations. Indeed it was.

During the eight years we were engaged in litigation, sales grew at an average annual rate of nearly 20 percent, and profits increased significantly virtually every year. It has been suggested, not entirely in jest, that having "top management"—most notably me—engaged in matters other than the running of the company can be of great benefit to the company's prosperity.

There may be some truth in this, but I think the energizing of the company by menacing and powerful outside forces is the real secret. I have wracked my brains subsequently to come up with a management system ("Management by invasion from Mars"?) that can simulate this outside threat and produce the same esprit and cohesion. But of course it cannot be simulated. If the threat is not real, it produces no impact.

There's another irony, too. Our company's profitability was, without question, favorably affected by the decimation of our competitors. We, of course, deplored vociferously the tactics used to put such companies as PAK Ventures (Brussel) and CMG (Freedberg) out of business, and we were absolutely sincere in those protestations if for no other reason than the prospect of similar tactics being used against us. But it is also true that the multiple prosecutions of mail-order companies by the Justice Department put a lot of our competitors out of business and kept a lot of other potential competitors from coming into business. This, naturally, made it easier for us to make money. It was fun to take note of the fact that much—if not all—of our legal bills were being paid from the increased profit margins made possible by the frenzy of federal prosecutorial activity.

THE BONES OF OUR DEFENSE

Our defense against the Utah indictment mirrored our previous strategy about not being a "tasty morsel," but included important new elements from our civil suit. We maintained and believed that the Utah indictments were in considerable part motivated by vindictiveness over our lawsuit, and intended to inhibit the discovery process in that litigation. The indictments had been handed down just six months after the filing of our suit with the District Court, and just two months from the issuance of the preliminary injunction prohibiting the government from using its multiple-prosecution strategy against us. Now the basic point undergirding our civil suit—that the government's intention was the elimination of companies whose activities they disliked, irrespective of whether the materials at issue were obscene—would form the basis of a motion to dismiss the Utah indictments on the grounds of bad faith.

Apart from these legal issues, my personal distaste for the Department of Justice was growing steadily. I was occasionally philosophical, and would say to Peggy, "Well, the people elected Reagan, Reagan appointed Meese, Meese let the loony-birds loose in the Justice Department, and that kind of thing happens, even in democratic and lawful societies." But we got angry, too. Peggy would insist, "How can they get *away* with it? Lying and cutting corners, and there's nothing in the system to stop it!" I said that we were stopping it. If nothing else, we were throwing massive amounts of sand into the gears of this juggernaut. Peggy agreed, but she pointed out that not very many parties were willing to fight, and that, most likely, the DOJ would get away with these probably unlawful tactics with most defendants most of the time.

Legal battles are fought, in considerable part, with motions, and in Utah we filed dozens of them.

Two of our motions were "dispositive"—that is, if decided in our favor, they would dispose of the case, eliminate it completely. One was the motion for dismissal of the indictments for bad faith and vindictiveness. The other was a motion to dismiss the indictments for preindictment delay, on the grounds that the indictments had been improperly postponed, deliberately making it more difficult for us to defend ourselves.

The delay motion contained some pretty strong arguments. We pointed out that it had taken only a few weeks for Richard Lambert to get the indictments returned against us once the evidence was provided to the grand jury. In other words, this was not a complicated case requiring four years to put together; if the authorities in Utah were seriously concerned about the "harm" being caused by PHE, they could have proceeded promptly.

The lapse of time in our case had been fifty-three months, very nearly running out the five-year statute of limitations. The only reason for this delay, we argued, was that the government was improperly holding the prosecution over our heads for the purpose of harassment and leverage and was using the delay for tactical advantage. This made it more difficult for us to defend ourselves, in violation of our right to due process and to free expression.

The prejudice to our case had occurred in considerable part because of the peculiarities of the *Miller* v. *California* standard. Because two prongs of the *Miller* test for obscenity depend on community standards, and because community standards change over time, we pointed out some important and dramatic developments in Salt Lake City between the time of the seizure of our materials in 1986 and the probable time of trial five years later.*

Our expert supporting testimony established that community standards regarding sexual activity in Utah (as elsewhere) had become more conservative in the four-and-a-half-year period of delay, primarily because of massive publicity about AIDS. As an expert sociologist had noted in an affidavit attached to our motion, there had been

---

*The five-year statute of limitations is met if an indictment is brought within five years of the putative crime; the trial may be delayed beyond that point.

a massive and unprecedented public information campaign about AIDS conducted over the past 5 years, geared in large part to changing people's sexual practices. During this time, literally hundreds of articles on the AIDS crisis had appeared in the Salt Lake Tribune alone. As a result, a substantial portion of the public has become far more conservative in their views of the acceptability of [sexual] practices. . . . [A] large percentage of people now feel that casual sex, sex with multiple partners, oral sex and anal sex are extremely hazardous because of the AIDS crisis, regardless of what their views on these subjects might have been in 1986, before concern about AIDS reached its present proportions. This will directly affect their attitudes about depictions of such behavior in magazines, videos, etc., making such depictions less acceptable to them.[2]

There were several precedent cases supporting this argument, including a 1979 case that found

[w]here . . . a case turns on a morals point of view, it is important that the trial be framed in terms of the community standards existing at the time of the alleged offense. . . . Consequently, it is impossible to say that the moral standards prevailing at the time of the trial over four years later were the same as those existing on the date of indictment.[3]

Another reason we pinned high hopes on the Delay of Indictment motion was that we hoped granting this motion might represent an attractive compromise for Judge David Winder, who had charge of our case in Utah. While our motion to dismiss for bad faith and vindictiveness was extremely well documented and supported by Judge Green's findings in Washington, we realized that granting our motion on the basis of bad faith would require Judge Winder to find that prosecutors in his own town had egregiously misbehaved, something it is always very difficult for a judge to do. Granting a dismissal on the grounds of preindictment delay, on the other hand, would require only a finding that our case had become prejudiced due to lack of timely action by the government, a far less onerous finding. The result would be the same either way; the case would be dismissed. If he found in our favor on the Delay of Indictment motion he would not have to make an official decision about the other one.

Still, we pinned our highest hopes, and certainly had our greatest body of evidence, on the Motion to Dismiss for Bad Faith and Vindictive Prosecution. Here we had been able to collect a substantial and growing amount of evidence in our civil case concerning the misbehavior of the government, particularly the close working relationship between William Delahoyde of the Eastern District of North Carolina office (who had spent so much time "visiting" our trial in Alamance County) and Richard Lambert in Utah. We were able to assert in the opening pages of our motion, with considerable evidence to back us up, that "DOJ's effort to force defendants to cease distribution of all sexually oriented speech is part of [a] larger, ongoing effort to suppress nationwide the distribution of constitutionally protected speech DOJ officials find personally offensive or objectionable."

In one of our civil depositions, Douglas McCullough, Delahoyde's boss in Raleigh, had admitted that he, other North Carolina prosecutors, and Utah's Lambert had discussed using multiple prosecutions against us to sap our "resources," "energy," and "psychological ability to contest the charges and defend" ourselves.[4] This constituted a bald admission on the part of a high-ranking federal official that the conspiracy to suppress nonobscene sexually oriented speech was well entrenched and very real.

We had testimony and documentary evidence that was particularly damaging with respect to the behavior of officials in the Eastern District of North Carolina, which we emphasized, though recognizing even then the dangers in letting Judge Winder shift the blame for improper government behavior from Utah back to North Carolina. The indictments our motions were designed to dismiss were Utah indictments, and we recognized that it might be problematic for the judge to link—though we believed he should—the misbehavior in North Carolina to the similar and closely linked pattern of behavior in Utah.

THE DEPARTMENT OF JUSTICE
MOVES TO DERAIL OUR CIVIL SUIT

The timing of the Utah indictments with certain other events made the government's posture particularly suspicious. As the following sequence of events shows, one of the reasons the Utah indictments were sought and obtained was to give the federal government an argument to block discovery proceedings in our civil case and to give them a weapon to hold over our heads in the disposition of that case. It was their way of fighting back against the perfidy of our civil suit.

Their effort to use the indictments to block discovery was particularly clear.

After Judge Green had granted our preliminary injunction on July 23, 1990, she had set an expedited briefing and discovery schedule. That same month, we had given notice to secure the depositions of Lambert and Delahoyde, among others. The DOJ had immediately attempted to block or delay these depositions and other, related, discovery procedures. However, the DOJ civil counsel, Michael Ambrosino, had confirmed Delahoyde's deposition for Tuesday, September 11, 1990, as part of the (new, revised) discovery schedule. Just prior to this assurance from Ambrosino, the DOJ realized that we had learned about a serious conflict being faced by Delahoyde as a result of evidence uncovered through documents turned over to us in the weeks just previous. They realized that at his deposition Delahoyde would be forced into an untenable position. If he admitted that he had made statements earlier to the FBI that he had favored the prosecution of "pornographers" even in circumstances where a successful prosecution would not be likely, on the grounds that it would deter others from being in the business, he would be confirming a central allegation of our civil case. But if he denied making those statements to the FBI (despite the corroboration of two FBI agents that he had, in fact, made them), he could very well trigger a perjury investigation because his statements were contradicted by the FBI agents. Furthermore, if he admitted that he had, in fact, made the statements the FBI said he had made, this would establish that he had lied in an August 24, 1987, letter he had sent to the FBI denying the making of the statements.[5] Either way, it was clear that Delahoyde would be in a very awkward position when he was deposed. The government therefore had a strong motivation to avoid his deposition. Accordingly, attorneys in the EDNC office filed a motion to quash our subpoenas★ and block the depositions of both Delahoyde and his immediate boss, Douglas McCullough.

Three days later, the U.S. District Court for the Eastern District of North Carolina denied the government's motion, freeing the way for us to depose McCullough and Delahoyde.

Because of the disruption caused by the Department of Justice's motion to quash, however, the DOJ requested that these depositions be delayed one day, McCullough's until Tuesday, September 11, and Delahoyde's until Wednesday, September 12. We had agreed.

McCullough's deposition began on Tuesday, September 11, as (re)scheduled. During the first portion of his testimony, McCullough was questioned about Delahoyde's desire to prosecute distributors of nonobscene sexually oriented material, about his own conclusion that we would not likely be convicted in the Eastern District, and about EDNC's discussions with Lambert on the use of multiple prosecutions against us. To accommodate a previous engagement, our attorneys had agreed to suspend McCullough's deposition at 2 P.M. that day

---

★Reluctant witnesses may be subpoenaed and thus forced to appear to give evidence in a civil case.

on the specific understanding that the deposition would resume early the following day, Wednesday, September 12, and that Delahoyde's deposition would begin immediately after McCullough's was finished. The following morning, DOJ lawyers informed us that they would not continue the McCullough deposition and that they would not begin the Delahoyde deposition. We immediately filed a motion for sanctions with the D.C. District Court.

Department of Justice responses to our then-current round of interrogatories (formal written questions) and document requests were due on that same Wednesday, September 12. At 4:30 P.M. that afternoon the DOJ's counsel informed us that the DOJ would not provide the required discovery. At 5:25 P.M. that day, the DOJ faxed a motion to delay their discovery responses until September 21. We could not have known it at the time, but September 21 would turn out to be two days *after* the DOJ expected to obtain, and did obtain, the indictments against us in Utah. That very same day the DOJ moved to stay *all* civil discovery on the grounds that it might prejudice the criminal case! In other words, the government had artfully (or not so artfully) postponed and blocked its most potentially embarrassing civil discovery requests until it could hurriedly obtain an indictment against us in Utah, thus providing fresh grounds for denying our right to discovery in the civil case. Adding insult to injury, just a few days after Delahoyde and the DOJ had refused to proceed with Delahoyde's deposition on September 12, Delahoyde had traveled to Salt Lake City to assist Lambert in obtaining the indictments against us. As our Utah Motion to Dismiss described it,

> On Friday, September 21, two days after the indictment, DOJ filed a motion to block discovery in the civil litigation, asserting that civil discovery would be inappropriate given the pendency of the Utah indictment. Lambert's decision, in conjunction with EDNC AUSA Delahoyde, to seek and obtain the Utah indictment, and the timing of that decision, were motivated entirely or in predominant part by a desire to prevent, delay, or restrict defendant's discovery efforts in the civil litigation and by a desire to retaliate against defendant for their filing of the civil litigation, and for their discovery effort.
>
> These actions, as were all of DOJ's threats of prosecution and bad faith efforts against defendants, were motivated by a desire to intimidate and suppress protected expression. The DOJ individuals involved in this concerted effort against defendants find sexually oriented expression personally disturbing and offensive. Based on that personal view they have set out to suppress *all* sexually oriented expressive materials, including constitutionally protected non-obscene materials. This improper motive directly led to the instant indictment.

Thus our Utah motion rested on two fundamental arguments: first, that the indictments were unconstitutionally motivated by a bad-faith desire to suppress nonobscene, constitutionally protected speech and to force us out of the business of distributing *all* sexually oriented speech, a violation of the First Amendment; and, second, that the indictments were vindictive because they constituted a form of retaliation against us for seeking relief in the D.C. civil court and were motivated by a desire to block or impede our civil action.

Bruce Ennis's team now added an interesting dimension by pointing out that the DOJ's demands that, as part of a plea bargain agreement, we cease distribution of all sexually oriented materials everywhere in the United States was particularly inappropriate in the case of Alamance County, North Carolina.

> . . . DOJ has tried to prevent defendants from distributing materials to jurisdictions in which those materials are *known* to be *non-obscene and constitutionally protected*. For example, Lambert knows that a jury in Alamance County, North Carolina, reviewed certain materials distributed by defendants and found *all* of them to be *non-obscene* under local community standards. . . . This attempt to prevent defendants from engaging in conduct *that has already been specifically adjudicated to be constitutionally protected* cannot be reconciled with the First Amendment even if it were constitutionally permissible to prevent distribution of the same materials in Utah.[6]

This is a somewhat fine point of the law, but it sheds a sharp light on the vicissitudes of the *Miller* definition of obscenity. If there were any sexually explicit items in all of the United States that were, by law, not obscene, they were those eight items in Alamance County that a jury had examined and exonerated.

LEGAL PRECEDENT

Our arguments rested on a solid history of case law, the most important of which were the Supreme Court decisions in *Bantam Books* v. *Sullivan* (1963) and *Dombrowski* v. *Pfister* (1965).

In the *Bantam Books* case, the Rhode Island legislature had created a commission that was charged with prosecuting violations of the obscenity statutes. The commission had demanded of several retailers that they cease selling certain "objectionable" publications, and the retailers complied.

The Supreme Court ruled that the commission's threats and demands constituted an informal system of censorship repugnant to the First Amendment, despite the fact that the commission had merely "exhorted" distributors to halt distribution and had not actually initiated prosecutions or otherwise given formal legal effect to their demands.

We argued that this was exactly what had happened in our case. DOJ prosecutors, including Assistant U.S. Attorney Lambert, had met to coordinate a plan of multiple prosecutions and threats of prosecution designed to force us to stop distribution of constitutionally protected, nonobscene materials. We reminded the judge that as part of any negotiated settlement Lambert had even wanted to suppress "mere nudity."

The *Bantam Books* decision noted, "People do not lightly disregard public officers' thinly veiled threats to institute criminal proceedings against them if they do not come around." In our case, of course, the threats had not been thinly veiled. They had not been veiled at all.

In *Dombrowski*, the Supreme Court had made explicit that it is not only threats of prosecution that impermissibly chill First Amendment rights but also actual indictments or prosecutions, as was now occurring in our case. In the *Dombrowski* case, Louisiana law enforcement officials had raided the offices of civil rights workers and threatened them with prosecution, much as we had been raided in May 1986. When the Louisiana officials' threats failed to suppress the speech the officials found offensive, indictments were returned against the civil rights workers. The Supreme Court held that the prosecutions must be stopped because they had been brought for the purpose of discouraging the exercise of the defendants' First Amendment rights. Several subsequent Supreme Court decisions had clarified and amplified this finding.

In response to our argument, the government asserted that there had been no attempt to improperly suppress speech in our case because the statements we characterized as threats were actually just part of the normal give and take of a plea negotiation process. "[V]irtually all contacts between representatives of the Department of Justice, and lawyers for the defendants, took place at the defendants' [i.e., our] initiation," they stated, not, of course, noting that it was their very rigorous actions that had made our requests for meetings necessary. The government also provided case citations upholding the propriety of plea bargain negotiations and the fact that such discussions could be "free-wheeling." The precedents appeared to establish that it was perfectly normal for plea negotiations to include a discussion of defendants giving up some of their constitutional rights.

It was March 1991 now, and Judge Winder had, by his own reckoning, more than ten thousand pages of briefs and documents from us and from the government in opposition. (I continue to be astonished at judges' abilities to digest such massive amounts of material. But when we appeared before Judge

Winder at a hearing the following June, he was fully conversant with the issues and with the facts of the case.)

We were asking the court to set aside indictments, to conclude that being put on trial itself constituted impermissible punishment because the prosecution was motivated by bad faith. We maintained that a trial, normally the bulwark of a defendant's rights, would be impermissible because it would require us to spend substantial amounts of money and effort defending against what we were certain was an impermissible proceeding.

Judge Winder took these matters seriously. He recognized that there were fundamental constitutional rights at stake as well as serious imputations about the federal prosecutors in his own community. Accordingly, he called for evidentiary hearings to take place on June 27 and 28, 1991. Both we and the government would be given an opportunity to question key witnesses from both sides, under oath.

NOTES

1. M. L. Hutchings, and G. W. Smith, "The Good, the Bad, and the Ugly: Crime and Punishment in Utah," *Utah Bar Journal*, September 1997, p. 19.

2. Affidavit of Prof. Edward Kick (Exhibit 5), Motion to Dismiss the Indictment Due to Pre-Indictment Delay and Incorporated Memorandum of Law, *United States of America v. PHE, Inc. et al.*, January 15, 1991.

3. *United States v. New Buffalo Amusement,* 1979.

4. Deposition of Douglas McCullough, September 11, 1990.

5. U.S. Department of Justice, letter from William D. Delahoyde, Assistant United States Attorney, to Paul V. Daly, Federal Bureau of Investigation, August 24, 1987. See also Deposition of Raymond Madden, March 21, 1991; and Deposition of Raymond Bernard, March 20, 1991.

6. Memorandum in Support of Motion to Dismiss the Indictment For Bad Faith and Vindictive Prosecution, January 16, 1991.

CHAPTER NINE

WHAT ARE WE AFRAID OF?

Sexuality and the Censors

Woman pollutes the body, drains the resources, kills the soul, uproots the strength, blinds the eye, and embitters the voice.

—Cardinal Hughes de St. Cher

Sex is less than fifty years old, yet it has upset the whole Western World.

—James Thurber

The government's massive campaign against us gave me more reason than usual to contemplate the nature of censorship and see its proponents in action. Just what is it that we fear about our sexuality? Why is sex at once so mysterious and so powerful that we seek boundaries, often prescribed by persons in the church or in government, to help us define and circumscribe this intensely personal part of our lives?

First, there is the unpredictability of sex. We tend to be apprehensive about the unknown, and our own sexuality can surprise us. That may be one source of concern.

Another source may lie in our genetic composition. After all, we are descended from people who survived as a species through efficient insemination of females by males, and by creating a relatively safe place where the young could be reared. This meant bonding between males and females in such a way that males defended a piece of turf, provided food, and (usually) demanded exclusive sexual access to their mates, to ensure the perpetuation of their genes. This suggests that we may be instinctively inclined to channel sex for reproduction and child rearing. Indeed, confining sex to situations in which reproduction is at least reasonably possible and desirable, usually in marriage, is the traditional conservative orthodoxy in most cultures. This argument suggests that, just as the human body is ill-suited for sedentary work combined with the consumption of high-fat foods (clearly true), the human body and psyche are ill-suited, or at least inappropriately evolved, for engaging in nonreproductive sexuality.

186

But humans are uniquely equipped to enjoy sex as an intimate and highly pleasurable process, quite apart from reproduction. Indeed, nonprocreational sex was one of the unique attributes of early humans. When we evolved beyond periodic estrus, the relatively brief fertile, sexually receptive cycles of most female mammals, nonprocreational yet pleasurable sex became part of our nature, part of the way that men and women bonded to one another for the rearing of young. So sex for its own sake—sexual intimacy—has been part of who we are for a long time.

FEAR OF LOVE

The overpowering attractions that men and women (and same-sex couples) feel for each other when they "fall in love" is another aspect of our sexuality that scares people; to both men and women, falling in love means relinquishing a substantial degree of control over our own lives. When we fall in love, another person is endowed with considerable power over us: Cleopatra's power over Antony, Romeo's over Juliet. Lovers' independence is curtailed by being in love. That these powerful emotional and sexual relationships can also be liberating takes time to learn. Meanwhile the prospect of granting another person such power over our lives (even as we resist it) can seem frightening indeed.

The urge to unite sexually, observed James Thurber, has survived for eons. "Its commonest manifestations are marriage, divorce, neuroses, and, a little bit less frequently, gun-fire."[1]

SEXUAL DEPICTIONS

Our fear of each other—woman's fear of man as man and males' fear of woman as woman—is surely part of what feeds some people's emotional discomfort and sometimes detestation of sexually explicit depictions. Today such depictions mostly portray sexual encounters between men and women as equals, with women—idealized perhaps—portrayed as sexually lusty, enthusiastically participative, and often taking the lead in sexual encounters. In these portrayals women are not afraid of men, men are not afraid of women, and their mutual lust knows no bounds. This is, of course, a fantasy world, where we can live vicariously as sexual equals and enthusiastic allies.

But human history also reflects strong themes of men and women as sexual antagonists, men as rapists and plunderers, women as defilers, debauchers, and debilitators of men.

In a remarkable passage in Shakespeare's *King Lear*, Lear sums up most graphically this historical view of women's sexuality "beneath the girdle," as a powerful force for evil in man's world:

> Down from the waist they are Centaurs,
> Though women all above;
> But to the girdle do the gods inherit,
> Beneath is all the fiends';
> There's hell, there's darkness, there's the sulphurous pit,
> Burning, scalding, stench, consumption; fie, fie, fie!

The fear of women's sexuality has seldom been so tellingly expressed. In a parallel vein, the comedian Eve Ensler sums up some contemporary (and apparently timeless) views about women's genitalia from her "Vagina Monologues" routine.

> It's a cellar down there. It's very damp, clammy. You don't want to go down there. Trust me. You'd get sick. Suffocating. Very nauseating. . . . There's rumbles down there sometimes. You can hear the pipes and things get caught there, animals and things and it gets wet and sometimes people have to plug up the leaks. Otherwise the door stays closed. You forget about it. I mean it's part of the house, but you don't see it or think about it. It has to be there though 'cause every house needs a cellar otherwise the bedroom would be in the basement.[2]

Women, through their sexuality, through the deployment of their power "down there," have often been seen and thought to sap men's strength, to enervate otherwise strong male leaders who could be assumed, but for the evil influence of women's sexuality, to achieve useful and important things in the world. Several historians, most notably Plutarch, have contended that Cleopatra thus undermined Antony to the detriment of all. "The unreined horse of concupiscence did put out of Antony's head all honest and commendable thoughts." And of course the biblical Samson's shorn hair was but a metaphor for his loss of strength to a powerful, sexual love. "His strength is useless against love," Delilah sings in Camille Saint-Saëns's opera. "He may be strong in battle, but [now] he is my slave, trembling in my arms."

More recently I saw some remarkable footage of Marilyn Monroe entertaining American troops in Korea in the 1950s. On stage, alone in a clinging gown, she had merely to raise her arms, or stretch her body suggestively, and a thousand troops were mesmerized, cheering, in thrall.

Given the potency of women's sexuality, their ability to so attract and mesmerize males, it is little wonder that they have often been accused of existential power, of making malevolent compacts with the devil. When the provocative flesh and flash of a woman can reduce men to virtual supplicants, is it a long reach to characterize women's genitalia as "hell . . . darkness . . . and . . . the sulphurous pit"? Fie indeed!

On the other side of the equation is the long history of literal rape by men. Men, who are generally stronger physically than women, have throughout the ages maintained control of society's political and cultural institutions, through which they have exercised power and control over everyone, including—some would say particularly including—women.

In the 1990s, the view by women of men as rapists was exemplified at the extreme by law professor Catherine MacKinnon and author Andrea Dworkin's contention that women are, by definition, victims of men, and that therefore all sexual activity between men and women denigrates and degrades women. Dworkin has gone so far as to assert that any form of sexual penetration by the penis is itself a form of rape, consent notwithstanding. Dworkin has written, "Force—the violence of the male confirming his masculinity—is seen as the essential purpose of the penis, its animating principle as it were. . . . This penis must embody the violence of the male in order for him to be male. Violence is male; the male is the penis. . . . What the penis can do it must do forcibly for a man to be a man."[3] In a like vein, Catherine MacKinnon holds that "the major distinction between intercourse (normal) and rape (abnormal) is that the normal happens so often that one can't get anyone to see anything wrong with it." And: "To be about to be raped is to be gender female in the process of going about life as usual. . . . Just to get through another day, women must spend an incredible amount of time, life, and energy cowed, fearful, and colonized, trying to figure out how not to be next on the list."[4] MacKinnon also asserts that there is no important distinction between real rape and depictions of rape or even depictions of consensual sexual intercourse in photographs, films, or drawings. Because women are by definition victims of men, depictions of sexual activity between the two, even when drawn from the imagination of an artist, is a form of rape or, at the very least, a deliberate attack on women who inevitably suffer as a result. MacKinnon's position, says appeals court judge and author Richard Posner, represents "the reductio ad absurdum of social constructionism applied to sex—that heterosexuality is itself a male invention and imposition."[5]

In the battle between the sexes, many of women's fears and hatreds toward men have been increasingly expressed in modern times, and that is understandable. Women's progress toward real equality is very recent. Even today, most women, especially in developing countries, are second-class citizens with conspicuously less education (today, perhaps the most important of all equalizers) and legal rights than their male counterparts. But even while the struggle for women's rights goes on, society is not well served by the promulgation of policies that automatically treat women as victims and men as satyrs. Consensual intercourse is not rape. Sexual activity between men and women is not—in the great majority of cases—denigrating to women or to men. Depictions of sexual activity do not conduce men (or women) to commit antisocial acts.

It is time to get past the characterization of women as "sulphurous pits" and men as rampaging rapists. It is time to treat each other with respect as equals, and to treat our sexuality and our sexual interaction with the positive enthusiasm it deserves.

WILL I LOSE CONTROL?

Certain kinds of order and control are absolutely essential for the functioning of civilization. Planes could not fly safely, supermarket shelves would not be stocked, telephones would not work without systems that rely on a high degree of order and at least some degree of control. I hasten to add that such control almost never need be imposed by government except for those laws that prevent the use of coercion and make agreements enforceable. The highly complex mechanism of the marketplace that stocks those supermarket shelves, for example, requires no government involvement at all and, indeed, to the extent that governments do become involved, the order of the system is usually distorted and undermined.

But the need for order and control is unquestioned. One need only think of the near panic that sets in when an aircraft is rolling along the tarmac and an uncontrolled element, such as a combative passenger or an audible mechanical problem, creeps into the scene. On these occasions we hope that the aptly named control tower will provide just that.

In many other areas of our lives, a certain degree of disorder and lack of control is appropriate and useful. In Washington's 1996 Folger Theater production of Shakespeare's *Antony and Cleopatra*, the depictions of life in Rome were presented in stark straight lines, soldierly, orderly, black-and-white, while the scenes in Egypt were full of color, soft lines, changing light and shadow patterns, sensuality, and a considerable degree of comfortable chaos. We all need a certain amount of "Egypt" in our lives, and sex is a major part of that, bringing the creative, pleasurable, disorderly element to the fore.

By its very nature, sex requires relinquishing control. The physical features of sexual congress require giving up control in exchange for sexual pleasure. Orgasm, for example, in both men and women, involves many kinds of involuntary muscular responses over which we have no control whatsoever. One rigorous description, from Sallie Tisdale:

> The rectal sphincter contracts between two and five times, each contraction lasting about 0.8 seconds; the neck, arm, and leg muscles cramp in involuntary spasms; the big toe juts out and the other toes bend back from the arched sole in a reflex called carpopedal spasms; the skin turns red—almost rashy, in the "sex flush"; breathing speeds up to hyperventilation; the heart races at 110 to 180 beats per minute; the face is distorted by grimaces and contortions. Both sexes do "full excursion pelvic thrusting." In women the vagina and uterus contract at the same speed as the rectal sphincter, as many as ten to fifteen times; in men the penis contracts at the same speed as the rectal sphincter, shooting semen out in several spurts. . . . [6]

All of this does not, of course, occur with every orgasm, nor can we control which of these involuntary spasms will occur, which not, or how many or how intense they will be. These, like many of our sexual responses, are often uncontrollable, and that is frightening to many people, perhaps physically, certainly metaphorically.

The loss of control symptomized by sex was apparently especially frightening to early Christian theologians. "What disturbed Augustine about sex," writes one historian, was that "it was involuntary, intense pleasure, in which various parts of the body began all on their own to expand, contract, throb, undulate, spasm, and generally go wild without so much as a word of permission from the conscious reason or will. Augustine . . . objected to the orgasm as such because it was not under the complete control of the conscious mind."[7] The Stoics feared sex for the same reason—it meant loss of control.

More recently, law professor Laurence Tribe has observed that sexual imagery "threatens to explode our uneasy accommodation between sexual and social custom—to destroy the carefully spun social web holding sexuality in its place."[8] President Richard M. Nixon, denouncing the liberalizing recommendations of his Commission on Pornography and Obscenity submitted to him in 1970, declared that we must "draw the line against pornography to protect freedom of expression[!]. Moreover, if an attitude of permissiveness were to be adopted regarding pornography, this would contribute to an atmosphere condoning anarchy in every other field—and would increase the threat to our social order as well as to our moral principles."[9]

Nadine Strossen cites author Walter Kendrick's description of Anthony Comstock, the famous nineteenth-century antipornography crusader:

> Like his more sophisticated contemporaries in France and England, Comstock at bottom feared nothing so much as the universal distribution of information. The prospect called up nightmarish images of a world without structure, where all barriers had been breached and all differences leveled. It was appropriate that sex should become the focus of such nightmares, since long before the modern threat arose, sex already stood for loss of control and the scattering of substance. . . . On the surface pornography threatens nothing but the unleashing of sexuality; but that unleashing, as Nixon [proposed], turns immediately into wantonness of every other kind, including the promiscuous redistribution of property.[10]

Does anyone really believe that sexuality and pornography threaten property rights? Apparently so. As sexologist Marty Klein points out,

> Authentic sexuality is ultimately revolutionary. It challenges gender roles by depicting women as lusty without being bad. It enfranchises us all as sexual beings. . . . It returns to us the right and means to own and evaluate our own sexuality, rather than referring us to social definitions of what is "normal." It challenges the role of monogamy and the nuclear family as the exclusive source of emotional comfort. It undermines traditional religions by refusing to make procreation the primary purpose of sex. . . . It trusts people to take care of themselves during sexual encounters. Finally, it sees sex as a positive force we can use to explore and expand our human horizons, rather than as a negative force we must control and restrict to protect ourselves.[11]

In the same vein, political tyrants almost always do their best to suppress sexuality. "[M]ost tyrannies have a puritanical nature. The sexual restrictions of Stalin's Soviet Union, Hitler's Germany, and Mao's China would have gladdened the hearts of those Americans who fear sexual images and literature. Their iron-fisted Puritanism wasn't motivated by a need to erase inequality. They wanted to smother the personal chaos that can accompany sexual freedom and subordinate it to the granite face of the state. Every tyrant knows that if he can control human sexuality, he can control life."[12]

George Orwell makes a similar point in his novel of a nightmare dystopia, *1984*. The masters of "Oceania" suppress sex, controlling all sexual instincts and activity. It was not just that "the sex instinct created a world of its own which was outside the Party's control and which therefore had to be destroyed if possible. What was more important was that sexual privation induced hysteria, which was desirable because it could be transformed into war fever and leader worship." Orwell's heroine Julia says, "All this marching up and down and cheering and waving flags is simply sex gone sour. If you're happy inside yourself, why should you get excited about Big Brother and the Three-Year Plans and the Two Minutes Hate and all the rest of their bloody rot?"[13]

Nadine Strossen concludes, "Just as *suppressing* sexuality speech plays an essential role in *maintaining* the political, social, and economic status quo, conversely, *protecting* sexual speech plays an essential role in *challenging* the status quo."[14]

Why is sexuality seen as so revolutionary? Why aren't we more concerned about things that directly attack the order of the state, or of the church? While there used to be laws against blasphemy, we have come to accept open criticism of the church as an important way to test eternal truths.[15] And criticism of the government is considered both integral and essential to a healthy democratic state. The vigorously criticized U.S. government is perhaps the strongest and is the oldest constituted government in the world. And the United States, where criticism of all religious institutions is both allowed and common, remains a highly religious society.

The Economist observed in 1992 that the religious commitment of the people of the United States "sets America apart from other modern democracies." In a 1981 Gallup poll, 57 percent of Americans reported affiliation with a church "while only 4% of French respondents, 5% of Italians, 13% of West Germans, 15% of Spaniards, and 22% of the British" did so.[16] Those who lament the decline of religion in the United States are simply out of touch with the facts.

If we have come to accept the utilitarian (and other) value of free political and religious speech, what is our basis for continuing to suppress sexual speech? If political speech, specifically speech that is directly critical of the government, is, as it appears to be by definition, more revolutionary than any form of sexual expression, why do we accept the one and not the other? Why is it legal to publish a treatise advocating the ouster of any and every person in the   government, but not a treatise that contains explicit and arousing sexual passages?

Part of the answer lies in our fear of the unknown. The unknown consists not only of what lies ahead, but sometimes, with what lies within ourselves. The forces of sexuality are mysterious. Those involuntary muscular contractions so well described by Sallie Tisdale may represent such *personal* potential chaos that part of us wants to "get it under control."

Marty Klein believes that such fears, for some people, are profound. From the perspective of his training as a psychologist, Dr. Klein traces a process that starts in childhood: our sexual fear is born from the conflict between our strong sexual nature and a learned belief that our sexuality is bad. As children we are taught that sex is bad, is wrong, yet even as children we know that we are sexual beings. We are interested in our own bodies, our genitals, the bodies of others. When we are told that our sexual feelings and impulses are bad, our own certainty of our own sexual nature leads us to conclude that we our-selves must be bad. Moreover, the "badness" of sex is something we are asked to take on faith, for our parents' conclusions and admonitions about sex cannot be challenged. Unlike many other values and lessons while growing up—lessons we expect to have supported and justified as we grow older—the myth about the badness of sex is usually labeled undiscussable.

Despite this, most of us gradually learn that others, too, have strong sexual feelings, fantasies, and "unacceptable" urges. As we come to understand that these urges and imaginings are normal, our fear of sexuality is at least some-what diminished.

But many adults, Klein observes, continue to feel that trusting their own sexuality is dangerous. "Unconsciously, they fear being punished . . . for their sexual fantasies, desires, and feelings. All therapists have heard heart-rending confessions about sexuality that patients are sure must never be shared with their partners."[17] For such people, whom Dr. Klein categorizes as "censors" because of their deep urge to suppress sexual images, the presence of pornog-raphy or other kinds of publicly acknowledged sex in their community increases their anxiety. And by suppressing pornography and other expres-sions of sexuality they can, at least to some degree, alleviate their own anx-iety about sexuality and their own fears about sex.

> Pornography invites viewers to get in touch with their fantasies, which are irrational. And it is used specifically to get aroused, i.e., uncontrolled. It depicts sex where people *relinquish* control. Actors are shown enjoying sex without the context or boundary of romantic love.
>
> The primitive fear is that getting too excited will destroy the ability to defer gratification in *other* areas; this is why the concept of 'morality' always seems to come down to controlling sex.[18]

Even while we are not "reasonable" when sexually aroused, we seem quite capable of segregating the irrational, sexual parts of our lives from the rea-soning parts. Sexual activity does not impede our ability to function in society as reasoning and reasonable persons. The five states with no obscenity laws, for example, are indistinguishable from the other forty-five as to the productive behavior of their citizens.[19] People who watch adult videos or enjoy other forms of nonprocreative sex show up for work on time, fulfill their duties to society and the community with the same vigor, and contribute to the advancement of science in pretty much the same proportions as those with less sexually active libidos. Indeed, the only apparent correlation, if there is any at all, between active sexuality and productivity would appear to be a positive one. "Psychologists agree that people with active and satisfying sex lives, including fantasy lives, tend to be somewhat happier and better adjusted, on average, than those who are sexually repressed. Sexual repression, like other attempts to curtail normal creative impulses, risks dampening creativity, imagination, and productivity in other spheres of life."[20] Those with active and healthy sex lives are likely to be more productive as a result rather than less so.

This does not mean, of course, that all forms of sexual expression should be tolerated. Communities may control the forms of expression, sexual and otherwise, that would otherwise be "thrust upon" members of the community in public places (to use a term from *Miller* v. *California*). Such expressions affect all members of the community and may be communitarily controlled. But what persons do privately is quite another matter. It is one thing for citizens to assert, with the force of law, "We will not have explicit pornographic depictions displayed on Main Street." It is quite another thing for a community to say, "We will enforce laws to make sure you are not indulging in any practices, even in private, of which we disapprove."

Marty Klein clarifies:

> There are a lot of people who just don't want sexual experimentation going on in the world. It reminds them that they have that desire themselves, desires that they are scared by or feel ashamed of or guilty about. Unapologetic sexuality opens up the possibility of a form of freedom—a choice—that sex-fearful people don't want to have. Rather, they try and shut down those sexual activities out there that they're scared of wanting to do themselves.[21]

I remember one incident during our years of negotiation with the government that illuminated this point. One of the prosecutors in our case, a man who had been consistently zealous in suppressing sexuality by prosecuting all forms of erotica, had, in the course of his work, watched many hours of explicit videotapes. In a moment of unusual candor during a meeting with our attorneys, he stated that, subsequent to viewing some videos he had found himself entertaining lustful thoughts about an attractive woman in his office. This experience seemed to trigger visions of the apocalypse. As described by one of the attorneys present:

He said that today, forty-three nations have wars, murder is out of control, and mankind is close to self-annihilation. He said the difference between a human watching violence and a sex film is significant. [He] . . . said that, as a prosecutor, he had been repulsed by photographs of autopsies and murder victims, but his viewing of [this] heterosexual obscene material has had an immediate [and worse] emotional effect on him. After viewing the films, he came away with a feeling of lust, and he viewed women as sex objects. . . . [He] said that obscene material is everywhere. . . . He continued for several minutes in this discussion, during which . . . he became red in the face and quite agitated.[22]

Marty Klein:

Some things by their very nature make sex public—I'll call it *public-ized* sexuality, for lack of a better term. These include, for example, sex education, contraceptive advertising, nude beaches, and the availability of X-rated videos for rent. When these exist, they are part of a community's public consciousness. Such activities declare that certain aspects of sex—pleasure, self-expression, high states of arousal—are legitimate, are not shameworthy, and are an integral part of emotional life for one's fellow citizens.

When sexuality is brought into the public arena in this way, it threatens sex-negative people. It undermines the community of cultural consensus in which they can feel safe. The very existence of this public-ized sex challenges the cherished belief that the community is not a sexual community, a pretense that sex-negative people need. By asserting that "everyone in this community is a sexual being, and that's OK," public-ized sex confronts and acknowledges *everyone*'s desire, not just the desire of the consumers of a particular sexual activity. . . .

The sexual "censors" are people who really believe that the world is sprinkled with sexual danger and that to be a good citizen means to spot these things, to challenge them, to disarm them whenever possible, to alert other people to the danger.

Such a person might say to himself, "I'm a terrible failure. I wasn't able to protect people, I wasn't able to protect the children, the innocent children." Children have nothing to do with it, but that's what they say. "I haven't lived up to what God wants from me. I haven't lived up to my own ideals." They feel depressed. They feel like, Why am I the only one? Why am I one of only a small number of people who realize what's going wrong here? I live in a community where the morals or the level of civilization is going downhill. I feel like I'm being overwhelmed by filth or degeneracy or reduction of morals. I'm frightened for myself but I'm also frightened for my community. I'm frightened for my fellow citizens who don't realize what's happening. . . .[23]

So the censors—and the censor's voice in all of us—want to control sex for everyone. What is still mysterious to me (though I follow Marty Klein's reasoning), is the urge to deprive all others of sexual images that feed the imagination, that spark fantasy, that stoke flagging libidos, and just plain make sex more pleasurable. It is as if, having sworn off sweets, or crossword puzzles, or television, we insist that every one of our fellow citizens should also be deprived of those things.

CONTRACEPTION, ABORTION, AND THE ROLE OF WOMEN

The suppression of sexual speech has always included in varying degrees the suppression of contraceptives, abortion, and information about these matters. Indeed, the infamous Comstock Law of 1873 classified contraceptives and abortion information as "obscene," prohibiting the mailing, importation, and transportation of "any drug, medicine, article, or thing designed, adapted, or intended for preventing conception, or producing abortion," as well as "any lewd, lascivious, or filthy book . . . or other matter of indecent character."

The inclusion of pornography and reproductive technology in the same law was no coincidence. Both represented to Comstock, as they do to the most ardent social conservatives today, a threat to the traditional family. Both have the effect of separating sexual pleasure from reproduction—pornography by its sex-for-the-sake-of-sex depictions, and abortion and contraception through their very availability and use. Such a separation threatens the established conservative view of how life ought to be lived.

The flip side of the coin is that the right to contraception and abortion—the right to sex without childbirth—became a centerpiece of women's struggle for equality. As women sought to escape from their inferior social status, unable to vote or enter into contracts or inherit property, they fought for the right to control their fertility. Birth control pioneers like Margaret Sanger and Marie Stopes sought equality and freedom from sexual oppression, but most of all they fought for women's right to control their reproduction.

These women understood the connection between fertility control and sexual pleasure. They demanded both. Sanger was repeatedly jailed under the Comstock Laws for operating a birth control clinic. She also asserted that "the magnetism of [sex] is health-giving and [it] acts as a beautifier and a tonic."[24]

Birth control measures always have attracted the opposition of the censors, for the very notion of contraception rests on the assumption that sexual pleasure, at least within the context of the marital relationship, is a positive human good, of value for its own sake and not just an activity that is necessary for procreation. Anyone who is enthusiastic about the dissemination of birth control therefore accepts, by clear implication, that sexual pleasure is at least acceptable, and more probably that sexual pleasure is, by itself, a good thing. "From the dawn of history, the fundamental reason for using contraception has never varied in the slightest for the billions of couples who have practiced it. Contraception is practiced in order to enjoy sexual relations without suffering the consequences of unwanted reproduction. . . . The part of the equation which never varies refers to the enjoyment of [sex]."[25]

To a certain extent our society is coming to accept this. Modern marriage counselors and sex therapists advise couples to pursue pleasurable sexual practices in a whole variety of ways. An active sex life is advocated as an important component of a healthy marriage; couples are urged to engage in "hot monogamy." Couples in their seventies, eighties, and nineties are encouraged to maintain active sex lives. If a middle-aged or elderly man is having erection problems, today's sex therapists will usually counsel the couple to try oral sex, a nonprocreational sexual practice considered so "bad" throughout our history that it is still actually illegal in nearly half the states in the United States.

Older Americans are having sex, enjoying it, and even using toys and watching explicit videos. As many hundreds of couples have reported on surveys, such activities provide pleasure and intimacy in their lives and their happiness is increased. Should we not all be delighted with this? I am, particularly as I enter these years myself, but it seems still difficult for those who think of sex as sinful to unabashedly applaud sex among our many and increasing millions of senior citizens.

Sex is good for people. It enhances the human condition. The fact that it is pleasurable honors rather than demeans us. We are lucky indeed that our powerful sexuality can be channeled so joyously into intimacy with a partner.

With this interlude accomplished, I return to the prosecution that was still facing us in Salt Lake City.

NOTES

1. James Thurber, *Is Sex Necessary?* (New York: Harper & Row, 1929), p. xxiii.
2. J. Bloomfield, M. McGrail, and L. Sanders, eds., *Too Darn Hot* (New York: Persea Books, 1998), p. 14.

3. Andrea Dworkin, *Pornography: Men Possessing Women* (New York: Dutton, 1979), p. 55; cited in Nadine Strossen, *Defending Pornography: Free Speech, Sex, and the Fight for Women's Rights* (New York: Scribner, 1995), p. 113.

4. Richard A. Posner, *Sex and Reason* (Cambridge: Harvard University Press, 1992), p. 32.

5. Ibid.

6. Sallie Tisdale, *Talk Dirty to Me* (New York: Anchor, 1995), p. 266.

7. G. Walsh, *The Role of Religion in History* (New Brunswick, N.J.: Transaction Publishers, 1998), p. 172.

8. Laurence H. Tribe, *American Constitutional Law* (Mineola, N.Y.: Foundation Press, 1996), p. 919.

9. Strossen, *Defending Pornography*, p. 177–78.

10. Ibid.

11. Marty Klein, "Censorship and the Fear of Sexuality," *Humanist*, July/August 1990, p. 15.

12. P. Hammill, cited in Strossen, *Defending Pornography*, p. 219.

13. George Orwell, *1984* (New York: Signet/Penguin, 1950), p. 111.

14. Strossen, *Defending Pornography*, p. 178.

15. It is worth noting that "blasphemy" can still be very dangerous. Salman Rushdie was forced into virtual house arrest for a decade following Iran's *fatwa* (death order), which condemned him for writing a novel, *Satanic Verses*, that Iran's Islamic leaders found to be insulting to Islam.

16. B. Kosmin and S. Lochmann, *One Nation Under God: Religion in Contemporary American Society* (New York: Harmony Books, 1993), pp. 8–9.

17. Marty Klein, "Censorship and the Fear of Sexuality" (mimeo, 1992), pp. 2–4.

18. Ibid.

19. The five with no obscenity laws are Alaska, Maine, New Mexico, Oregon, and Vermont. Hawaii's law restricts only obscene films in public theaters.

20. Lloyd Sinclair, personal communication, June 19, 2000.

21. Marty Klein, interview with the author, April/May 1997.

22. John Mintz, file memorandum, October 21, 1986.

23. Klein, interview, April/May 1997.

24. Philip Harvey, *Let Every Child Be Wanted: How Social Marketing Is Revolutionizing Contraceptive Use Around the World* (Westport, Conn.: Greenwood Publishing Group, 1999), p. 43.

25. J. Mayone Stycos, cited in ibid., p. 42.

CHAPTER TEN

DECISION IN DENVER

"I don't consider this letter a working concept," Postal Inspector Gary Jones is saying, under oath on the witness stand in Salt Lake City. He is having a problem with the definition of the word "concept" because he has used this term himself in a sworn declaration a few months previous. In an apparent effort to disprove our contention that the multiple-district prosecution strategy had been part of Department of Justice policy for many years, and that PHE's prosecution had been a direct result of that strategy, Inspector Jones had declared in his earlier statement that "the concept of targeting alleged violators of obscenity laws for multiple prosecutions did not occur until well after the PHE, Inc. search warrant and what was later to become known as Project Postporn." Now, confronted with a copy of U.S. Attorney Brent Ward's September 1985 letter to Ed Meese, a letter that spells out the multiple-prosecution concept in explicit detail, Jones allows that he was aware of the letter and the ideas it contained, and concedes that the letter was mailed to Washington a full eight months before the May 1986 raid on PHE. Given this, he must now insist that the Ward letter does not contain, as Dave Rudolf, who is questioning him, puts it, "an embodiment of that concept."

"I don't think it's an embodiment that was ever put into implementation," Mr. Jones says. "It is just something that has been written down as a proposal of something to be considered."[1] No concept there![2]

We were in Salt Lake City before Judge Winder at an evidentiary hearing on June 28, 1991. He had called the hearings so that both sides could present evidence in support of and in opposition to our motion to dismiss the Utah indictments for bad faith and vindictiveness. We also used this opportunity to present evidence in support of our motion to dismiss the indictments on the basis that they had been improperly delayed.

As the architect of our civil suit and of the ensuing Motion to Dismiss for Bad Faith, Bruce Ennis's job was to establish even more definitively than had already been shown in motions, in the discovery documents, and in depo-

sitions in the civil case, that PHE had been the victim of a coordinated, concerted, multi-year strategy on the part of the federal government, a campaign
designed to put us out of business or, at the very least, to so curtail it that the
result would be to suppress constitutionally protected materials as well as
arguably obscene ones. We would show that these indictments, and the im-
pending trial, were part of that strategy and were therefore utterly improper
as a matter of law.

On the witness stand Brent Ward, Utah's U.S. attorney, confirmed and
amplified the history of his role in the evolution of the multidistrict federal
strategy. His September 1985 letter to the U.S. attorney general had set out the
strategy in dramatic and explicit detail:"The heart of [the] . . . strategy calls for
multiple prosecutions (either simultaneous or successive) . . . in many loca-
tions." Ward was also pretty forthright about admitting that he would draw
the line "well below" the *Miller* obscenity standard in a plea bargain negotiation. Ward asserted that when he was negotiating a plea he could not accept
even an "average" definition of the kind of sexual explicitness that might be
permitted under a strict obscenity definition because some of his constituents
would still find the legally acceptable material offensive, and he did not believe
he could put the government's stamp of approval on any sexual material that
even the most conservative of his constituents would find obnoxious.

It was extremely useful for us to have Ward admit that he would insist on
the elimination of nonobscene and therefore constitutionally protected materials in any plea agreement. This meant that as a condition for a settlement in
our case, the government had been insisting on the suppression of constitutionally protected speech.

Ward also seemed to agree that negotiating about the nature of such
postplea materials was unlikely to be productive. The DOJ's standard operating procedure had always been to simply negotiate entire businesses out of
existence, as was done with Avram Freedberg, Karl Brussel, and at least five
other mail-order companies. By insisting on an out-of-business condition,
the government avoided the niceties of degrees of sexual explicitness, what
constituted "offensiveness," and what did or did not appeal to a prurient
interest. Instead, the companies' owners simply annihilated their own firms in
exchange for reduced sentences or fines. By giving up the right to ever sell
sexual materials in the future, they were knowingly relinquishing a constitutional right, but it is not unusual for persons under threat of prosecution to
bargain away some of their constitutional rights as part of the deal.

Ward's continuing testimony was a veritable litany about the astonishing
vagueness of obscenity laws. "By the way," he testified at one point, "we're
talking cases unlike the normal range of federal crimes where it's easy to

determine whether a crime has been committed, we're talking about cases where you don't know a crime has been committed until the jury has applied the *Miller* standard to the material and says so." On this point at least, Ward was exactly right. Asked whether "Adam & Eve would have to offer to cease the distribution of *any* material that a sizable portion of the public might find objectionable," Ward said, "I think that's correct; that's why the plea discussions became futile and unrewarding."

Ward's testimony also brought more confusion to the definitions of obscenity being used in the Justice Department. Asked whether "sexually explicit" necessarily meant "obscene," Ward replied "to me it would be—it would be possible that the term sexually explicit would be—would mean obscene, depending on the community examining the material." Bruce persisted, pointing out that, to be obscene, material "must be patently offensive, must appeal to a prurient interest, and must have no serious value, correct?"

"Well," answered Ward, "that's what sexually explicit may mean to some people."

Bruce repeated, "But sexually explicit is not necessarily obscene, correct?" Answer: "Well, may be or may not be."[3]

It would be generous to think that he was simply confused, that he did not quite understand that the term "sexually explicit" did not mean the same thing as obscene under the *Miller* standard. But Brent Ward was a seasoned U.S. attorney, a trained lawyer, and a man with a high degree of expertise in obscenity law. When he testified that "sexually explicit" may be exactly the same as "obscene," he was almost certainly being disingenuous, attempting to muddy an issue about which he was very well informed.

Even with the additional testimony emerging from the Salt Lake hearings, we were not optimistic about getting the Utah indictments dismissed on bad-faith grounds. One reason was that acceptance of our argument would require that Judge Winder, a Salt Lake City judge who would continue to administer jurisprudence in that city, would have had to find highly improper the behavior of an assistant U.S. attorney with whom he regularly did business. Richard Lambert had been a key player in the drama we had so carefully outlined, going all the way back to his participation in the 1986 raid, his collaboration with North Carolina authorities, and his active participation in all the plea bargain discussions at which he had insisted on our giving up the sale of nonobscene material. For Judge Winder to find in our favor, he would have to declare that the U.S. attorney's office, with which he routinely worked and with whose representatives he socialized annually at the Sun Valley Utah State Bar Convention, had egregiously misbehaved. That is very difficult for a judge to do.

On the other hand, the combination of evidence we had obtained from the government during the discovery process, the depositions given by numerous government representatives, including three FBI agents, supporting our contentions about a coordinated effort to put mail-order companies out of business, and the very declarations given by government representatives in opposition to our motion, built a very strong case. The hearing testimony, it seemed to us, was significantly strengthening this case, particularly because Judge Winder had had an opportunity to witness firsthand the evasiveness of several government witnesses on matters central to our position.

We were hoping that Judge Winder would find a way of derailing the existing indictments without actually determining misbehavior on the part of his Salt Lake City colleagues. He could, for example, dismiss the indictments due to preindictment delay. If he did so, the other motions would be moot and no one would be officially demeaned. The delay, after all, might simply have been the result of overwork at the U.S. attorney's office.

In response to our motion to dismiss for bad faith and vindictiveness, the government hammered away on the point that there was no bad faith involved in what had been normal plea bargain negotiations. Those meetings, they contended with a vehemence we found ironic, "were friendly, relaxed, and informal," and the conversations during plea negotiations "were free-wheeling, unrehearsed, and sometimes jovial." With just a little too much hurt in their tone, they asserted that "[t]here was no anticipation by representatives of the government that what was perceived as a courteous acquiescence to defense counsel's request for a meeting and the frank and friendly conversation that ensued, would four years later be transmuted into a claim of bad faith prosecution with the defendants' attorneys claiming near photographic recall of the spoken words."[4] We were pretty mean all right.

The government also argued (persuasively, as it turned out) that the indictments in Salt Lake City had been approved by a new U.S. attorney, Dee Benson, who had had no part in the earlier history of multidistrict prosecutions, and that these indictments had been handed down by an independent Utah grand jury, which found probable cause to believe that defendants had violated federal obscenity laws. They contended that "[d]efendants have failed to show that prosecutors in Kentucky, North Carolina, or Washington, D.C., had any role in the decision to bring the indictment in Utah; thus consideration of the motives of those prosecutors is irrelevant to this motion. . . . Mr. Benson made the final decision to proceed in seeking the indictment. . . . Defendants have presented volumes of information relating to events in Washington, D.C., and North Carolina, but have failed to connect any of those events in a significant manner to the prosecution of the defendants in Utah."[5]

While these arguments seemed, on the surface, persuasive, they contained a strong hint of what seems to me a serious tactical error: failure to present a united front. The U.S. government is so big and multifaceted that it can seldom present a coordinated, cohesive persona in situations of this kind. In this pleading the government was clearly trying to separate what its lawyers virtually admitted was misconduct by the government in other parts of the country from the supposedly pure indictment process in Salt Lake City.

There were to be several other examples of failure by the government to present a united front, most notably an assertion by one group of government lawyers that other government attorneys had erred in failing to dispute the facts we presented when we first filed our suit. An equivalent circumstance on our side would have meant that our civil attorneys would denigrate in their pleadings the actions or assertions of our own criminal defense attorneys. Such a course, to us, was unthinkable. The civil case was assiduously coordinated every step of the way with the actions and documentary pleadings of our criminal attorneys. For one to disparage the other in any way was out of the question. For the government, it was apparently routine.

We waited for Judge Winder's decision with some trepidation but high hopes. Dismissal of these indictments took on greater importance than it would have otherwise, because the indicted items had not gone through our outside screening process, and a few of them were pretty rough. One depicted some bondage scenes that would probably not have passed our current outside review process, a process that was instituted in 1986. In their pleadings, the government had taken great pains to describe these scenes in graphic detail.

During this period, as well as earlier, I had made a legal update part of our monthly employee meetings at PHE. One morning each month, we would all gather in the warehouse, surrounded by racks of merchandise, the conveyor briefly turned off, and discuss important events about the ongoing legal proceedings. I was as forthcoming as I could be within the bounds of what our lawyers would permit me to say about the status of our case. On a few occasions, I went beyond those bounds. On one occasion early on, I announced that we had earlier had in our midst an employee "plant," put there by the authorities in Alamance County to gather evidence.

"If there are any *new* spies among us," I stated at one August meeting, "I hope they will work diligently, just like our other employees, to make our operations succeed, and report to any prosecutors that we are good and honest people." I reassured the whole staff—by now about 150 people—that I would share all but the most sensitive information with them and said that if anyone had questions I could not answer in front of the group, they were welcome to come see me afterward.

On August 28, 1991, Judge Winder ruled against us, finding merit in the government's argument that the indictment had been cleansed by the involvement of Dee Benson and his screening committee, and using strikingly similar language to that included in the government argument. The key language of his decision stated

> Defendants have presented voluminous evidence, some contested, of questionable motives and zealotry exhibited by prosecutors and government officials in North Carolina, Washington, DC, and other points East. Defendants have failed, however, to connect such conduct in any significant way with the decision to seek an indictment against defendants in Utah in September 1990. The final decision to seek an indictment was made by an independent screening committee under the direction of United States Attorney Dee Benson, who played no role in the previous four-year investigation of PHE and the resulting plea negotiations.[6]

We were bitterly disappointed. Our motion to dismiss for preindictment delay was still in front of the judge, and he could still dismiss on those grounds. But this was now extremely unlikely since, had he been inclined to dismiss the indictments for preindictment delay, he would almost surely have done so without troubling to make the more difficult decision about bad faith and vindictiveness. We now saw little hope for dismissal.

RISKING A VERY LONG SHOT

Now Bruce Ennis's team had to consider formulating an appeal that put us at the very fringes of known litigation territory. I have a vision of Bruce and his colleagues, David Ogden, John Morris, and Julie Carpenter, huddled over rows of electronic dials representing litigation minutiae, turning the knobs tiny fractions in either direction, getting ever clearer signals about finer and finer points of the law.

What confronted us was the prospect of an interlocutory appeal, an appeal brought between indictment and trial based on the grounds that the trial itself would be a violation of our rights. This is seldom done, and even less seldom does it succeed. Our system of jurisprudence, as embodied in the Bill of Rights, builds in numerous strong protections for criminal defendants. Most of those protections have to do with the trial itself—the right to a trial by a jury, the right not to incriminate oneself, the right to confront one's accusers, and rules of evidence designed to protect the innocent from prosecutorial overzealousness. If we appealed before trial, we knew the government would point all this out. The dismissal we were seeking would be based on arguments that would be well answered in a trial itself, they would argue.

On the other hand, a trial would cost us a lot of money. It would subject us to months of work and interrogation. We believed we had a right not to be put through that hardship by prosecutors who were following an unconstitutional course.

The filing of the interlocutory appeal grew naturally out of our position that the First Amendment forbade the government's strategy and actions. But, as Bruce stated, the appeal was "highly, highly unusual." It had never been made in an obscenity case. To the best of our knowledge it has not been done in any other obscenity case to this day.

The idea that a prosecution can be stopped prior to trial had been confined to a relative handful of cases where courts have found that anyone with absolute immunity from prosecution could get the prosecution stopped early in the process because the prosecution itself violated their rights. This had come up mostly in civil cases, such as those relating to members of Congress, who are immune from *any* action, civil or criminal, for anything they say on the floor of the House or Senate. But could those precedents apply to us?

Bruce describes the principle.

If you can make a credible claim that you are immune from a particular legal proceeding, then the proceeding itself violates your rights. We had to craft an analogy to the prior cases concerning absolute and qualified immunity for government officials, to say that what the government was doing was violating our First Amendment right not to stand trial at all; our First Amendment right not to have to expend resources defending against what would be a violation of our constitutional rights. We had to analogize to those immunity cases. And that hadn't been done before.

Our interlocutory appeal was filed with the Tenth Circuit Court in Denver on May 26, 1992.* We reiterated our basic claims and spelled out why Judge Winder had erred in rejecting our motion.

It is undisputed that the First Amendment requires dismissal of a prosecution brought for the purpose of discouraging the distribution of lawful expression. . . . Whenever there is evidence, as here, that an impermissible desire to deter lawful speech is *a* motivating factor in a governmental decision, the *gov-*

---

*That nine months had gone by between Judge Winder's decision and our appeal is symptomatic of the snail's pace at which these proceedings moved.

ernment bears the burden of proving that it would have taken the same action even without the influence of the impermissible motive. This "but for" test requires a factual determination whether, in fact, the impermissible motive is a but-for cause of the governmental action.

Here, the district court failed to apply this constitutionally required test and erroneously failed to find whether an impermissible motive to discourage lawful expression was a but-for cause of this indictment. The district court apparently believed, incorrectly, that an absence of bad faith by then US Attorney Dee Benson, who at the last minute considered and approved Lambert's and Delahoyde's recommendation to seek indictment, would sanitize the indictment even if the indictment would not have been brought but for the bad faith of Lambert, Delahoyde, and other prosecutors. That is not the law. The Supreme Court and lower courts have repeatedly enjoined or dismissed prosecutions that were "recommended" or "set in motion" for bad faith reasons, even if "untainted" participants subsequently approved the indictment. And this Court [i.e., the 10th Circuit Court of Appeals] has repeatedly ruled in analogous contexts that governmental actions can violate the First Amendment if the persons *recommending* those actions were motivated by a desire to discourage expression, even if the persons who finally *approved* those recommendations were not impermissibly motivated. In each case, the First Amendment requires the court to determine whether an action, otherwise permissible, would have been taken but for the bad faith of the governmental agents who recommended that action. . . .

Here, there is overwhelming evidence that but for a bad faith desire to discourage the distribution of lawful expression, Lambert and Delahoyde would not have recommended indictment, . . . and that but for that bad faith recommendation, US Attorney Benson would not have considered, much less approved, Lambert's quest for an indictment. . . . Indeed, Benson's sole basis for approving the recommendation was the information Lambert and Delahoyde selectively chose to provide him. Thus, the district court's failure to make the factual findings required by the "but for" test was an error of constitutional magnitude.

. . . Accordingly, this Court should vacate the district court's denial of defendant's motion to dismiss for bad faith, and should remand with directions to determine whether defendants would have been indicted but for the bad faith of Lambert, Delahoyde, and other participants in the indictment process.

We were not asking the appeals court to overrule Judge Winder and dismiss the indictments (which they would never have done). Rather, we asked for a ruling that would require Judge Winder to address the fundamental constitutional issue, to determine whether Lambert's (and others') motives had been improper—an issue the judge had sidestepped in his decision.

In response, Lambert and his colleagues pointed out in their brief that most of the avowedly bad-faith discussions between our attorneys and the government's representatives had occurred all the way back in 1986, except for "fruitless discussions in the Spring of 1989" which they asserted involved no talk about curtailing the material we could sell.

The government restated, almost paragraph by paragraph, Judge Winder's decision, claiming that it contained not only his conclusions that the involvement of Benson and the screening committee at the end of the process was without bias, but also that the judge had concluded, at least by implication, that Assistant U.S. Attorney Richard Lambert had not brought any improper motivation to the process by which he sought and obtained the indictment. They tried, in other words, to demonstrate that the judge had already concluded, as a fact, that Lambert had not misbehaved. Judge Winder's language, however, contained no such conclusion. Rather, he had relied on what the appeals court later referred to as the "cleansing" effect of Dee Benson and the review committee.

In addition, the government argued that, on the law, Judge Winder's decision was not appealable. Relying heavily on *United States* v. *Hollywood Motor Car Co., Inc.* (1982), the government argued from that case that bad faith and vindictive prosecution charges are remedied by dismissal of the charges and are reviewable *after* conviction, not before trial.

"This case," the government asserted, "does not concern a claim that is unreviewable after conviction, because, contrary to defendant's argument, it does *not* concern a right not to be tried at all. . . . [T]he remedy for claims of bad faith prosecution based upon a defendant's exercise of his First Amendment rights and for vindictive prosecution is *dismissal of the charges* after conviction, even if it means that the defendant must first undergo trial and then appeal."[7]

Our appeal and the government responses were filed in Denver in March 1992. Supporting us, thirteen other organizations, including the American Civil Liberties Union and the Association of American Publishers, signed on as friends of the court, urging the court to hear our appeal and to grant the relief we sought.[8] Shortly thereafter, we learned that we would be allowed to argue our case orally before a three-judge panel in Denver, an opportunity we were very pleased to have. Bruce Ennis and his colleague David Ogden flew to Denver rigorously prepared, but knowing that they faced an uphill battle.

The three-judge panel was headed by Judge Ruggero J. Aldisert, who was senior judge, U.S. Court of Appeals for the Third Circuit, based in Philadelphia. He was sitting by designation in the Tenth Circuit in 1992. Bruce and

David's optimism rose; a visiting judge would likely show more flexibility than Tenth Circuit traditionalists.

From the beginning the hearing went well. Judge Aldisert appeared to be in charge and asked most of the questions. It was clear that he had some sympathy for our arguments and that, in particular, he put a good deal of weight on Judge Green's original opinion and findings, a very good sign.

It was also clear that these judges did not like the fact that Richard Lambert, who was at the center of contention in this case, had authored the government's brief and was arguing the government's position at the hearing. Lambert was in the awkward position of asserting, in effect, "I have done nothing wrong. How dare these folks impugn my integrity?" Coming from Lambert such arguments seemed self-serving and empty. Judge Aldisert made it very clear that he thought so, asking Lambert why he was arguing the case. "Isn't it your very own conduct that's in question here?"

Bruce and David left the hearing in an upbeat mood. Before these oral arguments, Bruce had put our chances of winning the remand at less than one in three; now he thought the odds had moved up to fifty/fifty, though there was a lot of uncertainty because we had heard very little from the other two judges on the panel, Moore and McWilliams. And they, like Judge Winder, might be especially reluctant to find misbehavior on the part of a government official in their own circuit.

On May 26, 1992, nearly six years from the 1986 raid on our premises, the Tenth Circuit decision was handed down.

It was a moment for all of us to relish.

The opinion was written by Judge Aldisert and joined by Judge Moore, with Judge McWilliams dissenting. It asserted that the First Amendment implications of the present case made a pretrial appeal appropriate. The court ruled that, in our case, unlike several cases cited by the government in which the Supreme Court had ruled the other way, there was "evidence of an extensive pattern of prosecutorial conduct dating back some five years that suggests a persistent and widespread campaign to coerce the appellants into surrendering their First Amendment rights." Further referring to "an uncontroverted, coordinated campaign of questionable prosecutorial activity," the court asserted we had a right to pretrial appeal.

Next, the court addressed Lambert's involvement in this "questionable prosecutorial activity," and whether or not Judge Winder had been correct in separating the process by which the Utah indictments had been obtained by Lambert and the more "questionable" prosecutorial activity at "points East." The opinion stated that Judge Winder "had judicial knowledge that Richard M. W. Lambert was a defendant in proceedings that enjoined him and other defendants in bringing multiple prosecutions against PHE, Inc., one of the defendants here." The opinion continued:

> Lambert's participation in what the District Court for the District of Columbia described as "a showing of bad faith" was described in at least *seven* separate instances in the court's [i.e., Judge Winder's] narrative of facts, and several of the instances involved Lambert's conduct outside the District of Utah. . . . [T]he district court reviewed voluminous testimony, including Lambert's deposition, describing Lambert's role, not only as a participant, but as an admitted leader in the instant prosecution. Faced with the uncontradicted testimony of Lambert's activities, the District Court's finding of fact that the "questionable motives and zealotry exhibited by prosecutors and government officials" in the Eastern United States did not find its way to Utah cannot survive our review. Lambert played a leadership role in this conduct "in North Carolina, Washington, DC, and other points East" as well as in Utah.
>
> There is substantial evidence, largely uncontroverted, that Lambert was involved in the multiple prosecution strategy from its inception. The appellants became the target of that strategy as early as 1986, when PHE's premises was searched by state and federal agents, including prosecutors from the Utah United States Attorneys Office. In that same year, Lambert and Ward met with appellant's attorneys. Lambert figured prominently in the investigation leading up to the indictment, and now appears as counsel for the government in this appeal.
>
> We therefore conclude that Lambert was extensively involved in the multiple prosecution strategy against the appellants, and the district court's finding to the contrary was clearly erroneous.[9]

Eureka!

The court then turned to the matter of whether the involvement of Dee Benson and his committee at the very end of this process had cleansed the indictment of any prior taint. Noting that "[t]he court may not permit vindictiveness to be hidden behind procedural cosmetics," the opinion came down squarely on our side.

> The government appears to be arguing for a rule that would permit the prosecution to precede an indictment with a campaign of harassment and prosecutorial misconduct, so long as a single administrative prosecutor remains aloof, in a *cordon sanitaire*, and thus is able to act as a cleansing agent to remove any past misconduct by his associates and assistants should an indictment be forthcoming.

... In effect, the district court re-invented a version of the discredited "silver platter" doctrine by holding that underlings who knowingly participate in an unconstitutional scheme to conduct an unlawful criminal prosecution may cure the constitutional taint by disingenuously presenting the fruits of their unlawful activities to their superiors on a "silver platter." However, where, as here, a prosecution is premised on the fruits of constitutionally tainted behavior, we cannot permit the prosecution to continue, notwithstanding attempts to launder the taint by presenting the fruits to an independent prosecutor.

... Accordingly, we conclude that the district court's apparent conclusion that Benson's participation in the indictment process cleansed any impropriety is erroneous as a matter of law.

All these words were, of course, music to our ears. So many of our arguments—arguments in which we believed so passionately—had been vindicated! The court summed up:

We conclude that appellants have already satisfied their burden of showing that the indictment is the tainted fruit of a prosecutorial attempt to curtail PHE's future First Amendment protected speech. ... [T]he burden now shifts to the government to "justify its decision [to indict] with legitimate, articulable, objective, reasons." In considering whether such proper reasons exist, the polestar to guide the district court on remand will be the controlling precept it recognized in its previous opinion in this case:

The inquiry is whether, "as a practical matter, there is a realistic or reasonable likelihood of prosecutorial conduct that would not have occurred *but for* the hostility or punitive animus towards the defendant because he exercised his specific legal rights."

This was exactly the standard we had requested. We were absolutely confident that no reasonable judge could conclude that these indictments would have been brought without the "punitive animus" of Lambert and the others. Clearly these indictments were part of a pattern, a pattern to "drive pornographers out of business," as the government itself had asserted. Such a pattern, it was now clearly established, was unconstitutional. Indeed, the Tenth Circuit opinion was redolent with language supporting this point. The court had found improper motivation on the part of the government and there would be no way now for the government to assert that each of these steps—Alamance, Raleigh, Utah, Kentucky—had been independent and therefore innocent. Indeed, it seemed less and less likely that the government would push ahead with a trial in Utah even if Judge Winder found a way out of the box he would now be in, because the Tenth Circuit opinion gave us such clear and immediate grounds to appeal a conviction, were the government to obtain one, that a trial would be hard to justify.

BASKING IN OUR VICTORY

We were ecstatic. Bruce and his colleagues had pulled off an astonishing feat. The country's first and only interlocutory appeal in an obscenity case had resulted in a reversal of the district court's opinion and a return of the case to the district court for reconsideration along very strict guidelines—guidelines that overwhelmingly supported our position.

I circulated a memo to all our employees the next day.

May 27, 1992

We won a tremendous victory in our Utah case yesterday. . . .

The Court of Appeals has held that companies like PHE have a "right not to be tried" in situations like ours where the government has engaged in "an extensive pattern of prosecutorial conduct dating back some five years that suggests a persistent and widespread campaign to coerce [PHE] . . . into surrendering [its] First Amendment rights."

Perhaps most important is an unequivocal finding that the current prosecution of PHE in Utah "is premised on the fruits of constitutionally tainted behavior" on the part of the government. In short, the Tenth Circuit has found that the government has been systematically violating our First Amendment rights! . . .

The result of all this is to put us in a much stronger position not only with respect to the Utah prosecution but also with respect to our civil suit in D.C.

The Tenth Circuit decision was widely reported in the press. The *Ogden* (Utah) *Standard-Examiner*, quoting an AP release, noted that "the US District Court in Utah was sharply criticized by the Tenth US Court of Appeals on Tuesday, saying the 'tainted indictment' had been served up on [a] 'silver platter.' "[10]

The Wall Street Journal noted that

[T]he decision by the 10th US Court of Appeals in Denver, will make it difficult for the Justice Department to pursue its controversial strategy of bringing simultaneous or successive indictments against distributors of sexually explicit materials in two or more conservative jurisdictions. . . .

The Justice Department under the direction of then Attorney General Edwin Meese, adopted the hardball prosecution strategy in 1985 to "test the limits of pornographers [*sic*] endurance," the court said, quoting from a government document. Once under indictment, distributors were told that they would have to stop selling all kinds of sexually explicit materials, including publications not considered obscene, such as *Playboy* and sexual manuals like "The Joy of Sex" available in mainstream bookstores throughout the country.[11]

Two weeks later the *National Law Journal* noted that

[d]efense attorneys in this case were particularly pleased that the court allowed an interlocutory appeal on a motion to dismiss—apparently a precedent in an obscenity prosecution. Such an appeal, the panel ruled, was critical, because the stakes involved "the right not to be tried."

"This case . . . presents an unusual, perhaps unique confluence of factors," observed the May 26 ruling by Senior Judge Ruggero J. Aldisert. There was, he wrote, "substantial evidence of an extensive government campaign, of which this indictment is only a part, designed to use the burden of repeated criminal prosecutions to chill the exercise of First Amendment rights. Under these circumstances we are persuaded that the district court's order implicates 'important right[s] which would be lost, probably irreparably, if review had to await final judgment.' "[12]

Finally in a column published in the *Washington Post* and other newspapers, columnist Nat Hentoff discussed the case.

> *Harassing those engaged in lawful activity is not*
> *a proper function of government.*

. . . The Adam & Eve company—which sells adult sexual materials only by mail order—had been found not guilty by a North Carolina jury. And in 1990, a federal district court in Washington ruled that the Justice Department had acted in "bad faith" by trying to force the company to stop distribution of every bit of sexually related material, including *Playboy*. Notwithstanding that setback, the national obscenity hit squad went after Adam & Eve in Utah, figuring that community standards there would at last bring this company its just and bitter deserts.

In an indignant editorial, the *Raleigh News & Observer* in North Carolina points out that all this close attention by the Justice Department has cost Adam & Eve $2 million in legal fees so far. And that is the intent of the Justice Department. As the original letter to Meese outlining the scorched earth plan said: "This strategy would test the limits of pornographers' endurance . . . as profitable as these enterprises may be, there is a limit to the prison terms, fines, and forfeiture of assets to which obscenity distributors will subject themselves."

Note the interchangeable use of obscenity (illegal) and pornography (which is not illegal, despite the strenuous efforts of law professor Catharine MacKinnon).

When the Justice Department pursued Adam & Eve into Utah, a federal district court there said that the defendants had presented "voluminous evidence, some contested, of questionable motives and zealotry exhibited by prosecutors and government officials." But, the court added, the defendants had not connected this pounding zeal to the particular obscenity indictment in Utah.

On May 26, however, in a 2 to 1 vote, a panel of the 10th Circuit Court of Appeals in Denver disagreed: "We conclude that appellants have already satisfied their burden of showing that the indictment is the tainted fruit of a prosecutorial attempt to curtail [Adam & Eve's] future First Amendment protected speech. . . ."[13]

The government recognized that this decision was a devastating setback for them. They appealed for an *en banc* review of the decision by the full Tenth Circuit panel. Ten sitting judges declined to grant such a review, however, and thereby upheld the panel's decision.

So many federal judges had by now found the government's tactics to be unconstitutional that we were convinced we had reached a watershed. Surely now we could find a way to put an end to all this.

The river looked a lot smoother now, and we were adding planks and armor to our liferaft. But the battle was not over. Even as the case was argued and won in Denver, intensive activity by new federal prosecutors was getting underway as a postal inspector from Alabama, posing as a mailman, prepared to take a reconnaissance tour of our building. Our breather would last just six months.

NOTES

1. Transcript of hearing before the Honorable David K. Winder of Utah, Central Division, *United States of America v. PHE, Inc., et al.*, Salt Lake City, Utah, June 28, 1991, pp. 52–107.

2. Bill Delahoyde was similarly forced to reinvent word definitions and other facts

in his open dispute with Raymond Bernard and Raymond Madden of the FBI. Delahoyde purported to be "outraged" that Bernard should have characterized his (Delahoyde's) views about some obscenity prosecutions as being worthwhile to deter pornographers even if the prosecutions would not likely result in guilty verdicts. Yet several of Delahoyde's other statements, as reported by Bernard, Madden, and others, clearly reflected just this position. See chapter 8.

3. Transcript of hearing, pp. 4–47.

4. Corrected Memorandum in Response to Defendant's Motion to Dismiss the Indictment for Bad Faith and Vindictive Prosecution, *United States of America* v. *PHE, Inc., et al.*, District of Utah, March 5, 1991, p. 22.

5. Memorandum of Points and Authorities in Response to Defendants' Pre-Hearing Memorandum of Fact and Law in Support of their Motion to Dismiss the Indictment for Bad Faith and Vindictive Prosecution and for Pre-Indictment Delay, *United States of America* v. *PHE, Inc., et al.*, District of Utah, July 17, 1991 (document misdated July 17, 1990).

6. Memorandum Decision and Order, David K. Winder, U.S. District Judge, *United States of America* v. *PHE, Inc., et al.*, August 28, 1991.

7. Brief of Plaintiff/Appellee, March 3, 1992, p. 27.

8. The other eleven who signed on to one of the two *amicus* briefs were the ACLU of Utah, People for the American Way, Playboy Enterprises, American Booksellers Association, Council for Periodical Distributors, the Freedom to Read Foundation, the Independent Video Retailers Association, the International Periodical Distributors Association, Magazine Publishers of America, National Association of College Stores, and the Recording Industry Association of America.

9. U.S. Court of Appeals, Tenth Circuit, *United States of America* v. *PHE, Inc., et al.*, [Opinion and Order], May 26, 1992.

10. *Ogden (Utah) Standard-Examiner*, May 27, 1992.

11. "Federal Anti-Pornography Tactic of Multiple Indictments Hits Snag," *Wall Street Journal*, May 29, 1992.

12. "Justice's Pornography War Suffers a Setback," *National Law Journal*, June 15, 1992.

13. Nat Hentoff, "The Justice Department's Tainted Fruit," *Washington Post*, July 25, 1992.

CHAPTER ELEVEN

SEX AND GOD

When churches talk about morality it always seems to come around to sex.
—Rev. Philip Wogaman

There is much evidence to support the conclusion that organized religion has caused more mischief in the world than it has done good. Certainly religious belief, particularly deeply held religious belief, has provided the context for an astonishing number of people to murder, maim, torture, and dismember their fellow humans. It can be argued that this carnage would have taken place even without a religious impetus, as a result of tribal or ethnic differences or simple greed for profit, for example. If that is so, it can be equally argued that those good things brought to the world by religion—and there are many—would also have taken place out of humanity's essential nature, without backing from organized religion.

Much of religion's negative impact lies in the fact that it has tended to divide us rather than bring us together. Humans have a powerful "We-They" nature. This quality, points out behavioral scientist Morton Hunt, causes us "to treat members of Us with humanity, Them with barbarity."[1] Religion tends to exacerbate the "We-They" phenomenon. By dividing us into sects, by creating believers (and thus nonbelievers), by defining the "true word," inevitably in contradiction to some other religion's "true word," religion provides us with more opportunities to make a "them" out of others.

History is, of course, rife with barbarities performed in the name of religion. Here is one small example.

In June 1099, when the armies of the First Crusade laid siege to Jerusalem . . . the leaders of the Crusaders . . . demanded unconditional surrender, and the defenders, after resisting for forty days, surrendered. The Crusaders entered the holy city; here is the joyous eye witness report of one Raymond of Agiles, a Christian—and a priest:

216

Wonderful things were to be seen! Numbers of the Saracens were beheaded . . . others were shot with arrows, or forced to jump from the towers; others were tortured for several days and then burned in the flames. In the streets were seen piles of heads and hands and feet. One rode about everywhere amid the corpses of men and horses.[2]

It is not just the followers of "other" religions who suffer from the murderous instincts of religious zeal. "Every flourishing religion has been intermittently watered by the blood of its own faithful, but none has seen more spectacular internecine butchery than Christianity."[3] This includes not only the niceties of the Inquisition, when heretics were tortured and killed for believing in the wrong kind of Christianity, but also the killing of Quakers by Puritans (who also cut off the ears of "heretics"), the persecution of "witches" by Christians, and the deaths of three thousand Christians at the hands of fellow Christians at Constantinople just a few centuries after the death of Christ, over a disagreement about the Nicene Creed. (Three thousand dead were more than all the Christian victims in three centuries of Roman persecution.)

All this took place some time ago and might be dismissed as the excesses of a bygone age. But at the close of the twentieth century we have had fundamentalist Muslims terrorizing their fellow Algerians, massacring thousands; violence between Catholics and Protestants in Northern Ireland, killing nearly two thousand in the 1970s alone, according to British Information Services; hundreds of thousands dead in Bosnia-Herzegovina with ethnically similar people deeply divided along religious lines; and Muslim versus Jew in the Middle East.[4]

HINDU VERSUS MUSLIM

Hindu nationalism boiled over in India in the late 1980s, taking the form of a campaign to build a Hindu temple at Ayodhya, on the site of a four-hundred-year-old mosque that desecrated, it said, the birthplace of the Hindu god, Lord Ram. Zealots duly destroyed the mosque in 1992, setting off a round of slaughter in which thousands of people, mostly Muslims, died.[5]

BUDDHIST VERSUS BUDDHIST

Even peaceful and self-effacing Buddhism can contribute to humanity's self-inflicted violence. In December 1998, hundreds of Buddhist monks, representing rival factions, rioted in Seoul, Korea, over control of a one-thousand-year-old temple. The monks smashed windows with two-by-fours, tipped over trucks, and tore part of the temple to pieces, all for religion's sake.[6]

JEW VERSUS JEW

Jerusalem. Conservative Jewish men and women who tried to pray together at the Western Wall during the Shavuot holiday early Wednesday morning and today said that they had been assaulted by hundreds of rigorously Orthodox [Jewish] men, evidently incensed by the sight of women praying with men.

The Conservatives said the strictly Orthodox Jews, known more commonly as the haredim, had spat on them and pelted them with garbage and feces, while calling them "Nazis," "Christians," "whores," and "goyim."[7]

MUSLIM VERSUS MUSLIM

Not to be outdone, the Taliban—the fanatical Muslim dictators of Afghanistan in the late 1990s—committed routine atrocities against that country's citizens, particularly women, all in the name of God. All Afghan women are forced to wear the *burqa*, which completely covers the face and body. One woman, reports the *New York Times*'s Bob Herbert, was dragged from a vehicle and beaten "because her arm accidentally slipped into view."[8] Meanwhile most Afghan women live miserable and abbreviated lives because the Taliban's interpretation of Islamic law does not permit male doctors to examine women, and women are not allowed to work as doctors (or at almost anything else).

The reason such abominations can be perpetrated by religious people in the name of religion is that all these devout people are certain that they are right, that only their particular belief system is privy to God's truths. Such misplaced certainty leads to "virtuous" violence; those who repented as their bodies were being broken during the Inquisition were, after all, being helped to find eternal life.[9]

The cornerstone of the intolerance that has so frequently led to cruelty and killing by deeply religious people is an absolutist position. If Salman Rushdie's book (*The Satanic Verses*) is blasphemous, then Rushdie should be killed; if God wants women in the home, then girls must not be educated; if homosexuality is bad, then homosexuals must be punished.

Man, noted Mark Twain, is the only religious animal. "He is the only animal who has the True Religion—several of them. He is the only animal who loves his neighbor as himself and cuts his throat if his theology isn't straight. He has made a graveyard of the globe in trying his honest best to smooth his brother's path to happiness and heaven."[10]

This belief in the absolute rightness of one's religion not only constitutes a religion's most dangerous tendency (the willingness to kill for the righteousness of one's cause), but also sets up the unresolvable conundrum: all the true believers cannot be right. For fundamentalist Christians, for example, Jesus Christ is the Savior, the only Savior, and anyone who does not turn to salvation through Jesus Christ cannot be saved and will not enter heaven. For devout Muslims, Mohammed is the prophet, and only Mohammed points the true path to God, righteousness, and the afterlife. They cannot both be right, and therefore "true" religion rests on very frail intellectual underpinnings. Of course, say the true believers, religion rests on faith, not intellect. But if all you need to do to prove I am wrong is to have faith that you are right, then no discussion is possible. If your direct hook-up with God trumps all reasoning, based solely on your faith, then the wounding and dangerous "We-They" conflict is assured. It is only by resort to what the Roman statesman Cicero called "right reason" that men and women can interact with each other amicably in a civilized society. When the faithful lock their minds, refusing to consider ideas that might conflict with some aspect of their faith, they (and we) lose the chance to interact with our fellow humans, the chance to engage in giving and receiving. Surrounded by religion-inspired slaughter in Algeria in the spring of 1997, an Algerian journalist noted on National Public Radio, "when we think, we can't be fundamentalists." But without thinking, we cannot be civilized.

Of course butchery of man by man does not require religion. Indeed, compared to the dark powers of government tyrants, religious murder is relatively minor. More people were killed by the organs of the state under Hitler, Stalin, and Mao Tse Tung than by all religious conflicts since time immemorial. But I believe it remains true that religion adds to the divisiveness among us, exacerbates our sense of "We-They," and gives us more reasons for splitting into groups whose enemies are other groups.

Hunt points out that the We-They tendency may be so persistent because it can be socially useful:

Hatred of Them unifies and solidifies the feeling of being Us, thereby strengthening the ingroup. It can also be personally useful: the sense of We-ness created by having a common enemy is reassuring, exhilarating, and feels good. Thus, for both societal and personal reasons We-They thinking is hard to combat.[11]

George Orwell's utopian nightmare in *1984* is built on this understanding. Oceania is constantly at war, either with Eurasia or Eastasia, and allied with whichever of the two is not the enemy. It doesn't matter who the enemy is and who the ally is; they switch regularly back and forth. But there is always a detested "They," a degenerate, repugnant "other" to hate and to fight.

Perhaps these We-They tendencies themselves feed the divisiveness of religion. But religion returns the favor, further dividing us, giving us yet one more reason to look down upon or otherwise distance those "others," and to believe in their wrongness.

Religion drives wedges between those with common beliefs, too, sometimes making We-They divisions over subtle differences. Sharita Alkhateeb, vice president of the North American Council for Muslim Women, notes that, for Muslim women in America, the issue of whether to cover or not to cover their heads is a "big topic." She goes on, "Unfortunately you have three groups: one who believe in covering, and about half of those who cover are very negative towards the ones who don't. Then you have the ones who don't cover and half of them are negative towards the ones that do. And the third group are the ones who feel comfortable either way and don't try to pressure anybody."[12] It is possible that these women would distrust others of their acquaintance without help from religious doctrine, but it is hard to believe that things have not been made worse by the religious requirement that all women must cover their heads (and, in some places, their faces and bodies as well).

I am gratefully aware that most Christians (like most others, including the third group of Muslim women who don't much care about head covering), are compassionate and tolerant, and that the New Testament message of love and charity has found a home in many more hearts than the We-They message of inerrancy, intolerance, and bigotry. Let us rejoice that this is so.

CHRISTIANITY AND SEX

The Christian church has been powerfully antagonistic to sex, almost from the start. As embodied by early clerics like Tertullian (c. 160–c. 230), who referred to woman as a "temple over a sewer," there appears to have been much of the same kind of fear of women's sexuality that we have seen noted earlier here. And those men who were most afraid of woman's sexuality seem to have dominated church thinking.

The Bible is not the source of this fear and denunciation. The Bible speaks of sex in many ways, most of them positive. It is entirely silent on the subjects of masturbation,★ abortion, birth control, oral-genital sex, and most other nontraditional sexual practices.[13] Sexual intercourse is routinely described in Genesis and is considered a "pleasure" by Sarah (Gen. 8:12); its unabashed recounting (Adam "knew his wife Eve") is almost routine in Genesis. The idyllic and lovely Song of Solomon is remarkably explicit in its erotic descriptions, a veritable paean to sexual love, and without reference to procreation or even marriage. The Old Testament does condemn homosexuality; it does so four times, but in contexts that suggest it is a relatively lesser matter than the problem of having sexual relations during menstruation (a condemnation that is repeated more than ten times) and other prohibited activities, like dietary proscriptions. Adultery is also condemned, but more as a violation of property rights than as a sexual sin.[14] But while the Bible sometimes celebrated sexual pleasure and sexual desire, the church condemned both; while the Bible said nothing about contraception, early Christian theologians treated it as a heinous sin, more sinful than early abortion:

> It is undoubtedly a tribute (if an ambiguous one) to such men as St. Jerome and St. Augustine that much of what the modern world still understands by "sin" stems not from the teachings of Jesus of Nazareth, or from the tablets handed down from Sinai, but from the early sexual vicissitudes of a handful of men who lived in the twilight days of Imperial Rome.[15]

It was these men—Jerome, Augustine, even Paul in the first century—and their followers who insisted that the flesh was inherently evil, that celibacy was preferable to marriage, that "woman as a whole and man from the waist down were creations of the devil." They were reinforced by clerics like Tertullian, who deeply feared women's sexuality. "Even natural beauty," he wrote, "ought to be obliterated by concealment and neglect, since it is dangerous to those who look upon it."

"It was Augustine who epitomized a general feeling among the church fathers that the act of intercourse was fundamentally disgusting. Arnobius called it filthy and degrading, Methodius unseemly, Jerome unclean, Tertullian shameful, Ambrose a defilement. In fact there was an unstated consensus that God ought to have invented a better way of dealing with the problem of pro-

---

★Onan was not observed to masturbate. He "spilled his seed on the ground" as a result of coitus interruptus to avoid impregnating his brother's wife (thus violating the Levite law).

creation."[16] Indeed, Augustine stated this explicitly. Would we not be better off, he asked rhetorically, "if it were possible to beget children without this lust, so that in this function of begetting offspring the members created for this purpose [i.e., the genitals] should not be stimulated by the heat of lust, but should be activated by [man's] volition . . . ?"[17]

That physical desire, presumably given to man and woman by God, became shameful and disgusting has led to generations of life-depleting guilt, needless torment, and probably a good deal of unnecessary violence. From its earliest days, the ideology of sexual shame and contempt has also created situations that are upside-down, hypocritical, and morally topsy-turvy. Since sexual desire was bad, for example, it became at times less sinful for a man to have sex with a prostitute than with his own wife, under the assumption that because he would desire his wife more, he would enjoy sexual relations more, and the act would therefore be more sinful. Such rules led early Catholic theologians to the conclusion that it was a worse sin to have anal intercourse with one's wife than vaginal intercourse with one's mother, and that masturbation (nonprocreative) was worse than rape (procreative).[18] Such zany nonsense may well be the inevitable result of dogma that denies man's and woman's very nature—the normal urge to engage in sexual relations.

In this climate, with sex approved only for procreative purposes and then only in the least enjoyable ways, contraception was considered beyond the pale, as were any physical positions for having sexual intercourse that the church deemed unorthodox. There were "atonements for almost every variant of sex other than the heterosexual, conception-oriented, man and wife, man superior position. And even that incurred a year's fast if practiced during Lent."[19] Anal or oral intercourse was considered "almost as culpable as homicide." Contraception was sinful in the extreme; abortion within forty days of conception was slightly less sinful, "possibly because abortion so often carried its own pains and penalties."

Historians do not much speculate on why these early Christian leaders so hated their own and others' sexuality. Sexual practices in Greece and Rome, traditions from which these men descended, were varied and interesting, certainly not always admirable, but not excessively burdened by the condemnation and guilt that marked early Christianity and has so burdened Western culture down the centuries. Newspaper editor and freethinker James Haught suggests that it would take "an army of psychiatrists and historians to pinpoint all the reasons western religions developed such hostility toward human sexuality."[20]

In Augustine's case, and with many others, the hatred of sexuality was grounded in his own stormy sex drives. In his *Confessions*, Augustine wrote, "Bodily desire, like a morass, and adolescent sex welling up within me exuded mists which clouded over and obscured my heart, so that I could not extinguish the clear light of true love from the murk of lust. Love and lust together seethed within me. In my tender youth they swept me away over the precipice of my body's appetites and plunged me in the whirlpool of sin."[21]

One historian suggests that the traditions of the Stoics—those who took such pride in enduring pain and abjuring pleasure—had a powerful influence. Stoics recognized that sex was an especially intense form of pleasure, "which is objectionable because it is so distracting. It causes a loss of control over both the mind and the body, and is therefore not conducive to sobriety or dignity." The second-century Stoic Sextus Empiricus asserted that all lust was bad, and he recommended self-castration "for those who found it difficult to practice celibacy."[22]

It is worth noting that this antipleasure syndrome is absent from the Jewish tradition. "The Torah, philosophically and historically, has always actively and enthusiastically encouraged both marriage and sexual intimacy. . . . A husband is required by Torah law to learn, know, and do what will give his wife sexual pleasure," observes one scholar.[23] Focusing on the positive implications of sexual intimacy, this perspective is quite at odds with the bitter view of sex embodied in the concept of woman as "a temple over a sewer."

Western civilization has paid a terrible price for the teachings of the early Christian clerics. For a hundred generations, Christians have been taught to respond with dread, disgust, and guilt to their natural urges. Given that human sexuality is in fact both pleasurable and beautiful, both a form of intimacy and an expression of love, healthy for the body and uplifting for the spirit, the toxicity of early Christian teachings on this subject is especially inexplicable.

SEX AND MORALITY

What *should* be the basis for moral sexual conduct? I believe that the foundation for sexual morality is the same as the basis for all moral behavior: to treat others as we would ourselves be treated. This principle is, of course, elucidated in the Bible at Matt. 7:12 and elsewhere. It is also found in the scriptural writings of all the world's major religions.★

★"This is the sum of duty: do naught to others which if done to thee would cause thee pain." *The Mahabharata* (Hindu)

"What is hateful to you, do not to your fellow men. That is the entire Law; all the rest is commentary." *The Talmud* (Jewish)

"No one of you is a believer until he desires for his brother that which he desires for himself." *Hadith* (Muslim)

"Hurt not others with that which pains yourself." *Udana-Varga* (Buddhist)

This precept provides a rich moral basis for human behavior, for the condemnation of murder and the punishment of murderers; for the condemnation of theft, robbery, and fraud, and the punishment of those who commit such acts; for the outlawing of all acts by which one human being may forcefully, fraudulently, or otherwise impinge upon the rights of another. It also forms a moral basis for treating Aleuts, Mongolians, Swedes, homosexuals, disabled people, heretics, rap artists, Muslims, Copts, Catholics, Protestants, prostitutes, gamblers, "sodomites," Cypriots, and even people who do not follow this rule, with dignity and respect. This simple rule, aptly called golden, thus forms a solid moral basis for the functioning of a free, democratic, open society.

NATURAL RIGHTS

I have observed that individual human beings are autonomous and entitled "by their very nature" to certain rights. This belief rests on the argument from natural law, to which I subscribe. The belief in natural rights—rights that depend on laws that are not man-made—is echoed from Cicero to Thomas Aquinas, from John Locke to Thomas Jefferson.

The Roman philosopher Cicero wrote, "There is in fact a true law—namely, right reason—which is in accordance with nature, applies to all men and is unchangeable and eternal." Cicero apparently believed, with Jefferson, that certain rights are "self evident" from our very nature, and that only reason is required to recognize those rights. A key theme of liberal thought has always been that natural rights flow directly from the characteristics of human nature.

But is this belief in natural rights itself a form of faith? Are the natural rights emanating from the very nature of human beings self-evident, and can these rights can be ascertained, as Cicero suggests, through reason alone?

"To me it is self evident that no person should initiate force against another person who has done him no harm," says David Boaz, vice president of the Cato Institute, who has written extensively on this subject.

"That would mean," I asked David, "that slavery is wrong not just because it doesn't work out very well in practical terms but because it is, ipso facto, wrong?"

"That's right," said David. "It seems clear to me, without any leap of faith, that the initiation of force without provocation is not only practically unworkable but morally wrong, and I do not need to have faith to reach that conclusion. To me it is self evident, from man's very nature. But I also recognize that others may see my convictions as a 'belief,' requiring faith. I don't agree, but I understand their point."

This makes sense. My own view is that the empirical evidence adds further to the self-evident nature of human rights. Freedom *works*, for the physical as well as the moral success of the human species. If we had not had many centuries to examine the relative success or failure of human societies that have existed in the context of respect for natural rights on the one hand, and the denial of such rights on the other hand, my convictions (and, I suspect, those of many others) about the self-evident nature of these rights would be less strong. But the evidence is in. Societies that recognize the natural rights of their citizens, that protect those rights from the depredations of others, are by far the most productive and successful societies as measured by prosperity, length of life, and other objective indicators of human well being. For editor and columnist Virginia Postrel, in *The Future and Its Enemies*, these practical arguments are transcendent.

> We have learned through sometimes bitter trial-and-error history that some behavior is compatible with human life, with peace and prosperity, and with increasing happiness and knowledge, and some is not. . . . We are well served to tolerate diverse personal goals . . . to avoid hurting people who hurt no one themselves, and to respect the bonds of life not because natural forms tell us to do so but because we have learned through long and difficult cultural evolution that these rules will, more often than not, improve the human condition.[24]

Following the same line of reasoning, the nineteenth-century classical liberals who asserted that natural rights flow from the characteristics of human nature also allowed that those rights flowed from "the conditions required for social cooperation." That sums it up pretty well. If we recognize natural rights, and organize ourselves in such a way as to protect them, life works. Societies in which the rights of individuals are respected culturally and protected by law, where individuals are prohibited from interfering with the equal rights of other individuals but are otherwise free to lead their own lives as they see fit, are societies that prosper.

This brings us back to treating others as we would be treated as the basis for the appropriate conduct of our sexual lives. All of us want to be treated with dignity and respect, sexually as well as otherwise. We hope that others will not betray our trust, sexually or otherwise, and we should therefore do our utmost not to betray others' trust.

This moral code does not lead to an across-the-board condemnation of sex outside marriage; it certainly does not discourage the enjoyment of sexual pleasure; and it does not denounce homosexuality. If two persons love each other and hold each other in respect, there is nothing immoral about their living together as lovers prior to marriage, for example. Indeed, such trial marriages have become commonplace in middle-class America and they often represent the most moral as well as the most rational of available alternatives in today's world, when marriage frequently occurs, for sound reasons, many years after sexual maturity. An estimated four million unmarried American couples were cohabiting in 1996, according to the U.S. Census.[25] On the basis of their marital status, these eight million citizens are neither less or more moral than others. The morality of their behavior consists in the extent to which they are treating others as they would be treated.

On the other hand, the rule of treat-others-as-you-would-be-treated discourages marital infidelity under most (though not all) circumstances, and it condemns all nonconsenting sexual activity.

Following these principles, what about the morality of employing stimulating erotica, the morality of pornography? If I myself desire the freedom to choose what books I shall read and what movies and videos I shall watch, I must grant to my fellow adult human beings the same privilege. Under the Golden Rule I cannot deprive others of their right to choose their own entertainment (assuming that their entertainment does not impinge on *my* rights), just as I would not want them choosing my entertainment for me, or forbidding any form of any entertainment to me. The Golden Rule demands tolerance.

Other aspects of the sexually explicit depictions issue are only slightly less straightforward. Depictions that are created from people's imaginations—drawings, cartoons, paintings, comics—should be permitted to those who want to have them. In the production of movies and videos by performers and producers, the treat-others-like-yourself principle requires that all performers participate voluntarily, that they be treated with dignity and respect, and that they treat others similarly.

Sex is not bad. Sexual activity, by itself, is not immoral, or even morally suspect. Sexual fantasy and the dissemination of materials that fuel fantasies are not wrong. But Americans are still living with the legacy of powerful leaders of the Christian church, who decried all that is sexual in human beings as disgusting, and who have persuaded generations of us to believe that all forms of sexual pleasure are sinful. These were foolish and dangerous men. It is time we outlived their malevolent legacy.

NOTES

1. Morton Hunt, *The Compassionate Beast: What Science Is Discovering About the Humane Side of Humankind* (New York: William Morrow, 1990), p. 88.

2. Ibid.

3. William Manchester, *A World Lit Only By Fire* (Newport Beach, Calif:. Back Bay Books, 1992), p. 7.

4. James Haught, *Holy Hatred* (Amherst, N.Y.: Prometheus Books, 1995), p. 11.

5. "Indecisive India," *The Economist*, March 7, 1998, p. 16.

6. *ABC News*, December 6, 1998.

7. "Orthodox Israelis Assault Jews Praying at Western Wall," *New York Times*, June 13, 1997.

8. "In America; A War on Women," *New York Times*, October 4, 1998.

9. Lester Thurow, *The Future of Capitalism* (New York: William Morrow, 1996), p. 266.

10. Haught, *Holy Hatred,* p. 19.

11. Hunt, *The Compassionate Beast*, p. 89.

12. "Islamic Emblem of Faith Also Trigger for Bias," *New York Times*, November 3, 1997.

13. Debra Haffner, "The Really Good News: What the Bible Says About Sex," *SIECUS Report*, October/November 1997, p. 3.

14. Ibid, p. 5.

15. Reay Tannahill, *Sex In History* (Lanham, Md.: Scarborough House, 1992), p. 138–148.

16. Ibid.

17. Saint Augustine, *The City of God*; quoted in G. Walsh, *The Role of Religion in History* (New Brunswick, N.J.: Transaction Publishers, 1998), p. 173.

18. Richard A. Posner, *Sex and Reason* (Cambridge: Harvard University Press, 1992), p. 17.

19. Or during Whitsun week, or on feast days or fast days. At one point, there were only, on average, five days per month when sex was acceptable. Tannahill, *Sex in History*, p. 151.

20. James Haught, "Sex and God: Is Religion Twisted?" *Free Inquiry* (fall 1997): 26.

21. Saint Augustine, *Confessions* (London: Penguin Classics, 1961), p. 43.

22. Walsh, *The Role of Religion in History*, p. 172.

23. A. V. Friedman, *Marital Intimacy* (Northrale, N.J.: Jason Aronson 1996), pp. 38–76.

24. Virginia Postrel, *The Future and Its Enemies*, (New York: Free Press, 1998, p. 166–66.

25. "Issues & Ideas—All in the So-Called Family," *National Journal*, September 19, 1998.

CHAPTER TWELVE

ALABAMA PILES ON

It was May 14, 1993, and we were being raided again.

Sitting at my desk earlier that morning I had been startled when the receptionist apologetically ushered four Alabama postal inspectors into my office. They showed me their badges. "Here we go again," I said.

My emotions seemed to be bungee jumping, from flashes of anger to resignation to feeling outright despair that this could still be going on after seven years.

This was the same investigative team from Montgomery, Alabama, that had already raided us the previous December. They had spent two days combing through our records, shutting down our operations, and confiscating our property. Now they were back, inventing new excuses to disrupt our business.

The sequence of raids and intimidation was exhausting and demoralizing, to say the least. First came the massive raid of May 1986, seven years earlier; we had been indicted and tried in 1987. We had been threatened by the Western District of Kentucky via a series of subpoenas calling for the production of huge amounts of documentation; two of our top managers had been required to appear before a grand jury in Louisville. Six of us had been indicted in the state of Utah, brought to Salt Lake City, and arraigned there—these indictments were still outstanding. Alabama's two-day raid in 1992 had included postal inspectors sleeping overnight in our customer service area, avowedly to preserve the "integrity" of the investigation, something I found especially invasive of our privacy.

By now the press seemed to be getting almost as weary of all this as we were.

On December 4, 1992, the occasion of the first Alabama raid, the Raleigh *News and Observer* headlined an editorial "GOVERNMENT'S DIRTY WORK."

A clique of hard-driving government prosecutors is after Phil Harvey of Carrboro. He hasn't robbed any banks, killed anyone or ripped off any savings and loans. The prosecutors simply don't like the business he's in, and they want to shut it down.

Just this week . . . 30 postal inspectors swarmed onto the premises of PHE's mail-order shop, Adam & Eve, to dig through magazines, videos and file drawers. This time, they said, Harvey is suspected of violating federal obscenity laws in Alabama.

The very idea of 30 federal officers spending days flipping through dirty pictures would be comical if it weren't so real. North Carolina workplace safety inspectors are stretched thin looking for firetraps and limb-threatening machinery. The police are getting shot at by violent criminals. The caseloads of local district attorneys brim with drug dealers and murderers. Yet the federal government has the time and money to harass a guy who sells "sensual accouterments."

The *Daily Tar Heel*, the student newspaper at the University of North Carolina in Chapel Hill, chimed in on December 9.

. . . Last week's raid investigating obscenity charges from Alabama came on the heels of charges from Utah . . . which came on the heels of charges in Alamance County . . . and in Kentucky.

. . . It's time for the government to get off [Harvey's] back.

We had been covered since July of 1990 by the injunction from Judge Green in Washington which forbade the government from indicting us in more than one jurisdiction during the pendancy of our civil case. But the Alabama group was bent on getting around the injunction. The postal inspector who led the team, Beryl (B. B.) Hedrick, informed us through press conferences that he believed we could be indicted for "money laundering" because the injunction from Judge Green covered only obscenity indictments. In addition Hedrick had searched out the case of Alexandria Quinn, a matter he thought he might be able to turn into a "child pornography" prosecution against us, and he was now determined to work this angle for all it was worth.

Alexandria Quinn was born Diane Stewart in (we now think) 1973. In 1989 and 1990, before reaching her eighteenth birthday, she had presented professionally forged identification (a birth certificate and a driver's license with her photo on it) to prove she was of age so that she could perform in adult videos. She appeared to be well over twenty-one (see Fig. 12-1), and

Figure 12-1.
Diane Stewart at 17.

her ID appeared to be completely valid. She had taken small roles in several dozen adult films and videos produced in California, and in October 1992 word began circulating that she had been underage when some of the videos were made.

The adult film industry takes this issue very seriously. The Free Speech Coalition, the trade association for adult film and video producers, has a standing $10,000 reward for anyone who can help convict real child pornographers. That reward has been paid at least once. Further, when there is ever a suggestion that a performer in a sexually explicit video may have been underage during the shoot, aggressive steps are taken. Phones ring all over the country, faxes are sent, titles of the films and videos concerned are immediately broadcast to all concerned distributors, cassettes are whisked off shelves, and research is done to ferret out the participation of such a performer in even the smallest role in the most obscure film. When we had gotten word about Alexandria Quinn's age in late October of 1992, we had immediately pulled all videos in which she appeared from our shelves, had segregated the videocassettes in an isolated corner of our warehouse, obtained a fire permit to destroy them, and, a few weeks later, burned them.

Postal Inspector Beryl Hedrick knew all this. In his December 1992 raid on our firm he had seen numerous memos expressing our urgent concern over this issue, documenting the immediate action we had taken to pull the Quinn tapes from our shelves, and the documentation of the destruction of the tapes, which included a Polaroid photo of the fire. It was on the record that we took the issue seriously and had done everything we could do to immediately cease the sale or dissemination of tapes that might include an underage performer.

The issue was complicated by the fact that Quinn had also appeared in numerous films shot after her eighteenth birthday, and these were perfectly legal. The producers in California did quite a responsible job of sorting this out. Indeed, Hedrick was quoted in the press as stating that "the industry [including PHE] generally responded well" to the Alexandria Quinn crisis.

For another prosecutor, these responses would have been sufficient. Indeed, the 1986–87 case in Alamance had at first included an indictment of our company for "exploitation of a minor" because of a similar age-falsification case involving another mature-looking actress named Traci Lords. Once the Alamance County prosecutors were convinced that we had had no way of knowing Lord's age, and that we had taken all appropriate steps to cease dissemination of the videos in a timely manner when we did learn of her age, they simply dropped the count.[1]

But Beryl Hedrick of Alabama knew he could hurt us merely by *accusing* us of child pornography, and if, as he seemed determined to do, he could catch us out in a mistake, such as having missed one or two copies of a Quinn video and let them slip through the system after the date on which we had learned about the falsification, he might even have the basis for an indictment. Such a mistake would normally be outside the legal definition of a proscribable act, particularly in the context of our very clear corporate policies and practices on this matter, but Hedrick was out to use his prosecutorial wiles in any way he could to harm us. It was his determination about the Alexandria Quinn matter that was the motive force behind the second Alabama raid.

In his first raid Hedrick had confiscated a magnetic computer tape containing the names and addresses of more than twenty thousand of our Alabama customers. Through subpoenaed documents, and material seized in the second raid, he was able to identify individual Alabamans who had purchased videos in which Quinn had appeared. He and his associates then went door-to-door in Alabama, confronting customers who had purchased these tapes and forcing them to turn over their copies of *Curse of the Catwoman* and a few other videos that featured Quinn. One customer was accosted by federal authorities in his office and forced to leave work, go home, and search for his *Catwoman* tape.

Now, in May 1993, my thoughts went something like this: *If this talentless little man can march in here with the full authority of the federal government, trespass on our property that we have worked for years to be able to purchase and use as our own; if he can confiscate even such private things as the names and addresses on our mailing list, violating our fiduciary responsibilities to our customers; if he and his automaton inspectors can come up here from Alabama and virtually shut us down, in our own building, in a dogged search for a mistake solely because they disagree with the content of our ideas, how can this be a free country?*

I was seething. Late in the morning, I saw two of Hedrick's inspectors chatting amiably with a couple of our artists, comparing notes on the capabilities of Apple Macintosh computers, which were fairly new to us at the time. On previous raids, our employees had surprised the inspectors by engaging in such friendly discourse with them and, on more than one occasion inspectors had remarked to me off the record about how friendly, capable, and loyal our employees seemed to be. Clearly they were impressed, and I have no doubt that such instances redounded to our benefit.

But I had reached the end of my tether that day, and I icily reminded both the inspectors and our employees that the sole reason for the raiders being there was to destroy the jobs of the very artists and designers they were talking to, to destroy our capacity to buy, let alone use, computers, and that their conversations should be conducted in that light.

Confronting Hedrick a little later I told him, between clenched teeth, that he would not, repeat not, steal from us the names of any more of our customers. He replied that he would take anything he wanted as long as it was covered by the warrant. "Go ahead," I said. "You've got the guns"—several of the raiders were armed—"take anything you want. Why not steal the furniture too?"

This sort of adolescent outburst did us no good, but I was no longer able to repress it. I even let my feelings show through in a couple of press interviews, something all of our attorneys had carefully warned me against. But I don't much regret the following remark, quoted in the *Chapel Hill Herald* on December 4: "I think it's clear that the religious zealots who are in charge of the US [Justice Department] simply persuaded the Attorney General's Office to continue their harassment. It's making me mad. When your government comes in and behaves like a jackass, you do get angry."[2]

Of course, the government was angry, too. Dave Rudolf's law partner Tom Maher is quoted in the same story: "It irritates them no end that they can't get Phil Harvey. . . . [H]e's been kind of a constant thorn in their side." The Raleigh *News and Observer* had similarly noted, following the December raid, "Harvey sells sexually explicit merchandise, and he evidently is driving the US Justice Department up the wall."[3] An observer suggested to reporter Melinda Ruley that I was particularly irksome to the government because "he leads a quiet life, doesn't live in a mansion with a succession of centerfolds. And he knows which fork to use."[4] "What infuriates prosecutors," added Dave Rudolf, "is [Harvey's] unwillingness to bow to the pressure. He's taken a very public stance, he's become a metaphor."[5]

Some of this may have been true (though I'm not so sure about the forks), but what we were doing, really, was hanging on. The current pretty well pulled us through the rapids, and we just kept repairing the raft and climbing back on it. By now, I didn't really feel we had a choice; simple honor demanded that we fight to the finish.

Hedrick and his Alabama colleagues explored every possible angle. They could not indict us on obscenity charges as long as we were under indictment in Utah and Judge Green's injunction was in effect. But Hedrick continued with his litany on "money laundering" and "child pornography" matters. He did a lot of prosecution by way of the press. Of all those who set out to intimidate and harass us, Hedrick was the most inclined to use interviews with reporters to keep the heat on. He was quoted in the Raleigh *News and Observer* on May 5, 1993, reiterating that "charges such as . . . money laundering could still be prosecuted under the injunction, because they are not grouped as obscenity charges." He told the *Chapel Hill Herald* that federal law allows distributors to be charged for child pornography even if they don't know the performers are under age.[6] While this issue had been the subject of litigation, the statement was wrong at the time Hedrick made it, and he knew it was wrong.*

The money-laundering angle was absurd. It would have been an obvious violation of the injunction barring obscenity indictments to bring an indictment for money laundering that, of necessity, would have to be tied to an obscenity charge. Like the RICO statutes, the grounds for bringing an indictment for money laundering are very broad; it can be brought if you simply deposit sales proceeds in the bank, if the government maintains that those proceeds were illegally obtained. Not even Hedrick, I think, had the chutzpah to try that, but he insisted he was working on it and he succeeded, in keeping with the government's overall strategy, in forcing us to defend against these fresh accusations, to spend more money on legal fees, and, in Rob Showers's phrase, to "keep us running around the country" defending ourselves.

But Hedrick's accusations were more than simply costly and demoralizing to us. The accusations of child pornography threatened our reputation, at least locally. Fortunately, most newspaper reporters took the time to get both sides of the story and to learn that the matter at issue did not concern children at all, but rather a mature seventeen-year-old.

Hedrick was also overstepping his legal bounds. He and his thirty agents seized a good deal of material that was not covered by their search warrant. The warrant was confined to corporate records and videotapes belonging to PHE, Inc., but Hedrick's team seized, in addition, a lot of material belonging

---

*Mr. Hedrick was well versed in the *scienter* requirements for child pornography prosecutions (see n. 1). At that time, a possessor/seller of sexually oriented expressive material was not legally liable under child pornography statutes if he or she did not know (and had not deliberately avoided knowing) a performer's age.

to other affiliated independent companies. To cover their tracks they claimed, wrongly, that these companies were merely trade names of PHE. We informed them during the search that this was not so, but they "did not have time" to call the North Carolina Secretary of State's office to verify the independent corporate status of the other companies. Instead they assumed their way to seizure of a considerable amount of material that was not covered by the warrant.

The discovery of independent affiliated companies (which, after the raid was over, he decided to recognize) gave Hedrick yet one more idea as to how he might skirt Judge Green's injunction and still get at us. In an interview with the *Chapel Hill Herald*, he pointed out that the injunction "only addressed PHE and Phil Harvey. There are certainly other facets to the company"—meaning the affiliate and subsidiary companies—"and other officers and directors" that could be the target of obscenity charges. In other words, Hedrick was now rattling his saber about the prospect of indicting people like marketing manager Peggy Oettinger and former vice president A. C. Bushnell, who were not individually covered by the injunction, or indicting one of our affiliate organizations, which would have required the same massive defense against simultaneous prosecutions that the injunction was intended to prohibit. We did not think that Judge Green would permit such a transparent violation of the spirit of her order, but this did not stop Hedrick from threatening us with it and from continuing an intensive investigation based on such far-fetched possibilities. Like the earlier Department of Justice activities against us, it, too, had the quality of a crusade by a true believer.

Peggy relates a story about Hedrick's way of dealing with people that still makes her tremble when she retells it. During the second raid, the Alabama postal inspectors had removed from the bulletin board in her office a memo marked "Attorney-Client Communication/Privileged." Such documents cannot be seized by prosecutors (or any opposing litigants), and Peggy demanded from Hedrick that he return it. He tried to bluff her; it would be too much trouble to locate for such a minor matter, the papers were all stored in boxes . . . why bother? Peggy was furious. She insisted, as was her uncontroverted right, that the privileged document be returned, and said she would enlist Dave Rudolf's help if necessary. After some delay, Hedrick grudgingly complied, and the document was returned. But he could not let this defeat go unpunished. Leaning close to her face, he asked Peggy, "How's your new house? I understand it cost over $500,000. . . . " He wanted her to know that he was investigating her personal life; that he had the power to embarrass her with her family and her friends and that he could crumble her personal world if he wanted to. "He was effective," Peggy admitted.

"Sounds like a slimeball to me," I said.

"That's being kind," Peggy said.

This is the sort of tactic that I fear is often employed against other parties to great effect. As Peggy noted, Hedrick and his colleagues "may not have ultimately gotten away with these kinds of tactics in our case because we fought back, but they get away with it all the time with others they're out to punish—even when there's no crime."

This time, it wasn't just our rights that were being violated; Hedrick and his fellow inspectors systematically invaded the rights of many of our customers as well. The *News and Observer* had criticized the Alabama inspectors for "snooping into the private business of law-abiding citizens," when they took our mailing list of Alabama buyers, and added "that's not out of character for this bunch [which has] never been too keen on the Constitution."[7] Our advertising manager, Mary Anne Kluger, reported numerous phone calls from Alabama customers who complained that postal inspectors had searched their homes and seized documents under threat of grand jury subpoena:

Customers have reported to PHE that the postal inspectors—including a postal inspector named Hedrick—took the following actions:

- an inspector appeared at a customer's place of business and gave the customer the ultimatum either to close and leave the customer's business immediately to travel home to produce documents and videotapes, or to appear before the grand jury.
- an inspector appeared unannounced at a customer's home at 9:00 P.M. . . . and without any warrant demanded—in front of the customer's wife—that the customer produce documents and videotapes. . . .
- in connection with several warrantless seizures made in customers' homes, postal inspectors insisted that customers view videotapes in the presence of the postal inspectors.
- postal inspectors have informed customers that the government obtained PHE's mailing list.[8]

To deliberately intimidate and embarrass private citizens who have done nothing other than engage in a voluntary transaction involving presumptively legal materials was unconscionable. Entering their homes without a search warrant was highly improper.[9] The immorality of this Big Brother snooping was all the more glaring because several postal employees had been murdered on the job that same year. "In the name of all that is holy," Peggy said in my office, "why can't they spend their time tracking down the murderers of their own colleagues?"

We were seeing again how easy it can be for rogue elements in a bloated government to inflict their personal values on their fellow citizens. Our business involved nothing worse than visual material that contained images and ideas that these prosecutors found distasteful.

Before all this took place, we had had over three thousand customers in the Middle District of Alabama, people who had ordered materials of various kinds from us and who were, I have every reason to believe, decent and honorable people who were satisfied with our services. Hedrick was well aware of the extent of his fellow Alabamans' interest in our products because he had confiscated portions of our mailing list. There had also been twenty or thirty prohibitory orders entered by citizens of the Middle District of Alabama, formal requests to the post office that we be instructed not to mail them anything further. Most of these requests were in response to the "Free Adult Catalog" postcards we use to help screen out persons who are not interested in getting our catalog—by now our consistent policy. For Hedrick and his boss Terry Moorer, the thirty "complaints" carried a great deal more weight than the three thousand customers who wished to do business with us. For them the urgent need was to shut down the availability of sexual materials for *everyone.*

And now, if they could catch us in a mistake of having let a Quinn tape slip through our system after we had learned about the age problem, they could nail us. Many of our current and former employees were subpoenaed to testify before an Alabama grand jury, and two employees, Jerry Craig* and Hilda Eubanks, were required to go to Montgomery to testify pursuant to those subpoenas. Alabama inspectors interviewed nine employees and at least one former employee. They subpoenaed three copies each of 150 different video titles, and records—purchase orders and other proof-of-sale documents—from various producers that supplied us with video product. They conducted raids on five video producers in California in a further attempt to "catch" us shipping a Quinn video a day or even an hour after we had learned of the age problem. They subpoenaed records concerning PHE from independent packaging and mailing services. They searched another business run by a former PHE employee in pursuit of PHE-related records. They scheduled a second grand jury session for May 25, 1993, and subpoenaed a PHE employee to testify there. When I wanted to rub salt into my wounds,

---

*Jerry Craig retains the dubious honor of being the only PHE employee to serve time in jail in service of our cause, though it was not in Alabama. As the designated custodian of some subpoenaed corporate records, Jerry accompanied the documents to the federal courthouse in Jacksonville, Florida, in 1993. On the advice of our legal team, he withheld some of the documents from the court, our side maintaining that the prosecutors (in a largely unrelated case) did not have a right to them. The judge found PHE and Jerry in contempt and ordered him to jail. He spent most of the day there until, as nightfall approached, we capitulated and relinquished the records.

I contemplated how much tax money we were paying to cover the cost of such activities.

All this was done in the hope that we had failed to round up, confiscate, and destroy every single copy of every one of hundreds of copies of the many dozens of videotapes in which Alexandria Quinn had appeared before her eighteenth birthday. It is unlikely that, even had we made such a mistake (and we did not), we would have been culpable for it as a legal matter. At an evidentiary hearing with Hedrick and Alabama Assistant U.S. Attorney Terry Moorer, attended also by Dave Rudolf and his colleague Tom Maher, U.S. Magistrate Judge Russell Eliason had asked Moorer and Hedrick if they really expected to find evidence that we had *deliberately* shipped a Quinn tape after learning about the performer's age: ". . . not mistaken shipment but intentional shipment."[10] Judge Eliason made it clear that he was not likely to support further searches in pursuit of nothing more than an honest error. Confronted with this challenge, Moorer testified, under oath, that Mr. Hedrick had uncovered some evidence of just such a deliberate act. I am sorry to have to say that this representation was a lie. There could have been no evidence of such an act because no such act occurred, nor has any evidence of it—even suggestive evidence—ever come to light in any of several subsequent proceedings or negotiations. The Alabama postal inspectors, apparently desperate to find a way around Judge Green's injunction, were simply inventing nonexistent facts to support their case.

Before commanding his first raid on us, Hedrick had gone undercover at our local post office, posing as a mailman, a fact he subsequently revealed to a reporter at the *Chapel Hill Herald*. After helping load 205 sacks of outgoing mail at PHE, he persuaded two of our employees to give him a "ten-cent tour" of the building, a venture Hedrick found "interesting and informative."[11] I'm glad he did this. The willingness of our employees to show interested outsiders around our premises is a policy of which we are proud. Our company has always dealt openly with law enforcement authorities and with post office employees and with any other interested parties who conduct themselves cordially. In fact, the more people know about us the better. As Fred Harwell, the lawyer who represented most of our unindicted employees, pointed out, the early effort to get our employees to spill the beans about the supposedly nefarious goings on at our firm produced additions to the record of more and more information that reflected well on us and therefore weakened the government's case. So let the sun shine in.

In the midst of all this, a bombshell: Utah dropped its case! On November 2, 1993, the U.S. Attorney's Office in Salt Lake City, now under the direction of newly appointed U.S. Attorney Scott Matheson Jr., who had taken Dee

Benson's place the previous August, cancelled the indictments. Whether it was because the new U.S. attorney simply had no stomach for a five-year-old case of doubtful legality, whether Judge Winder's predicament had convinced him to move on to other things, thereby letting the judge off the hook of having to decide the hard questions about Richard Lambert's conduct as ordered by the appeals court in Denver, or for other reasons, Utah bowed out.

The reasons stated by two assistant U.S. attorneys from the Utah office were revealing, and seemed to vindicate aspects of our strategy. The government's motion for dismissal noted that the case "is not readily provable at this time," because a jury would have had to use the community standards of 1986 to determine, in a trial that could have occurred no earlier than 1994,[12] if the material we had shipped in was legally obscene.

This indicated that our motion for dismissal due to delay of indictment had made an impression. In addition Utah Assistant U.S. Attorneys David Schwendiman and Stanley Olsen told the *Chapel Hill Herald* that the prospect of "further legal maneuvering" by our attorneys was "a strong deterrent to a prosecution team that wanted to move on to other cases."[13] Further, they claimed victory for Utah because we had stopped shipping materials into the state many years previously. Our lawyers' decision that we should cease such shipments back in 1986 had provided some important cover to the U.S. Attorney's Office for the dismissal of the Utah case.

Again, we were ecstatic. This part of a seven-year war of attrition had come to an end. Utah's Lambert had been on our case from the start. From the coordinated raid in May of 1986 through all of the most tortuous negotiations, threats of annihilation, and out-of-business demands, Lambert had been at the forefront. Now it looked as if he would emerge from all this without trying a single obscenity case. More reassuring to us, Utah represented the last possibility of our being tried for materials that had not been cleared through our outside review process. This process had been well established early in 1987, and it was certain now, whether in Alabama or elsewhere, that anything we might be indicted for would be material shipped after that date, material reviewed by two sex therapists before we offered it for sale. The therapist reviews would constitute a very powerful defense at trial and represented a significant strengthening of our overall defenses.

Whole categories of worries were thus eliminated at a single stroke. Most relieved of all were Fred Fuller and A. C. Bushnell, whose actions as (now former) employees of PHE were all now beyond the five-year statute of limitations. This was true as well of former marketing director Ann Busenburg, whose indictment had been dropped, due to her lawyer's skillful persistence, several months before.

But for the rest of us—for me, Peggy, and other current officers of the company—Utah's decision posed another potential danger. Was Alabama now free to indict us? True to form, Hedrick notified the press that they could do so. "If Utah's been dismissed, that certainly leaves the door open for a new game plan" in Alabama, he asserted to the *Chapel Hill Herald*, four days after the Utah decision. I was now pessimistic about Alabama—perhaps more pessimistic than I should have been. The *Herald* reported:

> Federal prosecutors in Utah have dropped obscenity charges against PHE, Inc., but that doesn't mean company president Phil Harvey is ready to declare victory in his battle with the government.
>
> Why not? Because he expects a grand jury in Montgomery, Ala., to hand up indictments by the middle of the month against him, other company officials and a PHE subsidiary.
>
> That knowledge left Harvey ruing Friday what he called the "irony of what at first glance appears to be a very positive development" for PHE in Utah. The company's legal problems continue.
>
> "They tied us down for three years and made us spend $1.5 million, and they're getting ready to do the same thing all over again in twelve days," he said of the US Justice Department's effort to prosecute the mail order company. "It's not really much of a respite."[14]

Our attorneys were not so sure that Alabama could now indict. The temporary injunction from Judge Green forbade indictment of PHE "in more than one federal judicial district" during the pendency of the civil suit, and we'd already had one. Further, her injunction contained language supporting an argument that a single indictment was all Judge Green had intended to permit. "[I]t is clear that their [plaintiffs'] First Amendment rights cannot be adequately protected by defending themselves simultaneously *or seriatim* in each separate district in which they may be indicted" (emphasis added). The DOJ maintained that Judge Green had meant we could only be indicted in one place at a time; we were not so sure. This issue would have to be determined by Judge Green herself.

Meanwhile we girded for the prospect of an Alabama indictment. Hedrick's press strategy might now be transformed into serious litigation.

The civil case was set to go to trial in a matter of weeks. Both we and the government faced the prospect of huge workloads, massive expenditures, and, in the government's case, possible embarrassing revelations.*

It is under such circumstances that negotiations become possible. And

---

*We had nothing further to reveal, a situation I have always found salubrious.

indeed, Bruce Ennis and his team in Washington began to get tentative hints that the beginning of the end game might just be near.

Each side held a club. For a Justice Department under a new administration (President Clinton had been sworn in ten months before), the civil case represented an acute potential embarrassment. They would have to contend with the conflicting testimony from Bill Delahoyde and the two FBI agents; with embarrassing revelations about the government's "punitive animus" in pursuing us; with the now well-documented misbehavior of several Justice Department lawyers; and probably with other revelations about which we did not yet know. The civil trial was not likely to play well for the government in the press, and they knew we were not afraid of press coverage. All this gave us substantial leverage.

For our part, a trial in Montgomery, Alabama, was not a pleasant prospect. We were confident we could win if we put on another full-court press, but there is always a chance of losing, especially in a conservative venue. And we were weary. A trial in Alabama would cost us a half million dollars, minimum. The civil trial was going to cost us even more—perhaps much more and our resources were getting thin. We longed for a year or two when our bottom line would not be gouged by the huge legal expense in our accounting statement. If the government would give up the Alabama case and any other cases representing material shipped before a reasonably contemporaneous date, that would be something very important to us. I had told the *Chapel Hill Herald* the previous July, "There are a lot of strands in the tapestry, a lot of things going on. At some point it's in the interests of both parties to put an end to it. We're all getting tired of it."[15]

Both sides prepared to negotiate. I only wished I felt as calm as I was trying to appear.

NOTES

1. The law requires what is called *scienter* in situations of this sort. If a reasonable person has no way of knowing that a particular performer is under the age of eighteen (which applies particularly when the performer has systematically misrepresented his or her age and appears mature), a producer or seller cannot be held liable under the child pornography statutes, providing they have kept proper records that establish the performer's age.

2. "X-rated Firm Raid X-asperates Owner," *Chapel Hill Herald*, December 4, 1992. It was not until several years later that I learned about an incident that would have delighted me at the time, had I known about it. Two of Hedrick's inspectors—"suits" as they were thought of in the informal environs of Carrboro, North Carolina—stopped for

a beer at a local country bar run by a former employee of ours who called herself Booger. Booger's bar was a place where a good old boy in bib overalls might be found playing pool with a biker in shredded jeans and chrome-studded leather, so the suits were conspicuous. Booger was a guitar player, a composer of country music, a poet. She presided over the bar. "I hope you aren't two of the assholes who are up the road harassing my friends at PHE," she greeted them.

3. "Warrant Details US Agents' Search for Pornography," *Raleigh News and Observer,* December 4, 1992.

4. Melinda Ruley, "Trouble in Paradise, Making a Federal Case Out of Adam & Eve's Sex Toys," *Chapel Hill (N.C.) Independent Weekly,* March 27, 1991, p. 27.

5. "Warrant Details US Agents' Search for Pornography."

6. "PHE Probe Eyed," *Chapel Hill Herald,* May 8, 1993.

7. "Government's Dirty Work," *Raleigh News and Observer,* December 4, 1992.

8. Affidavit of Mary Anne Kluger, March 4, 1993.

9. It was also almost certainly unlawful. The Fourth Amendment states "The right of the people to be secure in their persons, houses, papers, and effects, against unreasonable searches and seizures, shall not be violated. . . . " This means that you may not enter people's homes and confiscate their property without a warrant, or the owner's consent. The threat of a forced appearance before a grand jury to coerce compliance gives new meaning to the word "consent." Supreme Court Justice Louis Brandeis (in *Olmstead* v. *United States*) stated that our Founding Fathers had "conferred, as against the government, the right to be let alone . . . the right most prized by civilized men." The Alabama searches were a clear violation of this right.

10. Transcript of Hearing on Motion for Return of Seized Property, *In re PHE, Inc.,* Civil Case No. 1:93M150 (M.D.N.C. August 30, 1993), at 4.

11. "Probe of PHE Has Produced No Indictments," *Chapel Hill Herald,* July 18, 1993.

12. The snail's pace at which these proceedings had moved was again evident. The Utah indictments had been handed down in 1991. Hearings, motions, and the interlocutory appeal had consumed more than two years.

13. "PHE Charges Dropped in Utah," *Chapel Hill Herald,* November 6, 1993.

14. Ibid.

15. "Warrant Details US Agents' Search for Pornography."

CHAPTER THIRTEEN

THE ANXIETY OF LIBERTY
AND THE TEMPTATION
TO CONTROL

Whoever would overthrow the liberty of the nation must begin by subduing the freedom of speech.

—Cato's *Letters*

I t is the dream of every dictator, and many conservatives and socialists, to create order. An orderly society of well-behaved citizens, marching toward a future with few surprises, seems enormously appealing to the cautious mind. It suggests that everything is under control and will remain so. Reason and order will guide us. Wise and appropriately trained people, each expert in his or her own specialty, will make the important decisions about our economic, political, and cultural life. The streets will be safe. Aberrant behavior will be swiftly but justly punished. The trains will run on time. Wealth will be reasonably distributed, no one having conspicuously and embarrassingly greater wealth than his neighbor. A discussion of unpleasantly disrespectful ideas will be confined to the academies and remain, by law, hypothetical. Everyone will be happy.

When you posit the case for freedom against the orderly ideal of the cautiously conservative, or socialist (in this respect conservatives and socialists are often in the same camp) way of organizing society, it is easy to see why so much of human history has been antifreedom. Certainly the idea of millions of people wandering around doing pretty much what they please, living under a government that does nothing more than protect them from the depredations of their fellow citizens and outside threats, but otherwise pretty much leaves them alone, is not very compelling. There is no plan. There is no framework. There is no overarching governmental design, no societal "ideal." How can people be happy if they aren't organized? Being inherently weak and imperfect, how can people be expected to behave if they are not made to behave?

Organization is necessary for economic activity, for the production of wealth; it turns out that human beings will organize themselves for such activity remarkably well. Indeed they do so much better if left alone.

As to the second matter, government is particularly inept at coercing private morality, and morality cannot be coerced in any event. Virtue requires freedom.

Let us address the matter of economic freedom first. All the government needs to do to "organize" economic activity is to provide a sound legal framework that prevents theft and fraud and makes contracts enforceable, and maintain a sound currency. Economic behavior consequently is remarkably orderly, and usually very complex, far more complex, intricate, and finely tuned than anything that can be engineered by any government. Consider the multifaceted actions required to put a seven-dollar bottle of good Australian wine on the shelves of an American supermarket.

It takes vintners and barrel makers and stave makers and ink makers and label makers, box makers, transport workers, ship captains, cork makers, the makers of the things that make it possible to make cork, the refiners of the oil that lubricates the pistons that drive the ships that bring the wine across the sea; one could go on for pages cataloging the components involved in bringing a bottle of Australian wine to an American supermarket. Yet all these things go on routinely, day after day, without any "plan," without any facilitating supervision. Indeed, government actions generally impede these processes, through taxes, tariffs, import quotas, export restrictions, and such indirect impediments as minimum wages and regulations that dictate everything from sulfite levels in wine (sulfites are harmless) to the shape of toilet seats in employees' restrooms. Still, the wine arrives, and is of good quality. Perhaps thirty thousand other products also show up on those supermarket shelves, through simultaneous, intricate networks of activity. They are utterly beyond the capacity of any plan.

The fact of spontaneous economic order is remarkable. The idea of millions of people going about their daily lives without instruction from some centralized authority, working together voluntarily and seeking their self-betterment to the betterment of all seems extremely unlikely. Yet the fact of this spontaneous order, a term and an idea first described by Adam Smith more than two hundred years ago, has been documented, observed, and commented upon for centuries. Smith's book *The Wealth of Nations* introduced the idea of the "invisible hand" in economic life, a hand that guides those who, seeking only their own self-betterment, end up, without intending to, benefiting the entire society. "It is not from the benevolence of the butcher, the brewer, or the baker that we expect our dinner," Smith sagely observed, "but from their regard to their own interest." And it was a contemporary of Adam Smith's,

Adam Ferguson, who first pointed out that many of the best organized components of civilized life were "the result of human action but not the execution of any human design."[1] The ironic result: when people are left alone with their innate propensity, in Smith's phrase, "to truck, barter, and exchange," a remarkably orderly society emerges. The orderliness of economic life, freely pursued, has often formed the basis for social progress in other spheres. The French philosopher Voltaire was quite astonished to find in eighteenth-century England that commercial intercourse was taking place in London between people of virtually all classes, religions, and nationalities. "Enter the London stock exchange," he wrote, "a place more respectable than many a court. You will see the deputies of all nations gathered there for the service of mankind. There, the Jew, the Mohammedan, and the Christian deal with each other as if they were of the same religion, and give the name of infidel only to those who go bankrupt."[2]

A key to the complexity, speed, and efficiency of spontaneous economic life is that *no party coerces another*. All trades are voluntary, with all parties to trading agreements benefiting (though not necessarily equally) from the process. When coercion creeps in, when a "plan" is imposed by the government, order begins to collapse. Trades are no longer voluntary. Prices may be fixed, disrupting the necessary flow of information in the marketplace. People begin trying to beat the system. Economic activity based not on mutual trading advantage but on connections and politics starts to take over. The morality of the marketplace suffers accordingly. Instead of free citizens engaging in voluntary trades, less-than-free citizens engage in various forms of cheating. This normally convinces those in control of the government that even more control is needed. Thus have evolved the left-wing totalitarian states of the twentieth century.

Policies that permit people to do whatever they want short of interfering with the equal rights of their fellow citizens may hardly seem a coherent program for human societies, but it has been proven to be so. If we assume that the proper role of government is to enable human happiness and prosperity, then the lesson of history is clear. The happiest, most prosperous societies, whose citizens live the longest, are those societies where the government interferes least in the economic lives of its citizens. See, for example, Fig. 13–1, which shows the correlation between economic freedom and length of life. The economic freedom scale was constructed by James Gwartney and his colleagues[3] and is a carefully designed index of the extent to which governments leave citizens alone in the economic sphere, taking into account such matters as government-mandated prices, prohibitions on the movement of capital, barriers to trade such as tariffs and import quotas, restrictions that inhibit the start

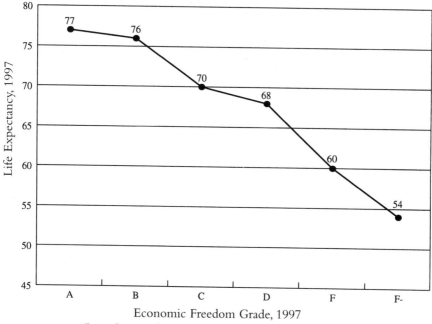

Economic Freedom Grade, 1997

(Sources: Gwartney and Lawson, Economic Freedom of the World, *pp. 22–23;*
Population Reference Bureau, World Population Data Sheet, 1997)

Figure 13–1. Average life expectancy and economic freedom.

up of new businesses, and the soundness of currency. The A and B countries are the freest in this regard, the F and F– countries are the most restrictive. The length of life data are from the Population Reference Bureau.[4] As can be readily seen, economic freedom is good for people. The wealth resulting from liberal economic policies improves health and lengthens life.[5]

If people in economically free societies live longer than people in economically repressive societies, why are governments so reluctant to let the invisible hand do its work? Why do governments persistently impose a heavy and coercive control on economic liberty?

Part of the reason is that governments are busybodies by nature. "What's the point of having this superb military . . . if we can't use it?" Madeleine Albright, then ambassador to the United Nations, once foolishly asked.[6] (The generals cringed. They knew the deterrent value of a strong military and Americans' reluctance to send their youth into battle.) Similarly, I suspect, governments—federal, state, and local—are, like the town busybody, predisposed by their very nature to interfere in other people's lives, using their power for no other reason than that they have it. I have been reminded of this by the Board of Directors of the Trails Property Owners Association in Chapel Hill, North Carolina. I own a home in this small development (called The Trails), which has perhaps forty households. Most of the houses are on half-acre lots or larger. The area is mostly in woods and is seven miles from the nearest town. The people who buy and live in these houses are not predisposed to the despoiling of their own property. The board of directors is elected from among the property owners in the development. Yet, even this tiny group of four or five people, "governing" a group of their own peers, has a persistent tendency to exert control. They examine requests for the building of a fence, the alteration of a wall, the decoration of a mailbox, or the cutting down of a single tree, for example, if it is "six (6) inches or more in diameter forty-eight (48) inches above ground level." It takes considerable time and effort for these people to exert their control over a few trees or a new fence. Unsupervised, the rest of us would almost certainly adhere to reasonable aesthetic and environmental standards. Yet because they have the authority, because other well-meaning people have earlier written rules into the bylaws, they seem to feel they must control the color of our fences and our mailboxes, just as Madeline Albright feels impelled to use the army.

If government on such a small scale tends to exercise and expand its powers, it is no wonder that larger governments—city, county, state, and federal—have a similarly innate tendency to grow, to control, to stifle. "The natural progress of things," said Thomas Jefferson, "is for liberty to yield and government to gain ground." How right he was.

Another reason for the persistent expansion of government power is the one James Madison particularly warned us of: the jostling at the trough of "factions," what we today call special interests, for favors from the government. Any group, any business, any group of businesses, any group of groups that has a strong economic motive to seek government assistance—favors that require government's coercive power—will inevitably seek such advantages. Adam Smith understood. He recognized that businesspeople, for example, will always seek ways of maintaining high prices at the expense of consumers. When they can get government to enforce policies that bring this about, they will facilitate the process with political contributions, persuasion, and outright bribes. Similarly, organized labor seeks minimum legal wages and government policies favoring unions, such as those that permit expenditure of union dues for political campaigns without members' permission. Sugar growers in the United States, through intense and successful lobbying, have gotten Congress to enact absurdly restrictive trade barriers that enable growers to sell sugar to the American public at twice the price at which it is available on the open international market.

This problem could be greatly ameliorated by making government smaller. The fact that the federal government takes two out of every ten dollars of national wealth and doles that money out in a whole variety of complicated and often dysfunctional ways means that the jostling at the trough is intense. It means that companies and unions and other factions will always be willing to pay very large sums of money to influence government policies. When there are hundreds of billions of dollars at stake, hundreds of millions of dollars will be spent pursuing them. This should surprise no one. The answer? Make government smaller. Many presidents have tried, but our government has kept growing, under Republicans and Democrats, under Ronald Reagan and George Bush as well as under Jimmy Carter and Bill Clinton. Government just gets bigger and bigger.

PRIVATE MORALITY

One of democracy's major flaws, one that probably led Winston Churchill to remark that democracy is the worst form of government except for all the others, is the tendency for the majority to impose its will on the minority. This has led to an astonishing array of coercive legislation in both the economic and the private (so-called moral) sphere.

It will be argued that people are sinful, that the government must make "bad" people less bad by forbidding behavior that is held to be improper or immoral by a majority of citizens. But when private peaceful behavior is interfered with coercively by the government, it is the coercers who are behaving immorally. "*Crimes* are those acts by which one man harms the person or property of another," wrote Lysander Spooner, a staunch champion of liberty, in 1875. "*Vices* are simply the errors which a man makes in his search after his own happiness. Unlike crimes, they imply no malice toward others, and no interference with their persons or property."[7] Spooner favored punishing the commission of crimes; he was adamantly opposed to the punishment of vices, in no small part because he recognized the enormous presumption it requires for one person to decide on behalf of another what constitutes the best path for seeking happiness. "In the midst of . . . [humankind's] endless variety of opinion, what man, or what body of men, has the right to say in regard to any particular action, or course of action, '*We* have tried this experiment, and determined every question involved in it? *We* have determined it, not only for ourselves, but for all others?"[8]

How can you, whoever you may be, decide for me, whoever I may be, what is the best and most appropriate path for me to take in seeking my own happiness and fulfillment? You cannot know. And I cannot know what is *your* best path to happiness. Therefore we must not interfere with each other. "The only purpose," to repeat John Stuart Mill's memorable phrase, "for which power can be rightfully exercised over any member of the civilized community, against his will, is to prevent harm to others." He was right. What my neighbor does in the privacy of his home is his concern, not mine, as long as it has no direct impact on me. If my neighbor chooses to consume alcohol or smoke marijuana or conduct (quiet) all-night poker games for high stakes, that is his concern, not mine. Indeed, I would be committing an act of immorality were I to enter his house, coercively, to prevent him from doing these things. It is equally immoral for the government to do it.

MORALITY AND PRIVATE BEHAVIOR

When government interferes in what the TV editorialist John Stossel calls "the private, peaceful" behavior of citizens, the government prostitutes the very function for which it was created. "Thomas Jefferson nailed three key points: Rights reside naturally in people. It is the job of governments to protect those rights. And the government that forgets the first two points can be replaced," notes Doug Esser in an Associated Press book review.[9]

When government interferes coercively in the private, peaceful lives of its citizens, it is also violating what I hold to be the most fundamental bedrock of morality, namely, that each of us should treat all others as we ourselves wish to be treated. Since all human beings wish to be left alone in the conduct of their private lives, they should not be interfered with in such conduct except to protect the rights of others. If you are following the Golden Rule, you cannot insist that the government should fine or incarcerate people for sodomy, smoking marijuana, or gambling. Indeed, when some citizens successfully work their will on others in such matters they invite reprisal. If Judge Bork, who advocates the abdication of the free speech clause of the First Amendment to the legislative branch of government, succeeds in depriving me of the right to read a "pornographic" book, he is inviting me to work through government to circumscribe what *he* may read in his own home.

There is yet another reason why government coercion of private, peaceful behavior is dysfunctional and that is this: morality coerced is not morality at all. "Virtue cannot exist without the freedom to make moral choices," notes author Doug Bandow. "Coerced acts of conformity with some moral norm . . . do not represent virtue."[10] Columnist Richard Hammer puts it even more forcefully: "[W]e can expect the individuals in a community in which government has legislated away all vices to have almost no moral standards whatever."[11] Attempting to make people virtuous by force results in a less virtuous society, because there are fewer opportunities to *choose* virtue, and, because the government has preempted moral decision making, we feel less obliged to behave morally. Instead, we begin looking for ways to beat the system.

WHAT OF THE FUTURE?

If government should, miraculously, learn to stay out of our economic lives and our private lives, would that not create great uncertainty? A future without a "plan" seems more uncertain than a future in which governments play a major role. But such an unplanned future is the only kind of future likely to be worth having.

As to the certainty of planning, consider recent history. The planned societies have had far less predictable and orderly futures than the societies that leave economic planning to the marketplace. The Soviet Union was planned, but from the vantage of 1950 or 1960, its future was most uncertain. And who would claim today that the planned economies of Cuba, or even of China in its apparently transitory phase, are as predictable, as likely to be as orderly, as the relatively unplanned economy of the United States? Thus we come to one of the enduring paradoxes of social systems: Planning leads to chaos; leaving people alone leads to order, and has the virtue of freedom as well. It has taken many centuries for humankind to grasp this awkward but fundamental truth, and many do not grasp it still.

Fearing the uncertainties of an unplanned future is natural. Admitting large numbers of immigrants, as the United States does, poses dangers and certainly a great many uncertainties. Yet a flow of immigrants also poses unpredictable wonders, diversities of mind and spirit, and unforeseeable accomplishments.

The establishment of women's rights, especially as expressed by ardent feminists, is frightening to many. What dangerous, anarchic forces will be unleashed? The Reverend Pat Robertson has suggested that feminism encourages women to "leave their husbands, kill their children, practice witchcraft, destroy capitalism, and become lesbians."[12] Yet most Americans recognize by now that women have the same unalienable rights as men, that they should be permitted full access to the political processes, and to equal employment opportunities at equal pay. And would less–than–equal rights for women mean greater order and predictability? I think not.

For those who revere rules and control, America's energetic, bubbling variety is a threat. The writer Grant McCracken calls this multiplicity of changes plenitude—"an ever-increasing variety of observable ways of living and being that are continually coming into existence." But instead of a benign plenitude, many, especially those on the Right, see "anarchic, willful, recklessly individualistic behavior everywhere. . . . [To them] the world feels tippy, puzzling, dangerous, and odd."[13]

Those who feel this way, says McCracken, try to stop the marvelous plenitude that is, in fact, America's tradition. They want to stop the cacophony, put an end to these revolutionary changes. "Suffer *this* and the world will come undone. 'This' has been the vote for women, access to high culture for those without educations, admission to law schools and medical schools for 'outsiders.' . . . [But] the world of plenitude is as accommodating as it is generative. It turns out the voice of grave and magisterial caution is almost always wrong."[14]

The economist F. A. Hayek, here cited by columnist James K. Glassman, argues that welcoming the future, embracing it, is the key to human happiness: "It is not the fruits of past success but living in and for the future, in which human intelligence proves itself. Progress is movement for movement's sake, for it is in the process of learning and in the effects of having learned something new, that man enjoys the gift of his intelligence." Hayek called the followers of this philosophy "the party of life, the party that favors free growth and spontaneous evolution." And, as Glassman observed, this is "the party that welcomes the future not because it's known but because it's unknown."[15]

Virginia Postrel, in *The Future and Its Enemies*, illuminates this tension between those who welcome the uncertainties of the future, whom she calls dynamists, and the "stasists" who, fearful of the future, want to turn to the past or, at the very least, keep things under tight control as we move along. As Postrel points out, government efforts to keep things under control usually have the opposite effect.

> [A] thicket of technocratic regulations stifles diversity and innovation. It also creates an alienated, confused, and sometimes terrified citizenry. Although they promise security, ever more complicated rules actually make the world uncertain. They deprive people of the benefit of their own local knowledge, of the reliable and familiar facts of how their immediate world works, while simultaneously creating new sources of instability: new rules to master, or to guess at, before acting.[16]

Leaving people alone is morally right because liberty is an ultimate human right and value. Leaving people alone is also right because freedom works.

People in free societies are healthier and live longer. P. J. O'Rourke, the humorist whose prognostications on human freedom are well worth reading, puts it very starkly. "We can't solve all the problems of life, but we can solve the problem of gross, worldwide material deprivation. The solution doesn't work perfectly. The solution doesn't work uniformly. Nonetheless, the solution works. If we can't fix everything, let's fix the easy stuff. We know how to get rid of poverty. We know how to create wealth. But because of laziness, fear, complacency, love of power, or foolish idealism, we refuse to do it."[17]

How do we eliminate material deprivation? O'Rourke: "If people are protected from coercion by other people, and from coercion by that agglomeration of other people known as the state, human brains and greed create economic growth." It is almost that simple.

Free people are unpredictable. Free people get in trouble, speak heresies, create great beauty, undergo a thousand agonies and great joys. Under such circumstances free people tend not to envy the accomplishments of others. They know that those accomplishments may redound to their own benefit, that they may accomplish similar things one day and that, in any case, accomplishments move us all forward.

Such persons are not afraid of you or me having the right to climb a hill, or importing duty-free sugar from the Dominican Republic, or getting drunk at home on Saturday night, or masturbating, or braiding hair for a fee without an irrelevant licensing procedure, or painting a controversial picture, or inventing a new way to increase milk production in cows, or having oral sex, or questioning the hegemony of the Christian church, or smoking marijuana. To deprive you or me of such rights through the deadening hand of government is to begin the destruction of the human spirit. I cannot know and you cannot know what some other person may gain (or not) from attending church or watching pornography, or creating pornography, or pissing in a bottle, dropping in a cross, and calling it art. These things are part of the privileges and burdens of free people, and must remain so.

NOTES

1. "Adam Smith's *The Wealth of Nations*," *The Cato University*, audiotape series (Washington, D.C.: Cato Institute, 1997).

2. Ibid.

3. James Gwartney and Robert Lawson, *Economic Freedom of the World, 1998/1999 Interim Report* (n.p.: Fraser Institute, 1998), pp. 22–23.

4. Population Reference Bureau, *1997 World Population Data Sheet*, wall chart, 1997.

5. Stephen Moore and Philip D. Harvey, "Freedom and Health: Life Under Tyranny Is Very Hazardous to One's Well-Being," *Investor's Business Daily*, May 5, 2000.

6. "The World; The Powell Doctrine Is Looking Pretty Good Again," *New York Times*, April 4, 1999.

7. Lysander Spooner, *The Lysander Spooner Reader* (San Francisco: Fox & Wilkes, 1992), p. 25.

8. Ibid., p. 29.

9. Doug Esser, Associated Press book review of David Boaz, *Libertarianism: A Primer* (New York: Free Press, 1997), May 23, 1997.

10. "Freedom and Virtue are Inseparable," *Orange County Register*, January 29, 1997.

11. "Temptation. What Might Jesus Have Said About PHE?" *Chapel Hill Herald*, June 6, 1993.

12. Grant McCracken, "The Politics of Plenitude," *Reason*, August/September 1998, pp. 34–35.

13. Ibid.

14. Ibid.

15. James K. Glassman, "Pundits, Not Prophets," *Washington Post*, August 13, 1996. The quotations from F. A. Hayek are cited in Glassman's piece.

16. Virginia Postrel, *The Future and Its Enemies* (New York: Free Press, 1998), p. 113.

17. P. J. O'Rourke, *Eat The Rich* (New York: Atlantic Monthly Press, 1998), p. 245.

CHAPTER FOURTEEN

TRUCE AND CONSEQUENCES

"I decided that we had to be more confrontational and risk it all," says Bruce Ennis.

So at one point in those negotiations at the DOJ in Washington with CEOS [DOJ's Child Exploitation Obscenity Section, the new name for the National Obscenity Enforcement Unit] and Alabama, I let myself get visibly angry and I raised my voice and I said that I thought they were jerking us around, their demands were too unreasonable, and we weren't going to get anywhere with rational discussion. I told them that if they wanted things that way we'd fight it out in court. "This is a waste of everybody's time," I said. "This is stupid. Start acting in good faith. I don't have time to mess around anymore." I slammed my notebook shut and got up and walked out of the room.

This was by no means the first time we had thrown down the gauntlet. Dave Rudolf is an old hand at confrontational tactics and had used them several times during our years of negotiating with the government. Even the softer-spoken Wade Smith has been known to roll the dice by walking out of a room where negotiations seem stalemated.

Such tactics are not just for show. You reach a point when the Chinese water torture, at which government negotiators are so adept, just drives you to the point where it no longer seems worth talking. The anger is real. Further, in these final negotiations, we knew that our club, the civil case, which was soon scheduled to be heard, was just as big as the one they were holding over us—the prospect of a trial in Alabama. We were not afraid to take on that trial if we had to, and Bruce was well aware of that.

After the government dropped its case in Utah, Bruce and Dave Rudolf had made some tentative contacts at the DOJ to sound them out. It was clear that George Burgasser, the new head of the CEOS unit, was interested in a settlement, as was Tom Millet on the civil side. God knows we were. The time, the expense, and the inevitable erosion of energy were taking their toll.

Our respective opening positions in the negotiating process looked like this: The government asserted that we must give up our civil case ("with prejudice"), and accept a corporate plea (no individuals) to an obscenity count in Alabama. In return the government would forgo any prosecution of any persons and would absolve me and all other employees and PHE itself of any obscenity-related charges for actions that had occurred prior to the date of settlement, except for the proposed Alabama guilty plea by PHE.

We were prepared to give up the civil case, but we were adamantly opposed to accepting a plea by the corporation or any other party to the crime of obscenity in Alabama or anywhere else. This would constitute a RICO predicate, and would greatly increase our vulnerability by making such a plea admissible at any future trial. It would also be a violation of every principle for which we had been fighting these eight long, bloody years. Our position was that we had not at any time violated any obscenity law, that the only time this had been put to the test a jury had vindicated us, and that we were not about to give up this point at the end of the game.

When Bruce stormed out of the negotiating room at the DOJ, he had nearly reached the elevator before George Burgasser reached him and asked him to hold on. "I'm sure we can talk this through," he said. "Everybody's got short tempers here but we can talk this through." Bruce said he didn't think so, but Burgasser got him back to the table.

It was a dicey moment. Bruce believes, as do I, that George Burgasser represented a far more reasonable voice than any of the previous heads of the NOEU/CEOS. From the time he was made acting director, it was fairly clear that Mr. Burgasser was prepared to negotiate in a forthright way. Bruce says, "If Burgasser had not been in that room, it all would have stopped then. There would have been no more discussion. The other guys were not being reasonable and I made the judgment that we were not going to get enough through continued talks to be worth it. So if Burgasser hadn't tried to patch things together, that would have been it."

"Been it" meant that we would have begun trial of the civil case with Bruce in charge in Washington, and we would almost certainly have been indicted in Alabama and gone to trial there, defended by Dave and Wade and Joe.

As it was, we began looking for the ingredients of a compromise.

The government insisted that "Alabama has to get something." This was a position we tended to believe. After all, Hedrick and those thirty inspectors had spent thousands of hours in the two raids on our premises, nine expensive raids on the premises of video production companies in California, and all the "house calls" in Alabama's Middle District that must have embarrassed even the law enforcement officers who had carried them out. Alabama's Middle District Assistant U.S. Attorney Terry Moorer had made at least two trips to North Carolina personally to interrogate Adam & Eve employees and to support Hedrick's position before a North Carolina judge. So Alabama had a lot invested, financially, psychologically, and emotionally in our case; it would be hard for them to simply give it up in exchange for a civil suit that was about matters in which they had been involved only at the very last stages. No Alabama authorities were named in the civil suit, for example. So we surmised that the Alabama prosecutors would not consider our dropping of the civil suit to be adequate compensation for their dropping the criminal case.

"We've got to throw them a bone," Dave Rudolf concluded after the first round of discussions. "We've got to come up with something we can plead the corporation to, something that can't hurt us in any future confrontation, something that won't violate the basic First Amendment principle we've been fighting for."

This was not the first time we had engaged in what seemed to me to be a very cynical search for a "crime" to which we could plead guilty. In our several rounds of negotiations in Utah, we had similarly tried to find a compromise plea, some relatively unimportant offense that would not involve obscenity or the First Amendment but which would give some concession to the other side by means of a fine and a settlement—a form of closure that might be satisfactory to them and their supporters. In the Utah case, PHE's Skip Loy had found a product we had shipped for several months in the early 1980s, a liquid pheromone called Rush Liquid Incense that turned out to be just flammable enough to violate a postal statute about using the mails for shipping flammable materials. We had not known the material was flammable at the time and we had shipped it, but, since doing so had violated a perfectly reasonable regulation, we were prepared to plead the corporation guilty to a misdemeanor or minor felony in connection with shipping that product. As it turned out, this was not an acceptable compromise in Utah at the time we discussed it and the subject was dropped.

Now we were looking again. "Rush" was ancient history, and might never have been shipped to Alabama anyway, so we were searching for something else.

During the course of scouring all our practices for possible violations of even the most obscure postal regulations, we had learned that sexually oriented unsolicited mailings had to carry the legend "sexually oriented ad" on either an outer or an inner envelope, printed in a type size no smaller than that used for any other word on the envelope and never smaller than 12-point type. This regulation was of little concern to us in 1993 because by then our unsolicited mailings were going only to a relatively small number of persons who had already purchased sexually oriented material through the mail and, in any case, all contained an inner sealed envelope with the "sexually oriented" warning in type more than double the 12-point minimum requirement. However, Peggy recalled that in the late 1980s we had sent out several sizable mailings with the legend "sexually oriented ad" printed in 6- or 8-point type, noticeably smaller than the 12-point type called for by the regulation. We began to search our records to be sure.

This was a bizarre form of research. Here were Peggy and I and our colleagues at PHE, under instruction from our lawyers, searching for a "crime" that no one was accusing us of but which we might have committed many years before, and to which we could voluntarily plead guilty! Such are the wondrous ways of the law.

Our research revealed that there was at least a possibility that we had sent mailings in an "illegal" envelope (type size of "sexually oriented ad" too small) into the Middle District of Alabama in 1985. We had had a "D" mailing in January of that year. (The "D" was our designation for "direct mail," meaning a prospecting mailing to purchasers of sexually oriented merchandise who had not yet bought from Adam & Eve.) We had mailed more than one hundred thousand such envelopes nationwide; Alabama zip codes had been included. It was therefore highly likely that at least one such envelope had been sent into the Middle District of Alabama in that mailing.

But there was a hitch. The five-year statute of limitations had run out. Even though we might have committed this so-called crime, it had happened so long ago that we could not be prosecuted for it. Could we waive the statute of limitations? Some quick research revealed that we could.

This mailing offense—under Section 1735 of Federal Postal Regulations—seemed to meet many of the requirements for both sides in the negotiation process. It was a federal felony offense, which did not please me at all, but we recognized that the added gravity of a felony would make it more acceptable to the other side. The offense also carried a very heavy fine, a maximum of $500,000 (almost as much as the cost of a trial), which was a higher degree of risk than we wanted to take, but, again, the possibility of a large fine made this violation more palatable to the government and to the Alabama authorities. For our side, the bottom line was also met. The fine we'd actually have to pay would probably be much less than the maximum. Even more important, the offense was unrelated to obscenity, had no constitutional implications, and could not constitute a predicate under RICO for any future prosecutions, a point about which we had been adamant throughout our negotiations. The prospect of a plea to this offense was also satisfactory to us on an emotional level because it was so obviously a technical error involving nothing more than an incorrect type size on a printed message. We were able to ask each other, not unreasonably, "How trivial can you get?"

When this Section 1735 offense was put on the table at negotiations, it was immediately clear that it would likely satisfy the Alabama group. "Terry Moorer grabbed onto the 1735 offer like a drowning man grabbing a raft," reported Dave Rudolf. This was a matter of central importance because the federal negotiators had been insisting that, on their side of the table, Alabama's demands constituted the principle obstacle to settlement; the Washington players might have been satisfied with swapping our dropping of the civil suit for their dropping all criminal prosecutions against us up to that time. If Alabama would accept the 1735 offense, the path to resolution of this eight-year war appeared to be open.

I was very uneasy about this. Pleading guilty to something that I wasn't even positive we had done and that, in any case, we could never be prosecuted for, made me vaguely uncomfortable, and the prospect of a fine as large as $500,000 made me more so. But our lawyers, in whom I had vested enormous trust and faith over the years, were of one voice: This is a good deal. Take it.

In addition to the triviality of the offense, I was also mollified by the fact that settlement with a Section 1735 would preserve the crucially important component of our case, that the government's multiple simultaneous-prosecution strategy would remain dead as a dodo. While the settlement would not require the government to admit to any wrongdoing, and while we would have no permanent injunction against multiple, simultaneous prosecutions, it was already clear that this part of the battle was essentially won. There had been no multiple prosecutions against any company since we had filed our lawsuit in January of 1991, and the government's civil attorneys had informed us that the Justice Department expected to announce a new policy on this matter very shortly. Even without such a change in policy, we believed we had sufficiently established the unconstitutionality of this practice through several judges in two districts (including a court of appeals) to permanently undermine its efficacy. If all the government could get, after hitting us with obscenity prosecutions in the Middle and Eastern Districts of North Carolina, plus Utah, Kentucky, and Alabama, was a plea to a type-size postal violation, their multiple-prosecution policy would almost surely remain defunct.

Indeed, at the last hearing before Judge Green prior to our settlement, the DOJ had promised that "the existing policy on multiple prosecutions for obscenity cases [is] under review, and it is anticipated that within the near future, that policy will be changed and . . . the policy will no longer encourage multiple prosecutions in obscenity cases."[1]

So we accepted. On December 2, 1993, I arrived at the offices of Jenner & Block, Bruce's law firm in Washington, and sat down in their cherrywood-paneled "B" conference room at a long table with Bruce and his colleagues and nearly a dozen representatives of the federal government. I signed the agreement on behalf of PHE, myself, and my fellow employees. James Eldon Wilson, Terry F. Moorer, and J. Robert Flores signed on behalf of the United States government. This ended the war. We waived the statute of limitations, and agreed that "on or about January 10, 1985, the exact date being unknown to the United States, in the middle district of Alabama . . . [PHE] did willfully use the mails for the mailing, carriage in the mails, and delivery of a sexually oriented advertisement, offering the sale of videotapes, which were delivered by mail in violation of Title 39 United States Code. . . ."

And we dropped our civil suit.

In exchange, the government agreed that we would not be prosecuted for any obscenity-related violation* anywhere in the United States for any act occurring prior to November 18, 1993, a date two weeks prior to the settlement.

It was over. The battle had begun in May of 1986 and ended in the last month of 1993. For a while, at least, we could hope for a period of peace.

The settlement was widely covered in the press, especially in the jurisdictions where the war had been fought. The Raleigh *News and Observer* reported:

> After spending more than seven years and about $3 million in legal fees, PHE Inc. has apparently secured a truce with the federal government over distribution of its mail-order erotica.
>
> In an agreement that allows both sides to save face, the Carrboro company pleaded guilty Monday to a single felony charge over the size of the words on an advertisement for sexually explicit videos in Alabama.
>
> In return, the government promised not to prosecute PHE for possessing or distributing sexually explicit materials before Nov. 18, said David Rudolf, a Chapel Hill attorney representing PHE.[2]

The Utah press gave the story an important local flavor:

> [Salt Lake City] A company that distributes sexual materials has dropped its lawsuit against former [Utah] US Attorney Brent Ward and assistant US Attorney Richard Lambert.

---

*We made sure to include all related crimes, like money laundering, and all related companies, like VideoMail, so that the government couldn't repeat Hedrick's tricks in these areas.

"It's a relief to have it over with," Lambert said.

PHE, a North Carolina company also known as Adam & Eve, dropped its suit against the federal government and the two Utah prosecutors as part of a deal struck with the US Department of Justice.

Justice officials agreed not to prosecute PHE on pornography charges in several states—as it has tried to do—if PHE would drop its lawsuit against the government. . . .

The deal sounds the death knell of multi-jurisdictional prosecution, [Utah PHE attorney Jerry] Mooney said. Multi-jurisdictional prosecution—the practice of filing identical criminal charges against a company in several states at once—was Ward's brain child, according to court records.

He recommended the practice to the then–US attorney general, who implemented the policy. The theory was to drive companies like PHE into bankruptcy defending all the charges, Mooney said. . . .

Four dozen members of Congress—mostly Republicans—urged Clinton to stand by multi-jurisdictional prosecution. Abandoning that approach "takes the teeth out of anti-porn enforcement," said Rep. Bill Baker, R-Calif.[3]

The *Washington Post*'s Jim McGee had followed our eight-year struggle closely:

US SETTLES OBSCENITY CASE WITH MAIL-ORDER DISTRIBUTOR
Firm Drops Lawsuit on Multiple Prosecutions, Pleads Guilty to Single Postal Violation.

A key chapter in the Justice Department's long pursuit of a major distributor of sexually explicit films and magazines ended quietly in federal court yesterday when the government agreed to drop further prosecution in exchange for a guilty plea in Alabama.

Facing the prospect of a contentious civil trial in Washington, the Justice Department agreed not to prosecute PHE, Inc. for any crimes committed before Nov. 18 [1993]. In exchange, the corporation pleaded guilty in Alabama to one count of violating postal regulations, for which it will pay a fine.

The civil trial, prompted by PHE's challenge to the government's prosecutorial tactics, was scheduled to begin Monday. It was to examine the unusual practices of a group of federal obscenity prosecutors who used the tactic of successive multiple prosecutions of the same defendant in different districts to attack mail-order firms that sell sexually explicit material. The agreement did not contain "an admission of liability or wrongdoing" on the part of the government.

The Justice Department had long considered PHE a primary target. "This is a victory of judicial fairness and for everyone who doesn't want the government to decide what they should read and do in the privacy of their own homes," said PHE President Philip D. Harvey.

In a hearing last month, a government lawyer told US District Judge Joyce Hens Green, who was to preside over the civil trial, that the Justice Department was reviewing the use of multi-district prosecutions in obscenity cases. That review continues, a department spokesman said and was not part of yesterday's settlement.

Under the agreement, PHE dropped its civil suit against the Justice Department. Harvey appeared in US District Court in Montgomery and entered a plea of guilty to a charge that a 1985 mailing by PHE failed to include the words "Sexually Oriented Ad" in sufficiently large type and in the correct location on the mailing envelope.

Harvey said his company spent nearly $3 million fighting the multi-district strategy, which has led to two injunctions and an adverse ruling by an appeals court. "The evil of the multiple prosecution strategy was that it was used to circumvent the law, not uphold it," Harvey said. "And I am frankly proud of the part we played in putting an end to it."[4]

We were all too aware that there was nothing to prevent the government from starting the process all over again, from ordering one of our videos into some conservative jurisdiction, opening a new investigation, and bringing us to trial. But we didn't think there would be much enthusiasm for such a course of action, for several reasons. It couldn't be done in Utah or Alabama, because we were not doing business there. The cutoff date meant that any videos or magazines the government might investigate would have been cleared through our review process. The government now understood, in great detail, how this process worked, and we knew that at least some people in the Department of Justice appreciated the value of this system. They knew that material certified nonprurient by objective experts would not likely be found offensive in many communities. They understood also, I think, that juries were likely to be impressed by the fact that our materials were reviewed and certified before we sold them, that this was as good a way as any company could establish for conforming with a terribly vague law.

They knew one more thing. Our "we-won't-be-a-tasty-morsel" strategy had been followed rigorously for more than seven years. Any new investigation would be fought tooth-and-nail, and the government would have to win every inch of ground it might gain at considerable effort and expense. They had seen and experienced some of the costs of such a battle (as had we) and we believed that this, combined with the olive branch of the continuing review process, would act as a powerful deterrent. (Shortly after the settlement, I wrote George Burgasser, the acting head of the obscenity unit at Main Justice, assuring him that we would maintain the review system as a permanent part of our company policy.)

A new era began. What would it be like to run the business without the constant threat of imminent indictment? What would I talk about at the monthly employee meetings with no news from the legal front? Could we maintain such high employee morale and organizational unity without that invigorating outside threat? (It may be coincidental that sales and profits grew more, on a year-by-year basis, during our eight-year struggle than they have in the eight years since, but I'm not so sure.)

And, I confess, I miss the sounds and smells of battle. We had been shot at, as Winston Churchill put it, without result, and there is indeed nothing quite so exhilarating. The moat around our castle is deep. The drawbridge is up and our archers' quivers are full of arrows, and no one comes.

NOTES

1. Thomas Millet, Hearing before Judge Joyce Hens Green, D.C. District Court, November 18, 1993. It took some time for this change to be formalized; finally in June 1998, the U.S. Attorney's Manual was revised to reflect the reversal: In obscenity cases "Generally, multiple prosecutions are not favored." (USAM§9-75.100.)

2. "Erotica Firm, Government Reach Truce," *Raleigh News and Observer*, December 7, 1993.

3. "Federal Prosecution of Firm Called Vindictive," *Deseret (Utah) News*, December 10, 1993.

4. "U.S. Settles Obscenity Case with Mail-Order Distributor," *Washington Post*, December 7, 1993.

APPENDIX A

The following are guidelines promulgated by Orange County District Attorney Carl Fox in 1987. They are significant particularly for the fact that they state a policy concerning what kinds of sexually oriented materials are likely be prosecuted in this jurisdiction and, by implication, those which are likely to be left alone.

(Orange County, North Carolina)

GUIDELINES FOR OBSCENE MATERIAL

I. The Test for Obscenity.

A. Patently offensive: material which describes or depicts sexual conduct in a clearly or obviously offensive way.
B. Contemporary community standard: average person applying contemporary community standards relating to the depiction or description of sexual matters would find that the material, taken as a whole, appeals to the prurient interest in sex.

    1. Prurient interest: a twisted, morbid, improper or unhealthy interest in sex.

C. Value: material lacks serious literary, artistic, political or scientific value.
D. Unprotected: material as used is not protected or privileged under the Constitution of the United States or the Constitution of North Carolina.

II. Regulated Conduct.

E. Sexual Conduct.

    2. Vaginal, anal or oral intercourse, whether actual or simulated, normal or perverted; or

3. Masturbation, excretory functions, or lewd exhibition or uncovered genitals; or
4. An act or condition that depicts torture, physical restraint by being fettered or bound or flagellation of or by a nude person or a person clad in revealing or bizarre costume or in undergarments.

F. Business Conduct.

5. Unlawful for any person, firm or corporation to intentionally disseminate obscenity as follows:
   a. sell, deliver or provide or offer or agree to sell, deliver or provide any obscene writing, picture, record or other representation or embodiment of the obscene; or
   b. publish, exhibit or otherwise make available anything obscene; or
   c. exhibit, present, rent or to provide: any obscene still or motion picture, film, filmstrip, or projection slide, or sound recording, sound tape, or sound track, or any matter or material of whatever form which is a representation, embodiment, performance or publication of the obscene.
6. Unlawful to create, buy, procure or possess obscene material with the purpose and intent of disseminating it unlawfully.
7. Unlawful to advertise or otherwise promote the sale of material that is represented or held out as obscene.
8. Unlawful to intentionally hire, employ, use or permit a minor under age of 16 to do or assist in doing any act or thing constituting an offense under Article 26 or G.S. Chapter 14 involving any obscene material, act or thing that the defendant knows or reasonably should know is obscene within the meaning of G.S. 14-190.1 when the defendant is 18 years of age or older.
9. Unlawful to disseminate to a minor under the age of 16 years obscene material that the defendant knows or reasonably should know is obscene within the meaning G.S. 14-190.1 when the defendant is 18 years of age or older. (Stiffer penalty if the minor is under 13 years of age.)

III. *Material Subject to Prosecution.*

G. Child pornography.

    10. children under 16 years of age depicted in sexual conduct either alone, with other children or adults in any material.

    11. adults cast in roles as children or minors involved in sexual conduct alone, with other children or adults in any material.

    12. Incest: sexual conduct between siblings, between parents and children, related adults and children. (This will include stepchildren as well.)

H. Beastiality [*sic*]: any sexual conduct involving human beings and animals.

I. Violence and restraint.

    13. torture: inflicting pain for sexual gratification.

    14. flagellation: whipping or beating another for sexual gratification.

    15. displaying or wearing of painful or harmful devices or paraphernalia for sexual gratification or as a part of sexual conduct.

    16. bondage: physical restraint of another, unnecessary to the sexual conduct, for gratification.

    17. forced sexual conduct against the will of and without the consent of another.

J. Excretory functions performed during or after sexual conduct or for the purpose of sexual gratification.

IV. *Duties and Enforcement.*

K. Proprietors and Employees.

    18. Screen materials before they are displayed for sale or rent.

    19. Determine whether they contain obscene material.

    20. If you believe the material to be questionable, call the police or the district attorney so we can make a preliminary determination as to whether it is obscene.

    21. In addition, I recommend that this material be kept separate from other videos in a distinct, readily identifiable area with a posted age restriction of 18 years of age and identification be required.

L. Law Enforcement.

22. Check video establishments to determine whether they are in compliance with the law.

23. Examine material selection and view questionable material.

24. Contact district attorney if material is believed to be obscene.

25. District Attorney will view material and determine whether it appears to be obscene.

26. District Attorney will request issuance of a search warrant or criminal process if material is found to be obscene.

These guidelines are subject to revision and modification at any time and copies will be delivered prior to search or arrest under any changes which may have been instituted.

APPENDIX B

There have been many studies, commissions, and reviews that have investigated the relationship between sexually explicit materials ("pornography") and antisocial behavior. Here is a summary from Marcia Pally:

> Between 1968 and 1970, the Commission on Obscenity and Pornography (also known as the President's Commission) studied the relationship between sexually explicit material and anti-social behavior. Over this two-year period, it conducted controlled laboratory studies and national surveys on pornography consumption and crime rates. The budget of $2 million in 1970 dollars exceeded by several times the $500,000 allotted Attorney General Meese's Commission on Pornography in 1985. Below are a few of the President's Commission's concluding remarks:
>
> - "Empirical research designed to clarify the question has found no reliable evidence to date that exposure to explicit sexual materials plays a significant role in the causation of delinquent or criminal sexual behavior among youths or adults" (p. 139).
> - "Studies of juvenile delinquents indicate that their experience with erotica is generally similar to that of nondelinquents. . . . There is no basis in the available data however for supposing that there is any independent relationship between exposure to erotica and delinquency" (p. 242).
> - "If a case is to be made against pornography in 1970, it will have to be made on grounds other than demonstrated effects of a damaging personal or social nature" (p. 139).[1]

"There is no warrant," stated this commission, "for continued government interference with the full freedom of adults to read, obtain, or view whatever material they wish." The commission further found that sex offenders were more likely than average Americans to have been raised in conservative, religious households.

THE MEESE COMMISSION

The 1985 attorney general's commission was loaded for bear almost from the moment of its organization. Part of the motive for its convening was to counteract the report of the 1970 commission. That report had been rejected out of hand by President Nixon, but remained the latest official government word. The very mandate of the Meese Commission was to recommend "more effective ways in which the spread of pornography could be contained," making clear that the commission was not meant to reach an unbiased conclusion.[2] Several Meese Commission members were known to be staunchly opposed to pornography and the commissioners were characterized by the ACLU as, "on the whole, quintessential censors, sharing all the elitism of censors of the past."[3] They included Father Bruce Ritter of Covenant House, a Catholic priest whose views on the subject of sex were known to be punitively conservative, and commission chairman Henry Hudson, a U.S. Attorney for the Northern District of Virginia, a well-known antipornography prosecutor. Alan Sears, who would take time a year later to attend our trial in Alamance County, was selected to be executive director of the commission. Sears had devoted much of his career to censoring sexual content in art. He went on to become legal counsel for Charles Keating's censorious Citizens for Decency Through Law.[4] Other members of the commission were less biased and two of them, Judith Becker and Ellen Levine, issued a minority dissent to many of the conclusions the commission reached.

The surprising thing about the Meese Commission's findings is that they were so universally assumed to be 100 percent negative on the subject of sexual materials. While it is true that the commission recommendations generally deplored the availability of sexually explicit and other sexually oriented materials, they did not do so categorically. Of particular note to PHE, given the standards we were adopting at that time, was the commission's findings that "pure" sexual depictions did no demonstrable harm. While insisting that nonviolent, nondegrading sexual portrayals were not the norm in mainstream "pornography" (they were wrong about that), they conceded that such straight sex depictions on the "preponderance of evidence" did not lead to sexual crimes or antisocial conduct. "The fairest conclusion from the social science evidence is that there is no persuasive evidence to date supporting the connection between non-violent and non-degrading [sexually explicit] materials and acts of sexual violence, and that there is some, but very limited evidence, indicating that the connection does not exist. The totality of the social science evidence, therefore, is slightly against the hypothesis that non-violent and non-degrading materials bear a causal relationship to acts of sexual violence."[5] The obvious reluctance with which the commission issued these words not only underscored its bias but also constitutes strong evidence of the fact that, as Lloyd Sinclair puts it, "the effects on adults from viewing [such] materials [are] neutral or mildly positive." In other words, the consensus among social scientists as described by Sinclair was so strong, even in 1986, that the Meese Commission was forced to concede this point.

Some commission members, clearly feeling that their report had created a more biased and negative impression than they had intended, went out of their way to make this point. Commissioner Frederick Schauer, for example, wrote in the *American Bar Foundation Research Journal* in 1987, a year after the commission report's release, that "I do not make the claim, nor does the report, that . . . sexual explicit material bears a causal relationship to acts of sexual violence. . . . As the evidence so clearly indicates, . . . the causal relationship is independent of the degree of sexual explicitness."[6] Dr. Schauer further stated that he did not "find the possibility of total deregulation [of pornography] troublesome, and I never have."[7]

Another generally conservative commissioner, Dr. Park Deitz, even had some good things to say about *Playboy* magazine, following an embarrassing incident. Alan Sears, demonstrating both his antipornography zeal and his lack of understanding of First Amendment law, had sent letters on the commission letterhead to twenty-three companies, owners of convenience store chains like 7-Eleven, informing them that they were considered distributors of pornography and would be so listed in the commission's final report unless they contested the accusation. "The companies had been identified by Donald Wildmon, leader of an up-and-coming religious right pressure group called the National Federation of Decency (its name was later changed to the less puritanical-sounding American Family Association). The Meese Commission's [or at least Sears's] not-so-hidden message was to get rid of *Playboy*, *Penthouse*, and similar soft-core erotic magazines."[8] *Playboy* and *Penthouse* took the matter to court and successfully argued that the commission had acted unlawfully by attempting to restrain presumptively protected speech, a form of "prior restraint" impermissible under the First Amendment. The whole incident was a matter of considerable embarrassment to the commission, and Dr. Deitz went on record stating that "I believe that *Playboy* centerfolds are among the healthiest sexual images in America, and so are many of Mr. Guccione's [*Penthouse*] centerfolds."[9]

The commission had also called for an independent review of the social science data on pornography by Dr. Edna Einsiedel of the University of Calgary. Dr. Einsiedel's review found no link between sexually explicit material and sex crimes, and did not support the conclusions of the policy recommendations that the Meese Commission later made.[10]

Still looking for damaging evidence after Dr. Einsiedel's not-very-encouraging report, the commission requested Surgeon General C. Everett Koop to gather more information. Koop conducted a conference of researchers and practitioners whose findings were summed up in the report of the Surgeon General's Workshop on Pornography and Public Health in 1986. This report found no evidence that exposure to sexual material leads to sex crimes:

> Pornography has been consistently linked to changes in some perceptions, attitudes and behaviors. These links, however, are circumscribed, few in number and generally laboratory-based . . . For instance, while it is a common belief that attitude changes lead to behavioral changes, research has consistently shown otherwise. Behaviors are as likely to influence attitudes as attitudes are to influence behavior.[11]

In sum, the best efforts of a biased commission to uncover proof that sexual images cause societal harm generally failed in this purpose. The degree of scientific rigor exercised by the commission in its investigations was so lax as to invite ridicule ("Who," the ACLU report asked rhetorically, "can forget the FBI agent detailing the obscene photographs he had seized in his career, including one of a 'vagina surrounded by a woman'?"[12] And the ancillary investigations requested by the commission, most notably those of the surgeon general and Dr. Einsiedel, had basically confirmed the 1970 commission report in its conclusion that sexually explicit materials were harmless. Indeed, the Meese Commission may have done us all a great favor by searching almost desperately for a connection between sexual images and societal harm and failing to find it. We can be even more confident than we were before that no such connection exists.

SEXUAL MATERIAL AND CRIME RATES

Other investigators have attempted to establish a correlation between the availability of sexual materials and rates of violent crime, particularly rape. Such claims are without support, as the following excellent synopsis from Marcia Pally sums up.

According to initial 1984 studies by Drs. Larry Baron and Murray Straus (Yale University, University of New Hampshire) and 1988 studies by Dr. Joseph Scott and Loretta Schwalm (Ohio State University), communities with higher pornography sales reported more rapes. Yet, on further research, Scott and Schwalm found higher incidences of rape in areas with strong sales of any men's magazines, including *Field and Stream*. . . . Pursuing the investigation further, Dr. Cynthia Gentry . . . found that the correlation between rape rates and pornography sales disappeared when the number of young men living in a given area was factored into the data. There is "no evidence of a relationship between popular sex magazines and violence against women," wrote Gentry. . . . The only factor that predicted the rape rate in a given locale was the number of men between the ages of eighteen and thirty-four residing there. . . . Scott and Schwalm . . . reported similar findings in their studies on rape rates and sexually explicit material.

In the early L. Baron and Straus research . . . which found a correlation between sales of sexual material and rape rates, the results are far from conclusive: Utah ranks lowest on the Sexual Magazine Circulation Index but twenty-fifth in number of rapes; New Hampshire ranks ninth on this index and forty-fourth in rapes. L. Baron and Straus then introduced into their data a "hypermasculinity" rating called the Violence Approval Index and found that the relationship between pornography circulation and rape disappeared. . . . Baron explained at the Meese Commission hearings: "The relationship [between sexual materials and rape] . . . may be due to an unspecified third variable. It is quite plausible that the findings could reflect state-to-state differences in a hypermasculated or macho culture pattern. . . . " Baron and Straus proposed not that pornography causes rape but that both the sale of pornography and rape occur in "hypermasculine" cultures that have long flourished in this country.[13]

Pally's review continues with coverage of international research:

[T]he Canadian Department of Justice completed a report on the effects of sexually explicit material, "Working Papers on Pornography and Prostitution, Report #13. The Impact of Pornography: An Analysis of Research and Summary of Findings" (McKay and Dolff, 1984, known as the Fraser Committee Report). It found,

> There is no systematic research evidence available which suggests a causal relationship between pornography and morality.
> . . . There is no systematic research which suggests that increases in specific forms of deviant behavior, reflected in crime trend statistics (e.g., rape) are causally related to pornography.

... There is no persuasive evidence that the viewing of pornography causes harm to the average adult ... that exposure causes the average adult to harm others ... that exposure causes the average adult to alter established sex practices. On the contrary, the research supports the contention that exposure, although possibly producing a short term, transient alteration in patterns, has no effect in the longer term. ...

The British Inquiry into Obscenity and Film Censorship (1979, known as the Williams Committee) also found no link between sexually explicit material and crime. Its authors wrote, "We unhesitatingly reject the suggestion that the available statistical information for England and Wales lends any support to the argument that pornography acts as a stimulus to the commission of sexual violence" (p. 80). The British Inquiry noted that in a five-year period of increasing availability and explicitness of sexual material, sexual assault declined. Following a crackdown on hard-core pornography, sex crimes increased. ...

Studies by Dr. Berl Kutchinsky at the Institute of Criminal Science of the University of Copenhagen report that in European countries where restrictions on pornography have been lifted, incidence of rape over the last twenty years has declined or remained constant. ... In Kutchinsky's study, sex crimes against female children dropped from 30 per 100,000 to approximately 5 per 100,000 between 1965 and 1982, after Denmark liberalized its obscenity laws, making sexually explicit material more accessible to the public. In 1987, Kutchinsky wrote,

Not only is there possibly a direct causal link between pornography and the decrease in certain types of sex crimes, but also and more importantly, sex crimes in Denmark, including rape, did not increase—as advocates of censorship had expected—despite the appearance and subsequent legalization of hard-core pornography. ... Since it was clear from the onset that most offenses involving homosexuality and prostitution have no obvious victims ... the detailed analysis of the decrease was restricted to "regular" heterosexual sex crimes, that is, sex crimes committed by a male offender against a female (adult or child) victim. In Copenhagen ... these crimes constituted 85 percent of all sexual offenses and had an overall drop from 96 reported cases per 100,000 population in 1966 to 25 per 100,000 in 1973. ...

Confirming Kutchinsky's data, Howitt and Cumberbatch . . . wrote, "Kutchinksy's (1990[l]) analysis shows a growth of up to 300 percent in nonsexual violent crime in Denmark, Sweden and West Germany from 1964 to 1984 compared with very modest changes in the rate of rape. . . . " In West Germany rape rates declined since bans on pornography were lifted in 1973. "I am aware," wrote Kutchinsky ". . . that rape also decreased in Italy (where pornography is very easily available) and that most of the European countries have unchanged rape levels."

Like the European research, studies in Asia find no link between the commission of sex crimes and the availability of sexual materials, including those with violent content. Singapore, with tight controls on pornography, showed a greater increase in rape rates (28 percentage points more) between 1964 and 1974 than did Stockholm, with liberalized pornography laws.[14]

More recently, Dr. Milton Diamond of the University of Hawaii has completed a study on the possible correlation between the increasing availability of pornography in Japan and the incidence of sexual crime. His findings are quite interesting. Dr. Diamond reports, "It is certainly clear from the data reviewed that a massive increase in available pornography in Japan . . . has been correlated with a dramatic *decrease* in sexual crimes and most so among youngsters as perpetrators or victims."[15]

After documenting the very substantial increase in the availability of sexually explicit materials (SEM) in Japan between the mid-1970s and the mid-1990s,[16] Dr. Diamond analyzes trends in sex-oriented crimes in Japan. Reported rapes were over 3,500 in the 1970s and dropped to 1,548 in 1990 and to 1,500 in 1995. Juvenile rape offenders dropped from more than 1,000 to just 346 in 1990 and 264 in 1995. Sexual assaults remained roughly constant at 3,139 in 1972 dropping to 2,730 in 1990 but rising to 3,644 in 1995. But even this small increase represented a slight decrease in the rate (from .0292 to .0290 per 1,000 persons), due to an increase in the Japanese population.

Because sexually explicit comics had been among the most rapidly increasing forms of sexual material available, and because Japanese authorities had essentially ignored age restrictions on the availability of SEM during the latter part of the period of review, Dr. Diamond was particularly attentive to crime statistics among juveniles. He reports that "the number of juvenile offenders dramatically dropped every period reviewed from 1,803 perpetrators in 1972 to a low of 264 in 1995; a drop of some 85%." Summarizing his data, Diamond notes that over this period of change, sex crimes in every category, from *rape* to *public indecency*, sexual offenses from both ends of the criminal spectrum, significantly decreased in incidence. Most significantly, despite the wide increase in availability of pornography to children, not only was there a decrease in sex crimes with juveniles as victims but the number of juvenile offenders also decreased significantly.[17]

The striking nature of these findings led Dr. Diamond to examine earlier data suggesting that the wider availability of pornography actually leads to a *decrease* in sexual crimes, whether because sexually explicit materials provide an alternative, nonviolent outlet to would-be sexual predators, or for other reasons. He notes that sex offenders, for example, as reported in several U.S.-based investigations,

> typically had *less* exposure to SEM in their background than others and the offenders generally were individuals [who were] deeply religious and socially and politically conservative. . . . Since then, most researchers have found similarly. . . . The upbringing of sex offenders was usually sexually repressive, often they had an overtly religious background and held rigid conservative attitudes towards sexuality; . . . their upbringing had usually been ritualistically moralistic and conservative rather than permissive.[18]

While no responsible researcher would claim that these correlations between an increase in the availability of sexually explicit materials and a decrease in sex-related crimes constitutes positive proof that one causes the other, the opposite claim appears even more far-fetched, i.e., that the availability of sexually oriented materials leads to an increase in antisocial behavior. Indeed, there appears to be more evidence to support the hypothesis that the availability of pornography decreases crime rather than increasing it.

SOME OPPOSITE RESULTS

A few investigations have reached quite different conclusions. As Pally points out, the Australian parliament, after conducting hearings on the subject, concluded that nonviolent and violent sexual material yield antisocial and violent effects. And an investigation in Hawaii turned up a two-year period when sexual material was restricted and rape rates declined. In both of these cases, however, the science was weak. The Australian parliament did not include any review of the available literature and in general its review is not considered rigorous. The Hawaiian study was conducted by Dr. John Court, a self-proclaimed Christian psychologist and onetime leader of the antipornography Festival of Light, who was found by the Williams Committee in the United Kingdom to have been both "misleading and intellectually dishonest."[19]

In any case, complete unanimity is rare in the social sciences, and would be especially unlikely in an area so fraught with emotionality as the social impact of sexually oriented materials. As Lloyd Sinclair points out, the preponderance of scientists agree with the preponderance of scientific evidence: The availability and perusal of sexual imagery do not cause harm.

NOTES

1. Marcia Pally, *Sex and Sensibility* (Hopewell, N.J.: Ecco Press, 1994), pp. 25–26.

2. Hendrik Hertzberg noted in the *New Republic* ("Big Boobs," July 1986): "The Meese Commission lacked the financial and staff resources of its predecessor, but since its conclusions were preordained, it didn't really need them."

3. American Civil Liberties Union (ACLU), *Polluting the Censorship Debate*, Public Policy Report, Washington, D.C., July 1986, p. 4.

4. Marjorie Heins, *Sex, Sin, and Blasphemy: A Guide to America's Censorship Wars* (New York: New Press, 1993), p. 148.

5. Attorney General's Commission on Pornography, *Final Report*, U.S. Department of Justice, Washington, D.C., July 1986, pp. 337–38.

6. Marcia Pally, *Sense & Censorship: The Vanity of Bonfires. Resource Materials on Sexually Explicit Material, Violent Material, and Censorship* (New York: Americans for Constitutional Freedom, 1991), p. 12.

7. Ibid., p. 13.

8. Heins, *Sex, Sin, and Blasphemy*, p. 70.

9. Pally, *Sense & Censorship*, p. 12.

10. Ibid., pp. 13–14.

11. Ibid.

12. ACLU, *Polluting the Censorship Debate*, p. 1.

13. Pally, *Sex and Sensibility*, pp. 54–55.

14. Ibid., pp. 57–60.

15. Milton Diamond, "The Effects of Pornography: An International Perspective," in *Porn 101*, eds J. Elias et al. (Amherst, N.Y.: Prometheus Books, 1999), p. 248.

16. Dr. Diamond also made sure that his findings were not biased by any changes in the way such crimes were reported in Japan during this period.

17. Diamond, "The Effects of Pornography," pp. 223–25.

18. Ibid., p. 243; citations omitted.

19. Pally, *Sex and Sensibility*, p. 61.

APPENDIX C

The following memorandum concerns the vagueness of the current definition of obscenity as laid down by the Supreme Court in *Miller v. California* (1973). The analysis was prepared by the Washington, D.C., office of the law firm of Jenner & Block at my request.

[In analyzing the vagueness of the *Miller* statute] we should note that the Supreme Court itself has repeatedly rejected the contention that the *Miller* standard is unduly vague, most recently in *Fort Wayne Books* v. *Indianapolis*. But the Court's discussion of vagueness in *Fort Wayne Books* is ironic when considered in connection with *H. J. Inc.* v. *Northwest Bell Tel. Co.*, a case decided later in the same Term (1989).

As you know, in *Fort Wayne Books* a publisher argued that Indiana's RICO statute (similar to the federal RICO statute) was unconstitutionally vague insofar as it criminalized a "pattern" of obscenity violations. Five Justices[1] dismissed this argument in a footnote, saying that if punishing a single act of obscenity was not unconstitutionally vague (as the Court had previously held), then it automatically followed that punishing a pattern of obscenity acts could not be unconstitutionally vague. The Justices asserted that a "pattern" of obscenity is inherently *easier* to discern than a single act of obscenity.

H. J. Inc. involved an alleged RICO pattern of bribery rather than obscenity. In *H. J. Inc.*, three of the five Justices who dismissed the vagueness argument four months earlier in *Fort Wayne Books* strongly suggested that the "pattern" requirement is unconstitutionally vague because no one can know what conduct will be sufficient to constitute a "pattern" of bribery with any degree of precision. (Scalia, J., concurring, joined by Rehnquist, O'Connor, and Kennedy.)

Of course, the law has long punished *single* acts of bribery, so here these Justices seem to be saying it is more difficult to identify a *pattern* of bribery than to determine a single act of bribery. Why, then, is it easier to identify a

277

pattern of obscenity than to determine a single act of obscenity? Given the obvious incompatibility of these two opinions, one can suggest that these Justices have a blatant double standard. Apparently, they prefer businessmen who engage in bribery over those who distribute literature sought by consenting adults. This hierarchy of values can be said to turn upside down our constitutional order, in which the distribution of literature is supposed to occupy a "preferred position" *(Wallace v. Jaffree,* [1985]).

There are other relevant ironies. The *Miller* standard itself, which relies on not one but *two* "local community standards" to define the offense, is not too vague for the Justices. Yet in a seminal void-for-vagueness case, *Connolly v. General Const. Co.,* (1926), the Court struck down a minimum wage statute because, in part, the minimum wage was based upon local community standards. The Court held that the concept of "locality" was so "equivocal" as to violate "[t]he constitutional guaranty of due process," as did the notion that a single standard could be derived from disparate wage structures and varying circumstances within a locality. The *Miller* standard has the same difficulties. *Connolly* and *Miller,* like *Fort Wayne Books* and *H. J., Inc.,* reveal the Court's double standard when sexual literature is at issue.

The Court's opinion in *Connolly* contains some language that is worth quoting to highlight just how hypocritical the *Miller* obscenity standard really is:

> [A] statute which either forbids or requires the doing of an act in terms so vague that men of common intelligence must necessarily guess at its meaning and differ as to its application violates the first essential of due process of law.

The Court has repeated this theme again and again over the years. For example, in *Lanzetta v. New Jersey,* (1939), the Court stated:

> No one may be required at peril of life, liberty, or property to speculate as to the meaning of penal statutes. All are entitled to be informed as to what the State commands or forbids.

More recently, the Court reiterated "that the void-for-vagueness doctrine requires that a penal statute define the criminal offense with sufficient definiteness that ordinary people can understand what conduct is prohibited and in a manner that does not encourage arbitrary and discriminatory enforcement." *Kolender v. Lawson,* (1983).

Over the years, the Court has emphasized the importance of the void-for-vagueness doctrine for restrictions on expressive activity—another fact that makes the *Miller* standard and the *Fort Wayne Books/H. J. Inc.* paradox appear even more ironic or hypocritical. Thus, in *Ashton v. Kentucky*, (1966), the Court asserted:

> Vague laws in any area suffer a constitutional infirmity. When First Amendment rights are involved, we look even more closely lest, under the guise of regulating conduct that is reachable by the police power, freedom of speech or of the press suffer.

See also *Cramp v. Board of Public Instruction*, (1961) ("The vice of unconstitutional vagueness is further aggravated where, as here, the statute in question operates to inhibit the exercise of individual freedoms affirmatively protected by the Constitution.") And in *Grayned v. City of Rockford* (1972), the Court explained that the void-for-vagueness doctrine is designed to counteract the chilling effect on expression caused by imprecise regulation:

> [W]here a vague statute abuts upon sensitive areas of basic First Amendment freedoms, it operates to inhibit the exercise of those freedoms. Uncertain meanings inevitably lead citizens to steer far wider of the unlawful zone than if the boundaries of the forbidden areas were clearly marked. [Internal quotation marks omitted.]

Because self-censorship of constitutionally protected speech is an especially pernicious evil, the void-for-vagueness doctrine serves an important First Amendment objective. Indeed, according to the Court, the very purpose of the vagueness doctrine "is to insure that the government treads with sensitivity in areas freighted with First Amendment concerns." *Chicago Teachers Union v. Hudson*, (1986).

In other times, the Court paid some attention to these First Amendment concerns in the area of sexually explicit speech. In *Winters v. New York*, (1948), for example, the Court struck down New York's antipornography statute on vagueness grounds. The Court stated:

> The failure of a statute limiting freedom of expression to give fair notice of what acts will be punished . . . violates an accused's rights under procedural due process and freedom of speech or press.

And in *Smith v. California* (1959), the Court relied on the void-for-vagueness doctrine to hold that a person cannot be prosecuted for obscenity without knowledge of the allegedly obscene materials:

[S]tricter standards of permissible statutory vagueness may be applied to a statute having a potentially inhibiting effect on speech; a man may be the less required to act at his peril here, because the free dissemination of ideas may be the loser.

But the promise of *Winters* and *Smith* have been lost. Several Justices—Brennan, *Paris Adult Theatre* v. *Slaton*, (1973) (dissent); Marshall id.; Stevens, *Pope* v. *Illinois*, (1987) (dissent); and Scalia, id. (concurrence); and at least one state supreme court (Oregon), *State* v. *Henry*, (1987)—have indicated that one or more prongs of *Miller* are unworkably vague. The only thing clear about the current *Miller* regime is that it contradicts the void-for-vagueness doctrine articulated in *Winters* and similar cases. Moreover, the knowledge requirement articulated in *Smith* has been limited in *Hamling* v. *United States*, (1974). Thus, today magazine and video distributors act at their peril unless they examine every page and every frame of what they sell—and even then they can only guess at whether a particular item will be found legally obscene. This situation inevitably breeds the self-censorship feared by the Court in earlier cases and other contexts, and starkly reveals the Court's double standard on vagueness: one standard for obscenity and another for everything else.

NOTE

1. The Justices in the *Fort Wayne* majority were White, Rehnquist, Blackmun, Scalia, and Kennedy.

APPENDIX D

US DEPARTMENT OF JUSTICE, WASHINGTON, DC, MEMORANDUM

Subject "Project Postporn" and the Danger Of Multiple District Prosecutions	Date
Coordinated from Washington, DC	September 14, 1988

To:	H. Robert Showers	From:	Paul C. McCommon III
	Executive Director		Special Attorney
	National Obscenity		National Obscenity
	Enforcement Unit		Enforcement Unit

Over the past year, I have become increasingly concerned about "Project PostPorn" and the practice of "simultaneous multiple-district prosecutions" generally, but particularly where such a project is controlled according to DOJ policy guidelines from Washington. On several occasions, I have advised you of my concerns, but I don't feel you have taken my warnings seriously.

Pursuant to your request, I drafted a letter for Assistant Attorney General Ed Dennis' signature, which is to give US Attorneys the authorization to proceed with their investigations and indictments. In my judgment, these US Attorneys are being given the "green light" to proceed without sufficient guidance from you as to the inherent risks involved in these cases. Therefore, it is the purpose of this memorandum to place my previously communicated comments and objections relating to this project in writing. I trust that these comments will be of assistance not only as to "Postporn," but as to other projects as well. Much of what I state herein relates to your conduct during the previous eighteen months. The reason for this is that it will always be your conduct which will form the factual basis of a lawsuit, motion to transfer, or motion to dismiss (i.e., *Freedberg*).

1. *History of "Postporn."* I first became involved in the project on May 22,

1987. My involvement was initiated by you, because of your concern and concerns expressed to you by Dan Milhalko and others that Cindy Christfield was lacking experience in the areas of First Amendment, constitutional, and obscenity law. Although I was to be a co-coordinator of the project, the project was already well underway by May 22nd—targets had been selected; most participating districts had been selected; planning conferences had been held in Utah with you and Cindy in attendance; memoranda on legal issues had previously been prepared by Jan and Cindy at your direction; and Cindy was in the process of working with you to send out letters, exhibits, and policy guidelines from you to the USAs in the participating districts.

At the time I entered the project, I relied on your judgment and those of the other organizers that it was a good project. Also, based on "my understanding" of the project and its purpose, I didn't see evidence that the project was flawed, although we were undertaking a novel approach. My original understanding of the project was: (1) the targets were large mail-order businesses dealing in "sexually oriented advertisements" and "hard core" materials; (2) the venues for these investigations were appropriate based on citizen complaints, i.e., "prohibitory orders;" (3) these were middle-level targets in terms of importance; (4) the cases would be handled by the US Attorney's offices with assistance from us; and (5) our role was to be "coordinating" in nature, as opposed to an "authorizing" or "approving" function.

In the months following May 22nd, it became clear that my original understanding of the project and how it was to work were not accurate. First, we sent out additional letters and guidelines under your signature that expanded the NOEU role. Each target was assigned an NOEU co-counsel, and I had several conversations with you concerning your suggestion that I be "lead counsel" in Louisville. Being "lead counsel" on these cases was encouraged by you to me and to the other NOEU attorneys. Next, as we moved into the search warrant phase it became clear that our role in these matters was now in the nature of "authorization." The first search conducted was the "Bijou" search in Chicago on November 18, 1987, and you will recall the various problems that we had regarding authorization of the warrant, communication, and coordination.

It also became known to me for the first time last Fall that we had a policy regarding multiple district prosecution, stated in USAM §9-75.320. This policy, that we sent to the USAs in our correspondence, stated in part: (1) the NOEU must be "consulted" prior to initiating a case; (2) the NOEU must "coordinate" the investigations; (3) a law enforcement agency "must consult" with the NOEU prior to referring the case to a USA; and (4) indictments must be "approved" by the NOEU prior to filing. The last sentence of the first paragraph of §9-75.320 also indicates that these cases will *originate* with the NOEU, presumably working with law enforcement agencies, and that USAs will then be notified by the NOEU that an investigation is permitted in their district.

Also, since at least March, 1987, you have given speeches heard by many AUSAs and others, where you have stated your purpose for multiple-district cases which is to keep the defense attorneys busy and running around the country. You have also used the "bat and ball" analogy, that we want them playing in our ballparks with our bat and our ball. I think a judge could easily find improper forum shopping, based on this expression of prosecutorial motivation and based on your degree of control as provided by DOJ policy.

On December 17, 1987, we held a "Postporn" planning conference here at DOJ for primary district AUSAs and their postal inspectors. At this meeting, we informed the AUSAs for the first time of the indictment approval process through the NOEU, and the specific requirement of a prosecution memorandum. We also discussed the schedule for indictments, the need for pre-indictment conferences, and the coordination of publicity here at DOJ with the USAs working with you. Eventually, a major press conference was held here at DOJ by Assistant Attorney General Ed Dennis on July 1, 1988.

Following the USAs' conference in San Diego on February 19, 1988, you came back with the policy that would place a primary responsibility on you in the area of pleas in these cases. The way I originally understood the new policy, you would resolve problems with a plea if (and only if) the districts involved were unable to agree. After my recent review of the other USAM draft proposals, however, I now understand that you are to sign off on *all* plea agreements. These policies went out in a letter to USAs from you and Brent Ward dated March 11, 1988.

The final development in "Postporn" was the indictment approval process. A memorandum was sent by Marcella to all "Postporn" AUSAs requiring that they send their draft indictment and a prosecution memorandum to her in Miami for review and approval. This memorandum was sent by Marcella immediately following our seminar which ended May 25, 1988. Marcella was then to forward a copy of the indictment to us here at DOJ, and then a committee of three Task Force lawyers would review the indictment.

Therefore, "Project Postporn" evolved as it progressed, and throughout this evolution toward control and authorizations, Cindy and I were continually made aware of additional policies that were to be communicated by us to AUSAs. These policies resulted in more control being exercised over these cases by the NOEU. Therefore, "Project Postporn" can be summarized as follows:

(1) AUSAs indicated an interest in participating at the March 3–5, 1987 conference in Washington, DC;

(2) Targets of the investigation were selected by the NOEU;

(3) Venues were selected by the NOEU based on prior AUSA interest and citizen complaints;

(4) Project was coordinated by NOEU (ultimately yourself);

(5) NOEU (Rob Showers) set all policies, guidelines, and timetables;

(6) Search warrants were required to be approved by the NOEU;

(7) Every target had an NOEU co-counsel;

(8) Searches were coordinated by the NOEU;

(9) Pre-indictment conferences were held at the urging of the NOEU;

(10) NOEU indictment approval was required;

(11) Publicity must be coordinated between USAs and yourself;

(12) Main press conference held at DOJ;

(13) All pleas must be approved by you;

(14) Your expressed motivation to put pressure on the targets and their attorneys through simultaneous cases, and taking away their home field advantage.

2. *Legal Ramifications.* The above facts, considered together, indicate a serious problem. Because the vast majority of USAs on your subcommittee do not have extensive First Amendment experience, they should be made aware of this problem *before* the decision is made by Ed Dennis to send out the "go ahead" letter to USAs. I believe we are derelict in our duty if we do not warn them that, considering the above facts, additional *Freedberg*-type lawsuits and/or granted motions to transfer are foreseeable.

The problem here is *not* multiple-district prosecution. Case law and legislative intent is clear that venue in federal obscenity cases is proper in either the district of shipment/mailing or in the district of receipt. Had these cases originated in these districts, and had DOJ policy and practice not mandated NOEU's control, we would be on firm legal ground. However, the issue here is the appearance of an improper prosecutorial motive, and the effect such appearance will have on federal judges.

Cannon 9 of the Cannons of Ethics of the State Bar of Georgia reads: "A lawyer should avoid even the appearance of professional impropriety." I believe this is the primary reason for Judge Jackson's order in *Freedberg*—he observed an "appearance of impropriety" and he reacted accordingly. Although Judge Jackson clearly overreacted, I can foresee other judges acting similarly. For example, in the case of *United States* v. *Luros*, 243 F. Supp. 160,

177 (N.D. Iowa 1965), the Court properly denied a Rule 21(b) motion to transfer in a case brought pursuant to 18 USC §1461, but stated:

> If this prosecution were initiated here at the direction of the Department of Justice in Washington, rather than at the instance of the local United States Attorney, it may well represent an attempt at forum shopping.

Also, in the case of *Arcara* v. *Cloud Books, Inc.*, 92 L.Ed.2d 568 (1986), the Supreme Court upheld the closure of an adult bookstore based on a nuisance rationale and use of the premises for prostitution and lewdness, but Justice O'Connor stated in her concurring opinion:

> If, however, a city were to use a nuisance statute as a *pretext for closing down a book store because it sold indecent books* or because of the perceived secondary effects of having a purveyor of such books in the neighborhood, the case would clearly indicate First Amendment concerns and require analysis under the appropriate First Amendment standard of review.

At 579 (emphasis added). The above cases demonstrate that judges will look behind the use of a valid law, and will act to prevent the use of even a proper law to achieve an improper or illegal result.

In the present matter, the facts raise an "appearance" of an improper motivation. Moreover, I am concerned about your "bat and ball" speech, and whether that information would come out in a *Freedberg* deposition, whether it has appeared in newsclippings from your speeches, or whether an AUSA somewhere might admit having heard you say that.

CONCLUSION

There are issues that must be discussed by you and Marcella before a letter goes out from Ed Dennis. First, the USAs' Subcommittee must reevaluate its multi-district policies in relation to the *Freedberg* and *Luros* decisions. Second, any USA who is told to proceed should be given the whole story as to multi-district cases where Washington has coordinated so closely. Third, we should reevaluate whether each of our targets is worthy of multi-district prosecution. And fourth, districts should be authorized to proceed independently and at their own pace, to minimize the appearance of Washington control.

cc: Marcella Cohen

BIBLIOGRAPHY

Aristophanes. *The Acharnians, The Clouds, Lysistrata.* Translated by A. H. Sommerstein. New York: Penguin Books, 1973.

Attorney General's Commission on Pornography, *Final Report.* Washington, D.C.: U.S. Department of Justice, 1986.

Augustine. *Confessions.* London: Penguin Classics, 1961.

Bloomfield, J., M. McGrail, and L. Sanders, eds. *Too Darn Hot.* New York: Persea Books, 1998.

Boaz, David. *Libertarianism: A Primer.* New York: Free Press, 1997.

Bork, Robert H. *Slouching Towards Gomorrah.* New York: ReganBooks (HarperCollins), 1996.

Commission on Obscenity and Pornography. "The Report of the Commission on Obscenity and Pornography." Washington, D.C.: U.S. Government Printing Office, 1970.

Commission on Obscenity and Pornography. *Technical Report.* 1970.

Cowen, Tyler. "Is Our Culture in Decline?" *Cato Policy Report,* September/October 1998.

Diamond, Milton. "The Effects of Pornography: An International Perspective." In *Porn 101,* edited by J. Elias, V. D. Elias, V. L. Bullough, G. Brewer, J. J. Douglas, and W. Jarvis. Amherst, N.Y.: Prometheus Books, 1999.

Doctorow, E. L. *Loon Lake.* New York: Plume/Penguin, 1996.

Donnerstein, Edward, D. Linz, and S. Penrod. *The Question of Pornography.* New York: Free Press, 1987.

Friedman, A. V. *Marital Intimacy.* Northrale, N.J.: Jason Aronson, 1996.

Gwartney, James, and Robert Lawson. *Economic Freedom of the World, 1998/1999 Interim Report.* N.p.: Fraser Institute, 1998.

Haffner, Debra. "The Really Good News: What the Bible Says About Sex." *SIECUS Report,* October/November 1997.

Harr, Jonathan. *A Civil Action.* New York: Vintage Books, 1995.

Harvey, Philip. *Let Every Child Be Wanted: How Social Marketing Is Revolutionizing Contraceptive Use Around the World.* Westport, Conn.: Greenwood Publishing Group, 1999.

Haught, James. *Holy Hatred.* Amherst, N.Y.: Prometheus Books, 1995.

———. "Sex and God: Is Religion Twisted?" *Free Inquiry* (fall 1997).

Hayek, Friederich. "Why I Am Not a Conservative." In *The Constitution of Liberty.* Chicago: University of Chicago Press, 1960.

Heins, Marjorie. *Sex, Sin, and Blasphemy, A Guide to America's Censorship Wars.* New York: New Press, 1993.

Hunt, Morton. *The Compassionate Beast: What Science Is Discovering About the Humane Side of Humankind.* New York: William Morrow, 1990.

Hutchings, M. L., and G. W. Smith. "The Good, the Bad, and the Ugly: Crime and Punishment in Utah." *Utah Bar Journal*, September 1997.

Interview with Drew Carey. *Reason*, November 1997.

Kimball, Spencer. "The Teachings of Spencer W. Kimball." Salt Lake City: BookCraft, 1982.

Kipnis, Laura. *Bound and Gagged, Pornography and the Politics of Fantasy in America*. New York: Grove Press, 1996.

Klein, Marty. "Censorship and the Fear of Sexuality." *Humanist*, July/August 1990.

Kosmin, B., and S. Lochmann. *One Nation Under God: Religion in Contemporary American Society*. New York: Harmony Books, 1993.

Ladd, E. C. *The Ladd Report*. New York: Free Press, 1999.

Lord, M. G. *Lingua Franca*. April/May 1997.

Macy, Marianne. *Working Sex*. New York: Carroll & Graf, 1996.

Manchester, William. *A World Lit Only By Fire*. Newport Beach, Calif.: Back Bay Books, 1992.

McCracken, Grant. "The Politics of Plenitude." *Reason*, August/September 1998.

Mill, J. S. *On Liberty*. New York: Penguin Classics, 1985.

O'Rourke, P. J. *Eat the Rich*. New York: Atlantic Monthly Press, 1998.

Oaks, Dallin H. "Challenges for the Year Ahead." Speech given at Brigham Young University, September 6, 1973. Quoted in "Statements by Leaders of the Church of Jesus Christ of Latter-Day Saints Concerning Pornography." Brochure. Corporation of the President of the Church of Jesus Christ of Latter-Day Saints, 1986, 1988.

Orwell, George. *1984*. New York: Signet/Penguin, 1950.

Pally, Marcia. *Sense & Censorship: The Vanity of Bonfires. Resource Materials on Sexually Explicit Material, Violent Material, and Censorship: Research and Public Policy Implications*. New York: Americans for Constitutional Freedom, 1991.

———. *Sex and Sensibility*. Hopewell, N.J.: Ecco Press, 1994.

Peterson, Mark. "Steps in Overcoming Masturbation." Council of the 12 Apostles, circa 1989.

Posner, Richard A. *Sex and Reason*. Cambridge: Harvard University Press, 1992.

Postrel, Virginia. *The Future and Its Enemies*. New York: Free Press, 1998.

Rigby, Julie. "Oh! Oooh! Ewww! 7 Women Review the New Sex Movies." *Redbook*, October 1995.

Ruley, Melinda. "Trouble in Paradise, Making a Federal Case Out of Adam & Eve's Sex Toys." *Chapel Hill (N.C.) Independent Weekly*, March 27, 1991.

Sheridan, Danny. "*Playboy's* Pro Football Forecast." *Playboy*, September 1997.

Simon, Julian. *How to Start and Operate a Mail-Order Business*. New York: McGraw-Hill, 1965.

Spooner, Lysander. *The Lysander Spooner Reader*. San Francisco: Fox & Wilkes, 1992.

Strossen, Nadine. *Defending Pornography: Free Speech, Sex, and the Fight for Women's Rights*. New York: Scribner, 1995.

Tannahill, Reay. *Sex In History*. Lanham, Md.: Scarborough House, 1992.

Thurber, James. *Is Sex Necessary?* New York: Harper & Row, 1929.

Thurow, Lester. *The Future of Capitalism*. New York: William Morrow, 1996.

Tisdale, Sallie. "Talk Dirty to Me." *Harper's*, February 1992.

———. *Talk Dirty to Me*. New York: Anchor Books, 1994.

Tribe, Laurence H. *American Constitutional Law*. Second edition. Mineola, N.Y.: Foundation Press, 1988.

Walsh, G. *The Role of Religion in History*. New Brunswick, N.J.: Transaction Publishers, 1998.

Williams, Linda. "The Visual and Carnal Pleasures of Moving-Image Pornography." Address to the Society for the Scientific Study of Sex, April 1997.

INDEX